Essentials of Management
A Behavioral Approach

Essentials of Management

A Behavioral Approach

Justin G. Longenecker

Baylor University

Charles E. Merrill Publishing Company
A Bell & Howell Company
Columbus, Ohio

Published by
Charles E. Merrill Publishing Company
A Bell & Howell Company
Columbus, Ohio 43216

This book was set in Palatino.

The Production Editor was Michael Robbins.

The cover was designed by Will Chenoweth.

International Standard Book Number: 0–675–08552–7
Library of Congress Catalog Card Number: 76–23935
1 2 3 4 5 6 7 8 9 10—80 79 78 77
Printed in the United States of America

Preface

This book presents a basic treatment of the process of management. As indicated by the title, it confines itself to the *essentials* of management and presents them with an emphasis upon the *human behavior* involved. The book is designed, therefore, for those who desire a condensation of contemporary management theory and practice.

Characteristics that differentiate the book from others include: (1) management functions—planning, organizing, directing, and controlling—provide the framework for the book; (2) discussion of these functions reflects an awareness of behavioral aspects of management; (3) one chapter considers the special features of international management; (4) the text includes such topics of current interest as contingency theory, systems theory, strategic planning, conflict management, assessment centers, and management by objectives; (5) a case problem at the end of each chapter permits application of the theory presented in the chapter; (6) the writing style and the use of real-life examples contribute to a sense of practicality; and (7) chapter outlines, objectives, summaries, and questions facilitate study.

I am indebted to my colleagues for permission to use their case problems and to the Dean and the Associate Dean of the Hankamer School of Business, Emerson O. Henke and Richard C. Scott, for their cooperation in many ways. I also appreciate the work of Jane Longenecker in typing the manuscript a number of times.

The patience and understanding of my wife, Frances, and daughters, Linda, Nancy, and Jane, were also most helpful in making this book a reality.

Waco, Texas   *Justin G. Longenecker*

Contents

1

Introduction to Management

Objectives

1. Identify the unique features of managerial activity.
2. Summarize the major developments in management thought and practice.
3. Describe four *managerial functions.*
4. Explain the *systemic* nature of organizations and the contributions of *systems theory* to the understanding of organizations and management.

Chapter

1

The Nature of Organizations and Management

In its "Fiftieth Anniversary" issue, *Forbes* applied the perspective of history to corporate management in this striking commentary:

> If a company has nothing going for it except one thing—good management—it will make the grade. If it has everything *except* good management, it will flop. That's the clear lesson of 50 action-packed years of U.S. business history.[1]

These dramatic comments indicate the importance of management to the proper functioning of today's social organizations. All types of organizations—hospitals, schools, government offices, foundations, and churches, as well as business firms—require good management to accomplish their objectives.

The Nature of Management

The Distinctive Skill of Management

We have come to recognize that management and the abilities of the manager are quite separate and distinct from the activites and abilities required of operating personnel. At one time, it was customary to promote the most proficient worker when filling a management vacancy. Although this procedure had much to recommend it, it ignored the fact that ability to direct the work of others is substantially different from that of doing one's own work. Capable employees who had performed outstandingly as craftsmen or office employees proved disappointing when moved into managerial positions. Gradually, it became clear that the manager requires talents or must exercise abilities that are quite different from those of nonmanagerial personnel.

The distinctive nature of managerial ability was further revealed by the discovery that managerial skills are somewhat transferable from one field of endeavor to another. Thus, managers can move from production to sales and do an effective job in either area. Other managers move effectively from business to government, and vice versa.

In 1975, George P. Shultz, former Secretary of Labor and of the Treasury, was named president of San Francisco's Bechtel Corporation, a large engineering and construction company.[2] Prior to federal service, Shultz had served as a business school dean at the University of Chicago. Admittedly, knowledge of the federal bureaucracy would be helpful to an engineering and construction company. However, the directors of the Bechtel Corporation must have believed that he also demonstrated relevant managerial ability in Chicago and Washington before naming him to the chief executive slot in a private corporation.

Although there is undoubtedly a desirable minimum amount of knowledge necessary concerning the field being managed, it is evident that the skill and ability of managers is distinct from the technical knowledge associated with the field. Certainly, managers do not need to be the greatest technical experts in the field in which they are managing.

---

[1] "Management," *Forbes* 100, no. 6 (September 15, 1967): 51.

[2] "Room at the Top for Ex-Cabinet Men," *Business Week,* no. 2396 (September 1, 1975): 19–20.

A manager provides the dynamic force or direction that combines static resources into a functioning, productive organization. He or she is *the individual in charge*, the one expected to get results and to see that things happen as they should. If a small business fails to achieve its objectives, a new proprietor appears, and a sign goes up: "Under New Management." In a large corporation, an organization shake-up occurs, with dismissals, transfers, demotions, promotions, and new appointments.

For example, Lockheed Aircraft Corporation directors in 1976 accepted the resignations of the company's top management team. This action followed the disclosure of $22 million in payments to foreign political or government figures and was taken as the company faced the possible loss of large overseas orders. Earlier, in 1971, the government had given Lockheed a $250 million loan guarantee to keep it afloat. At that time, many argued that the management team which had brought the company to the edge of bankruptcy should be replaced.

The term *management* is often used as a noun to denote individuals who exercise leadership in an organization, that is, the managers. It is important to recognize, however, that management may also be viewed as a *process*. In this sense, it is comprised of the manager's activities in decision making, coordination of group effort, and general leadership. Some have described management, rather tritely, as "getting things done through people." This distinguishes *managerial* from *nonmanagerial* work but tells us very little about the actual process of managing or how it gets results through people.

There is some similarity in the activities of all types of managers. Thus, the duties of a manager of an office or storeroom have something in common with those of the president of the organization. These activities are described as functions and are discussed later in this chapter. At this point, it should be clear that management consists of those activities necessary to secure the contributions of individuals and to regulate these contributions to achieve the organization's goal.

The Managers

Definition of Management

Trends in Management Thought and Practice

To develop a sense of perspective, we direct our attention in this section to a few of the major shifts or trends in management thinking. In later chapters, we consider more specific changes and developments.

Applying Science to Management

Frederick W. Taylor is known as *the father of scientific management*. This title recognizes his pioneering efforts in attacking the traditional approach to management by the substitution of more systematic and analytical methods. Although his work was primarily concerned with shop management, the general approach that he advocated is applicable to all varieties and levels of administration.[3]

---

[3] For a collection of Taylor's writings, see Frederick Winslow Taylor, *Scientific Management* (New York: Harper & Row, Publishers, 1947).

Taylor learned the machinist and patternmaker trades in the 1870s in Phila-
delphia and in 1878 went to work for the Midvale Steel Company. In this
plant, he progressed to positions of machinist, gang boss, and higher positions
in the management hierarchy. In 1890, Taylor left the Midvale Steel Company
to engage in consulting work, and, in 1898, he entered the employment of
Bethlehem Steel Company.

During his early years in management positions of the Midvale Steel Company, Taylor applied a fresh and novel approach to the practice of shop management. He was quick to question traditional techniques of management and
ready to devise and experiment with different methods. During his years as a
consultant, he continued many of the same type of studies, and he later followed the same scientific management approach in his work with the Bethlehem Steel Company.

Taylor's Studies of Pig Iron Handling

It is enlightening to examine some practical examples of Taylor's revolutionary approach to shop management. One of the classic examples associated
with Taylor's work is his study of pig iron handling at the Bethlehem Steel
Company. According to Taylor, the circulation of this particular illustration
was so widespread that some people equated scientific management with handling pig iron! Taylor cited this particular example because pig iron handling
represented the simplest kind of human effort. It was his idea that proof of advantages from scientific management of such simple tasks would demonstrate
the general advantages that might accrue from scientific management.

The pig iron study occurred at the Bethlehem Steel Company, which had
five blast furnaces and a gang of seventy-five men manually handling pig iron.
A railroad siding ran into a field with pig iron in piles alongside. A plank was
placed against the side of the railroad car, and the worker picked up a pig of
iron weighing about ninety-two pounds, walked up the inclined plank, and
dropped the pig in the car. In studying pig iron handling, the motions and
steps of the workers were analyzed minutely, and attention was given to the
proper distribution of work and rest.

Employees were then carefully selected and given detailed instructions in
the new method. Management insisted upon exact performance according to
prescribed methods. Employees could earn substantially more than their average rate by following the prescribed methods. At the time the experiment began, each worker in this gang was loading an average of about twelve and one-
half tons a day. After the study and changes, the output of these men was increased almost four times to forty-seven and one-half tons of pig iron a day!

Taylor was careful to differentiate between scientific management and the
techniques associated with its early applications. Workmen in the experiments
were paid on a piece-work basis, but Taylor insisted that scientific management was not a scheme of incentive wage payments. Neither was it the use of a
stopwatch, the study of motions, nor the instruction of workmen in the proper
methods of job performance. Viewed more broadly, he saw scientific management as the systematic or scientific investigation of all the facts and elements
connected with the work being managed. It was the very opposite of management by tradition and rule of thumb.

There were many criticisms of Taylor's work and the scientific management movement. An employee's work was analyzed as one might analyze the operation of a machine, and the goal was maximization of efficiency of this human "machine." Over several decades, many people came to realize the serious inadequacies of such views concerning labor.

Another notable change in management thinking and practice has occurred in the area of human relationships. In this development, the work by Elton Mayo and his research group was unusually significant.

Recognition of Human Relationships

Mayo's best-known research, occurring in the late 1920s, was conducted at the Hawthorne plant of the Western Electric Company. In this investigation he was assisted by F. J. Roethlisberger of the Harvard Business School and William J. Dickson of the Western Electric Company. The experiments in the Western Electric Company were originated to discover methods for improving the productivity of employees. These experiments were primarily concerned with the physical environmental aspects of the job, such as the effects of lighting and fatigue upon output. The most notable result of the research was its revelation of the great limitations of the engineering or physical hypotheses that provided the foundation for the studies. In the experimentation, employees failed to behave according to management's image of them as simple biological organisms. The experiments revealed the inadequacy of the traditional viewpoint concerning employees—the type of viewpoint that characterized management thinking in Taylor's day.

The practical impact of the work of the Mayo group was to reveal to management the significance of human relations in organizational behavior. Even though detractors have criticized certain extremes of the human relations movement, it has been impossible since Mayo's day for serious thinkers to shrug off the concepts developed during this period. Employees were discovered to be much more complex in their makeup and motivation than had been generally realized. The human aspects and relationships of industry were found to be of critical importance in the daily functioning of organizations.

In recent years, some management theorists have adopted a *contingency*, or *situational*, view of management. This view has terminated, or at least interrupted, the search for universal management principles. In the real world of business organizations, successful management patterns and practices proved too complex for resolution with simple universal principles. Although a supposed "principle" might explain one situation, other situations seemed to contradict the same "principle."

Contingency Approaches to Management

According to the contingency view, appropriate management practice depends on the situation at hand. More specifically, the best type of organization structure, leadership, or control system depends upon the circumstances and unique features of the particular situation. Democratic leadership, for example, may work in one situation but not in another.

Recognition of situational forces and contingencies is not the same as saying there is no better way or best way to manage or that a manager's intuition will produce results that are on the average as good as those of the professionally trained manager. Rather, we recognize that management is more complex than we once believed. The contingency concept will appear in various forms throughout this text as specific circumstances affect the application of management theory.

The Management Process

The management process in an organizational system is made up of the things managers do—that is, with activities performed by all managers, ranging from president to first-line supervisor. It also includes the activities of managers who function in different areas of business—production, sales, finance, research, and so on.

Managerial Versus Nonmanagerial Duties

Not all duties, even required duties, of managers can be properly classified as "managerial" in a strict sense. *Managerial* activities are those concerned with the functioning of the organization as an institution. They are related to the work and accomplishments of subordinate managerial and operative personnel. The distinctive contribution of a manager is the blending of individual work, just as a symphony conductor blends the musical efforts of individual musicians into a performance of harmony and beauty.

The Busy Manager

Observation of managers in action reveals a very active working life. There may be exceptions, but most managers are extremely busy. Such hectic schedules do not necessarily constitute an ideal behavior pattern for managers. They may be busy because they are inefficient or because they have never learned to delegate to others. Be that as it may, the typical executive is a busy and possibly overworked individual.

Studies of managerial behavior have confirmed this picture of the busy manager. The following example of the busy executive life reveals a little of the manager's life style and orientation:

> Horace A. Shepard, 53, CEO of TRW, Inc., in Cleveland . . . rises at 6 every morning, and is in his office by 7:30. "Inevitably, wherever I go the briefcase goes along, and I spend at least two hours in the evening and each weekend day with it," he says.
>
> But there is no complaint about the time put in. "Who wants to have a lot of leisure? Most people profess to want it, but most of them who retire wind up busying themselves on many outside activities," says Shepard.[4]

The fact that a manager works hard and spends long hours on the job tells us little about the patterning of managerial activities. We might surmise that an efficient manager would take one project at a time, complete it, and move on to the next project. Studies of managers in action, however, have shown that the systematic, orderly executive seldom exists in the real world.

In Mintzberg's study of chief executives, he found that they averaged 36 written and 16 verbal contacts each day.

> A subordinate calls to report a fire in one of the facilities; then the mail, much of it insignificant, is processed; a subordinate interrupts to tell of an impending crisis with a public group; a retiring employee is ushered in to receive a plaque; later there is discussion of bidding on a multi-million-dollar

---

[4] "Not Much Time for Anything but Work," *Business Week*, no. 2329 (May 4, 1974): 70.

contract; after that, the manager complains that office space in one department is being wasted. Throughout each working day the manager encounters
this great variety of activity. Most surprising, the significant activity is inter-
spersed with the trivial in no particular pattern. Hence the manager must be
prepared to shift moods quickly and frequently.[5]

Another approach to analysis of management activity identifies certain basic **Identification of**
management functions. A manager's discussions with subordinates, for example, **Management**
may have any of a number of different purposes. The manager, in some cases, **Functions**
is checking on work progress and, at other times, is outlining future work
projects. The manager also discusses the type of work assignments to be made
to different subordinates and the extent to which particular employees should
be allowed to make decisions. Each of these, and others as well, is different in
purpose and nature. In attempting to identify basic management functions, we
are seeking some fundamental categories or classifications that permit a logical
grouping of managerial activities according to their purpose and nature.

These is no universally recognized set of management functions. Different
theorists have cut the pie in pieces of different sizes and shapes. Some suggest
as few as three, while others propose a dozen or more. There is actually considerably less disagreement than might be imagined from a superficial exam-
ination of the various schemes of classification. A number of basic functions
are widely recognized, even though there is some variation in labeling them.

In this book, four functions—planning, organizing, directing and motivating,
and controlling—will provide the framework for our analysis of management
activities. Each of these functions is discussed briefly in the following sections
and also serves as the basis for a major section of the book. In practice, these
functions are intertwined in the day-to-day performance of a manager.

The Management Process   **Figure 1-1**

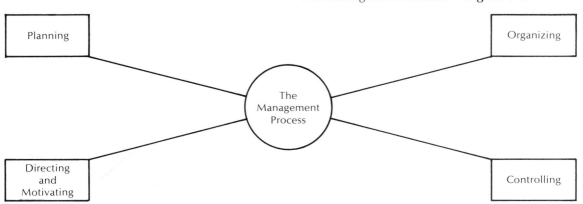

The general meaning of managerial planning is consistent with the common **The Planning**
usage of the term. It involves thought and decision concerning a proposed **Function**
course of action. The plan may be concerned with not only a decision to take

---

[5] Abridged and adapted from p. 31 in *The Nature of Managerial Work* by Henry Mintzberg. Copyright © 1973 by Henry Mintzberg. By permission of Harper & Row, Publishers, Inc.

action but also such aspects as "who," "when," and "how." Planning is concerned with the future. It anticipates and precedes action, as contrasted with reflective thinking about past events. How far a plan extends into the future varies, naturally, according to the type of plan.

By providing a factual basis for future action, planning aids or facilitates the action being planned. Otherwise, there would be little value in planning. Subjecting almost any unplanned activity to the process of planning demonstrates the general validity of this proposition. Students can discover the road to improvement in learning through properly planned study. Such planning involves the allocation of time to study versus other pursuits. It also requires thought as to the order of study and the environmental conditions for study.

Overall business planning for a company typically culminates in a financial budget, which may be thought of as the most basic business plan for the concern. It applies to a given period of time, typically one year, although it may be of any length. The budget is based upon sales predictions and incorporates the operational plans necessary to meet anticipated sales levels.

Use of forecasting and budgeting is one mark of an organization's sophistication in planning and in general management. Most large corporations, for example, would find it difficult, if not impossible, to operate without comprehensive financial budgets.

The Organizing Function

We might regard the organization function as breaking down an overall objective into the specific functions and assignments necessary for the accomplishment of that objective. Major divisions or departments represent major functions of the business, and these are further subdivided into individual jobs. The organizing function is also concerned with the relationships among functions and jobs.

Superior-subordinate relationships are of primary importance in organizing. The manager creates a structure of relationships that links each employee, directly or indirectly, to the organization head. The connecting lines running downward from top management to operative employees provide the channels for communication between superiors and subordinates and make possible a transmission of plans, instructions, problems, and progress reports.

Very small companies typically use a type of organization known as *line* organization. In this type of organization, each person is connected with a single line of responsibility to a superior. The subordinate is accountable to, and receives orders from, only one superior. It is a simple form of organization without special service groups or advisors. As organizations grow, however, they develop a need for specialists to furnish advice and service. This leads to a type of organization known as *line and staff*. In a line and staff organization, the staff experts and service departments supplement the basic line organization. Most large organizations are line and staff.

Another question confronting the manager as organizer is the extent to which authority and decision making should be delegated downward in the organization. Any manager finds it necessary to make some decisions personally, particularly with respect to the most important decisions confronting his organization. Other decisions may be made personally by the manager or passed to lower levels. In recent years the decentralization of decision making has been a popular movment in American industry.

Another subject that has received increasing attention in recent years is the social nature of business organizations. Organizations have come to be viewed as social institutions. Management has discovered the existence of an informal organization supplementing or conflicting with the formal structure. Many questions have been raised as to the discrepancy between the way organizations are supposed to function and the way they actually function.

The organizational machine must be activated or energized in order to carry out management plans. It is the function of directing that sets the organization in motion. We sometimes speak of a manager giving the "go ahead" or "green light" to a program or plan. This step authorizes subordinates to begin work in accordance with the program and constitutes direction on the part of the manager.

The Directing and Motivating Function

The term *directing* may carry a connotation of harshness or autocratic management. The military organization, for example, passes orders downward through its chain of command. It is not necessary to consider the function of directing as highly authoritarian, however. Some motivation beyond mere order giving may also be necessary to get the organization in motion as desired. This is becoming increasingly the case as managers come to realize the strength of positive motivation and also as organizations develop a more democratic atmosphere.

One of the principal variables in directing is the degree of autocracy in the manager's directions. Direction can range from quite direct commands to guidance through much less direct means. Subordinates may be permitted and even encouraged to contribute suggestions and ideas for consideration by the manager. In the extreme case, direction may appear to be largely self-direction on the basis of some common understanding of goals and objectives.

Closely related is the extent to which managers manage in detail. Some managers look over the shoulders of their subordinates almost constantly and insist on personally approving every change. Other mangers provide only general supervision, and subordinates enjoy considerable latitude in the discharge of their responsibilities.

Controlling refers to the regulation of the organization to insure the achievement of organizational objectives and the completion of organizational plans. It corresponds, in a sense, to the steering and braking of an automobile. The organization's performance must be examined and checked to insure that the organization is on the right track. Some organizations have an accounting executive, specialized in this function, who is called the *controller*, but controlling is also a part of the responsibility of every manager in the organization.

The Controlling Function

Perhaps the most obvious feature of controlling is the comparison of organizational or individual performance with standards. An automobile driver who reaches a particular town on a cross-country trip checks the location with the road map and schedule for the day. Occasionally, the driver may find that the trip is running behind schedule—or even going in the wrong direction! In the manufacturing plant, inspectors check manufactured products for compliance with product specifications. This is part of the quality *control* function, and the inspectors may be assigned to the quality *control* department.

The purpose of checking performance is to see that it meets expectations. The anticipated results may be thought of as standards. Such standards may take various forms. The preceding quality specification is one example. A schedule of output for a specific time period is another type of standard. Time standards, set on the basis of time and motion study, provide work standards for individual employees. The general quality objectives of an organization as a whole also provide a type of objective with which performance may be compared. The financial budget, as a comprehensive financial plan, provides a standard or set of standards that may be used to judge overall performance.

If deviations from standards are revealed, it is the responsibility of the manager to take corrective action. This means that he or she must get performance back up to the time schedule, get quality up to par, or make other adjustments necessary to meet the expectations previously established. Knowing of the deviation is futile if no corrective action is taken. It is here that a manager proves his or her worth as controller—by getting the organization back to standard performance.

The action necessary for correction takes many different forms. In the case of the deviation from quality control standards, for example, there may be a number of explanations for the deviation and, therefore, a number of points at which corrective action may be needed. A machine may require adjustment, or its speed of operation may need to be changed. It is also possible that the operator should be trained or, perhaps, replaced with an operator of greater ability. Another possible solution is the substitution of better material. Changes may be required in the physical environment to eliminate noise or dust that might contaminate the product or interfere with the operator in the performance of required duties.

The Systems Concept in Management

The Systems Concept

A *system* is basically a set of components related in the accomplishment of some purpose. A functioning physical organism is one type of system, and a machine is another type. Thus, dogs, mice, ball-point pens, watches, and typewriters are all systems.

The systems concept entails the idea of parts or units functioning in combination with other units. Collectively, these parts comprise a system that is either conceptual or physical. The economist's *model* is a system, as is the real economy it represents. The primary interest of systems researchers is in the type of system that is subject to manipulation or control—such as economic systems and business systems in contrast to systems of astronomy.

We should also note that some systems involve people as parts of the system whereas other systems do not. Medical research which studies the physical organs as a part of the functioning body system is an example of the latter. In the study of management, our principal concern is *social systems*—the type involving people. As a matter of fact, most *people systems* are really *people-equipment systems*.

A business organization, or any organization for that matter, may be viewed as a system of interrelated parts. The elements of such a system, as indicated by the following diagram, are input, process (or operation), and output.

The Business Firm and the Systems Concept

Input $\longrightarrow$ | Process | $\longrightarrow$ Output

In a business organization, employees, physical facilities, money, and the managers themselves are parts of the system. The outputs are the products, services, and satisfactions provided by the organization. Inputs are the materials, information, and energy flowing into the firm. Raw materials which enter the production process of a factory constitute an input. Automobiles and replacement parts are inputs in a repair shop. Other inputs are informational—for example, a customer's order or an outside auditor's report. The physical and mental work of employees may likewise be visualized as an input.

In reality, the business organization involves a series of systems or, perhaps more accurately, a complex system encompassing smaller or more specialized systems. The office typewriter and the milling machine in the factory are, in themselves, systems of component parts. These machines and the personnel who operate them are, in turn, parts of office systems and production systems. The processes of communications and decision making provide links for integrating the separate parts or specialized systems into the comprehensive business system.

The management team of an enterprise constitutes the decision-making or regulating subsystem of the organizational system. Managers are thus not only parts, but they are special—directing and controlling—parts of the total organizational system. Consequently, the managerial role should be seen in its relationship to the total organization. The manager's activities should, ideally, maximize the output of the total system.

Managerial Work and the Business System

The thread that binds together the seemingly disparate activities of managers is revealed by this view of the managerial task. Individual managers do not work in isolation, and neither is one function or activity performed without reference to another. The planning of Manager A must be harmonized with that of Manager B if organizational goals are to be achieved.

An observer may see either the parts of the system or the system itself. A manager who sees only the parts—be they products, departments, machines, or individuals—but fails to discern the broader patterns and relationships has defective managerial eyesight.

A business firm is one type of open system. Any living organism or organization, for that matter, is an open system. Openness simply means that the system trades with or interacts with its environment. The system imports something from the environment and exports something into the environment. In systems terminology, imports are called *inputs,* and exports are called *outputs.*

The Business Organization as an Open System

As is clear from Figure 1–2, the firm's interactions with the outside world are varied. Many types of inputs are received and a variety of outputs exported. The environment also establishes constraints within which the firm

Figure 1–2   *The Firm's Environment*

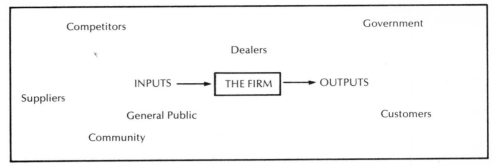

operates—law and culture, for example. The firm's operation entails contacts not only with customers but also with numerous other publics.

Total management responsibility thus entails a broad range of "boundary" issues or problems. Management is concerned, for example, with issues of social responsibility—an area of extreme importance. We must recognize, however, that the firm's economic contribution to customers—its products and its position in the marketplace—is one of its most crucial environmental problem areas. Importance of the firm's relationships in this area is evidenced by those avoidable market errors that sometimes destroy the firm itself.

The concept of the open system is, thus, directly relevant to the informational needs of the manager. To use fact and avoid fantasy, the manager must understand the environment. Effective management requires a constant flow of information about the product, its acceptance in the marketplace, competitive product modifications, pertinent economic and social developments, and related technological change.

Values of the
Systems Approach   A major contribution of the systems approach results from its stress on the interrelatedness of the parts of an organization. A manager is often tempted to see organizational problems and activities in isolation. In an extreme case, a manager may concentrate upon the efficient functioning of his or her own department and give only secondary attention to its relationships with other parts of the organization.

Any neglect of important relationships results in some degree of inefficiency. One General Motors executive pointed out an unfortunate example of such neglected relationships.[6] The Chevrolet sales department at one time conducted a major contest on four-cylinder Novas. Every dealership had banners, and advertisements appeared in magazines. However, nobody had bothered to tell manufacturing who, because of declining sales in four-cylinder engines, had gradually moved out most of the equipment!

The systems concept is useful, therefore, because of its strong emphasis upon these interrelationships. This emphasis avoids some of the pitfalls of a "components" mentality in which departments work out their own relationships haphazardly.

Another key value in systems theory lies in its treatment of the organization

---

[6]"A Battle but Not the War," *Forbes* 108, no. 3 (August 1, 1971): 49.

as an *open system*. This emphasis upon the firm's interaction with its environment is a prerequisite for successful adaptation to changing conditions in the outside world.

Summary

Management of organizations requires a type of ability and activity that is separate and distinct from the abilities and activities of operating personnel. *Managers* provide the dynamic force necessary to transform the resources of a business organization into a productive, operating concern. They are responsible for directing an organization in the achievement of its objectives.

The introduction and adoption of the *scientific method* has been a notable development in the history of management. Another major trend involves the increasing attention to *human relationships* in business organizations. Frederick W. Taylor and Elton Mayo were particularly associated with these two developments.

In theorizing about management and organization behavior, scholars have turned to *contingency theory* or a *contingency approach*. This theory means that *situational* factors affect management process and organization structure. Rather than following universal principles, managers must look for the set of variables that constrain management action in specific situations.

It is possible to define management as a *process* or group of related and continuing activites. In examining management in this manner, it is possible to identify the following basic management *functions: planning, organizing, directing and motivating,* and *controlling.*

Planning involves the determination of future courses of action. This entails not only a determination of what is to be done but also concerns the manner and timing of performance. Organizing is concerned with the determination of relationships among people, jobs, and functions. In directing and motivating, the manager sets the organization in motion. Such activities include issuing orders and instructions, but they also include other types of motivation. In the function of controlling, the manager regulates organization performance to insure achievement of objectives. This process entails a comparison of performance with standards and any necessary corrective action.

The *systems concept* provides an integrating view of the *functions* of management. This approach—that of *systems theory*—stresses the *interrelatedness of all parts and functions of a business organization.* The business organization is viewed as an *open system* with an emphasis upon both internal and external relationships.

Discussion Questions

1. What factors have encouraged the professionalization of management?

2. According to the best usage, should the word *management* apply to managers or to the process of managing?

3. What was the major contribution of Frederick W. Taylor to management thought?

4. Of what significance to management theory was Taylor's pig iron handling study?

5. What was the greatest contribution of the Western Electric studies to an understanding of the management process?

6. The *contingency* approach to management stresses the existence of significant variables in given situations. What are some types of variables that might affect proper management practice?

7. Of what possible significance is classification of activities as *managerial* and *nonmanagerial?*

8. Is it likely that the fragmented work schedule of executives is a reflection of a gregarious type of personality that is associated with management careers? Explain.

9. What relationships exist between the functions of *planning* and *organizing? Planning* and *controlling?*

10. How is a financial *budget* related to the functions of planning and controlling?

11. What is meant by the *degree of autocracy* in the performance of the directing function?

12. Explain the *systems* concept. What seems to be the distinctive feature of this idea?

13. Give several examples of systems that do not involve people as components.

14. How does the concept of the *open system* apply to a business organization?

Supplementary Reading

Drucker, Peter F. *Management: Tasks, Responsibilities, Practices.* New York: Harper & Row, Publishers, 1974.

Kast, Fremont E. and Rosenzweig, James E. *Organization and Management: A Systems Approach,* 2nd ed., Chapter 5. New York: McGraw-Hill Book Company, 1974.

Levitt, Theodore. "The Managerial Merry-Go-Round." *Harvard Business Review* 52, no. 4 (July-August, 1974): 120–28.

Mee, John F. "Changing Concepts of Management." *Advanced Management Journal* 37, no. 4 (October, 1972): 22–34.

Mintzberg, Henry. "The Manager's Job: Folklore and Fact." *Harvard Business Review,* 53, no. 4 (July-August, 1975): 49–61.

Organ, Dennis W. "Linking Pins Between Organizations and Environment." *Business Horizons,* 14, no. 6 (December, 1971): 73–80.

Stewart, Rosemary. "The Manager's Job: Discretion Vs. Demand." *Organizational Dynamics* 2, no. 3 (Winter, 1974): 67–80.

Wall, Jerry L. "What the Competition is Doing: Your Need to Know." *Harvard Business Review* 52, no. 6 (November-December, 1974): 22–38.

Wren, Daniel A. *The Evolution of Management Thought.* New York: The Ronald Press Company, 1972.

A Management Dilemma

Susan Williams, 53, had more departmental seniority than any other employee, including Ed Cook, the department manager in a major insurance company. She was considered one of the more capable employees, although her efficiency had declined somewhat during the past five years. Even so, Ed realized that she was extremely conscientious and that she earned every penny of her paycheck. As a result of her ability and seniority, she customarily received the choice work assignments and was the highest-paid employee in the department. Although there was no formal designation of various "special" projects as belonging to Susan, she handled them as a matter of course.

A problem developed when Ed employed Ann Bentley, 21, a personable, intelligent, and diligent employee. Ann's two years' prior experience in closely related work made it possible for her to catch on to work routines much more rapidly than was customary for a new employee. She was both hard working and aggressive. On several occasions, Ed became aware of tension or hostility developing between the two women. However, he did not wish to intrude into personal conflicts, and the work was being accomplished on schedule.

One afternoon, the controversy reached the boiling point when Susan Williams decided her personal duties were being taken over far too extensively by the new employee. She practically pulled Ann to the front of Ed's desk and demanded, "Will you please tell her once and for all which projects are mine and which are hers?" The office suddenly became quiet as everyone awaited Ed's reply. The abrupt confrontation made further procrastination impossible.

Questions

1. In what way has the manager's organizing function contributed to this problem? Could it have been avoided by better organization? How?

2. Evaluate the directing or motivational approach evident in this department.

3. Evaluate Ed Cook's performance as a "controller."

4. How should Ed Cook respond to the demand of Susan Williams?

2

Planning and Decision Making

Objectives

1. Distinguish between *individual goals* and *organizational goals* and explain their contribution to organizational effectiveness.
2. Show the need for achievement of the *profit goal.*
3. Define the *service goal* and explain the relationship of *strategy* and the *hierarchy of objectives* to the service goal.
4. Explain why business firms should assume *social responsibilities,* and provide examples of socially responsible behavior.
5. Cite the relationship of *ethics* to business activity, and explain ethical foundations.

Chapter

Goal
Setting

Most human activity is purposeful. Every organization is created to accomplish some objective or objectives. Individual members of organizations also contribute their services in order to achieve certain personal objectives. Such objectives may be visualized as targets or goals. These goals—those of the organization and its members—are examined in this chapter, which opens our consideration of the planning function.

The Nature of Organizational Objectives

Setting Organizational Goals

Organizations come into existence as a result of purposeful action by one or more individuals. It might seem, therefore, that organizational purpose would be obvious. *Organizational objectives* are often implicit, however, and require explicit formulation before they can be used for direction. Also, environmental conditions are constantly changing so that continuing redefinition of the firm's objectives is necessary.

A distinction must be made between "official" company objectives and those that are followed in operation. It is possible that these may differ. The president might say, for example, "We are doing everything in our power to protect the environment," while the company's plants dump pollutants into lakes and rivers.

Individual Objectives

Individual members of organizations—those contributing capital and services—have personal goals that induce them to make their respective contributions. Stockholders, for example, expect profits as a return on their capital. Employees seek compensation as a reward for their employment. Managers, the key members in setting objectives, also have personal objectives, which are not necessarily identical with those of the stockholder group. They work for salaries, bonuses, stock options, and other financial inducements.

Not all goals of organization members are financial, however. Some needs are social and are satisfied through associations provided in the organization. Other needs, such as the desire for accomplishment or for doing something worthwhile, are individual and may be satisfied through work.

The objectives of the various groups of individual members are compatible with each other to some extent and also conflict to some extent. For example, all participants desire a minimally satisfactory rate of profits. On the other hand, the stockholders' concern with earnings and dividends conflicts somewhat with the managers' desire for maximum salary and bonus.

Organizations and Coalitions

Those people with personal interests exert pressure during the process of determining organizational goals. Stockholders insist on profits. Employees demand compensation. Customers expect acceptable quality and service. Society, through laws and public opinion, requires protection of the environment and promotion of the general welfare.

In view of the numerous people involved in the process of forming objectives, some have suggested that an organization should be thought of as a *coalition of interests*. In other words, organizational objectives in some way represent a consensus that has been hammered out in a manner acceptable to the various participants. It is, therefore, unrealistic to think that a manager sets objectives solely for the benefit of shareholders, totally apart from the consideration of other interests. This is simply impossible. Any manager who attempted to maximize profits by lowering wage rates or reducing quality would immediately experience severe opposition.

Managers, particularly top-level managers, play a unique role in the establishment of objectives. They must strike a balance among the various interests and participants. In other words, they must balance the pressures from the coalition members so that the continuing participation of each is assured.

Successful operation obviously entails at least a minimal integration of personal and organizational objectives. By contributing to the achievement of organizational goals, an employee must be able to realize at least some personal objectives. This does not suggest that there is perfect integration of personal goals and organizational goals. The social approval of peers, for example, may require an employee to adopt an antagonistic attitude toward the company and to curtail production.

The environment presents dangers and opportunities to the firm. By careful selection of objectives, management may exploit those opportunities and avoid those dangers. One value of organizational objectives, therefore, is proper orientation of the firm to its environment.

Values of Organizational Objectives

Objectives also provide a focus for policy making and for management decisions of other types. The various activities and policies—in production, sales, finance, and so on—should be directed to the achievement of these objectives. As an example, suppose that a chemical manufacturer desires to lead not only in the production of standard chemicals but also in research and the introduction of new products. The company's personnel policies and practices must provide for the recruitment and retention of creative scientists for its research laboratories. The financial planning of such a manufacturer must permit the investment of large amounts in research and facilities over a long period of time before a dollar is ever realized from these investments. Production planning must be sufficiently flexible and imaginative to adapt to new production techniques and to assist in the development of production processes for new products. Marketing personnel must be able to assess and develop markets to permit exploitation of new discoveries originating in the laboratory.

Clearly formulated objectives enable all parts of an organization to work toward the same goal. Production and sales departments need not work at cross purposes if there is a common objective. If production policies call for a product of high quality, advertising will not stress price to the exclusion of quality. Nor will prices be set on the basis of a competitor's inferior line of products.

Clear objectives also encourage a consistency in management, planning, and decision making over a period of time. Long-run goals caution against action that is merely expedient in a short run. Recognition of a basic objective thus provides a stabilizing force in monthly and yearly management decisions.

Objectives are often vague and not explicit. Every organization obviously has some sort of goals that have brought it into existence and that keep it operating. Merely implicit recognition of goals, however, involves the dangers of inconsistency, lack of coordination among departments, and temptation to compromise. If a student is not thoroughly committed to a college education, the attraction of a good job or marriage may easily sidetrack that individual.

**The Profit Goal
of the Firm**

**The Universal
Profit Objective**

A sign on the wall of a neighborhood restaurant reads, "This is a nonprofit organization—although we didn't plan it that way!" A business organization never plans it "that way." The firm is in business to earn a profit. Profit is basic to the philosophy of the free enterprise system. Adam Smith saw profits as the device which transforms the selfishness of mankind into channels of useful service. "It is not from the benevolence of the butcher, the brewer, or the baker that we expect our dinner," wrote Adam Smith, "but from their regard to their self-interest. We address ourselves, not to their humanity, but to their self-love, and never talk to them of our necessities, but of their advantages."

Profits are essential for survival in a competitive economic system. The profit objective is important, therefore, to all participants in an organization system. In the following statement, William S. Anderson, chief executive officer of NCR Corporation, explained the fundamental importance of profits to NCR:

> The profit which we shall be reporting this year is important beyond the dollars involved. The reason is that profitability is the best single measure of any company's health and vitality. A company which cannot earn a profit, or earns only a marginal profit, is a sick company. Its future is clouded and everyone connected with it has cause for worry—shareholders, employees and customers alike.[1]

It should be clear that profits are absolutely necessary for all participants, even though profits reward stockholders most directly. Profits compensate stockholders for the use of their capital and for the risk they assume in the particular venture.

**Importance of the
Profit Goal**

Consideration of factors that complicate profit maximizing should not be allowed to obscure the importance of the profit goal. The quest for profit is a powerful driving force in a free enterprise system.

Profit goals are typically the most explicitly formulated goals of the enterprise. In more detailed form, they comprise standards of performance for the management of the organization. The overall profit goal provides the basis for performance standards throughout the organization.

**The Service
Goal of the
Firm**

**Nature of the
Service Goal**

Emphasis upon the profit objective tends to obscure the existence of other goals of the enterprise. Every business has another objective that it must accomplish, however, in order to make its sales and realize its profits. An electric utility must supply electricity to justify the dollars of the utility customers. A manufacturer produces some physical product of value to other business firms or to ultimate consumers. An insurance company provides protection. Marketing institutions transport and store products and arrange for the transfer of ownership. Each type of business firm thus performs some useful function desired by its customers.

This objective appears clear as we think of the business organization from

---

[1] William S. Anderson, "1975 Will Test Resiliency of 'The New NCR,'" *NCR World* (November-December, 1974).

the standpoint of society. Our society permits the existence of organizations that are harmless or that perform some constructive role. It prohibits or outlaws organizations whose functions are considered detrimental to society. Business organizations have a claim to existence because of their contribution of goods or services.

The service objective exists not only generally—the goal of providing *some* useful product or service—but it takes specific form as the firm chooses to produce specific goods and services. At the most basic level, this entails decisions concerning overall *strategy*. What type of business firm should this firm try to be?

The Basic Strategy of the Firm

Careful formulation of overall business strategy is essential for survival and growth and deserves the close attention of top management. Otherwise, changes in the environment and industry may leave the company without a successful business. The problem is complicated because problems in basic business strategy are often obscured by more pressing current problems. In pursuing operating efficiency, management may fail to observe the decline in its industry or the need to develop new products.

An example of a strategic error is the decision of Xerox to enter the mainframe computer field.[2] The cost of keeping up with computer technology and selling in competition with IBM proved too great. In 1975, Xerox retired from the field after a six-year effort that netted less than 1 percent of the market. Xerox Chairman C. Peter McCulough explained that a substantial investment—between $150 million and $200 million—would have been required to reach the break-even point by 1980.

This example suggests the need for an aggressive and objective attitude on the part of management in selecting and scrutinizing long-run service objectives.

The firm's overall strategy or broad service objectives are general and provide little guidance for such activities as internal audit, production control, and personnel research. Because of this fact, the general objectives for the company as a whole must be broken down into more specific objectives for the different parts of the organization.

The Hierarchy of Objectives

The result of factoring general objectives into more and more specific objectives is a *hierarchy of objectives*. A given company objective may typically be accomplished in a number of ways. For example, a decision to manufacture or to purchase a component part establishes a manufacturing or purchasing objective for some unit or individual. The hierarchy thus constitutes a *means-end chain* whereby the "means" at a higher level become the "end" at the next lower level. An example of a means-end chain is in Figure 2–1.

At lower levels of the hierarchy, objectives become more specific and narrow. Departmental objectives become the goals of departmental personnel. It is difficult for departmental members to look beyond its goals to those of the broader organization—to take a truly "systems" view of the total firm. Sales personnel tend to think in terms of sales goals, research personnel in terms of research goals, and so on.

Interdepartmental Conflict

---

[2] "What Xerox Salvaged from Its Big Mistake," *Business Week,* no. 2392 (August 4, 1975): 26–28.

Figure 2-1   *A Means-End Chain for a Travel Agency*

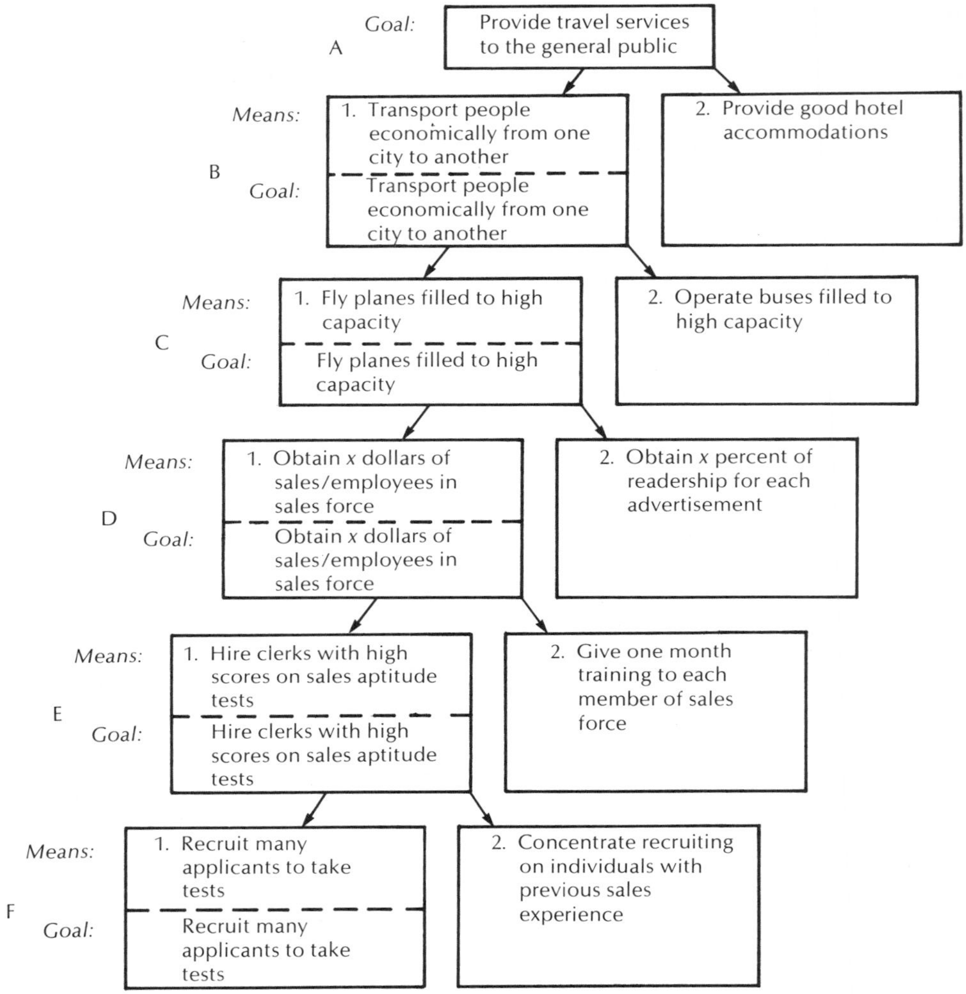

Source: Lyman W. Porter, Edward E. Lawler, and J. Richard Hackman, *Behavior in Organizations* (New York: McGraw-Hill Book Company, 1975), p. 84.

The limited departmental viewpoints that emerge tend to encourage inter-departmental rivalries. Further consideration of the problem of conflict and its resolution will occur later, particularly in Chapter 7.

Inversion of Ends and Means   One cause of interpartmental rivalry is the tendency of organizational members to substitute "means" for "ends." A specific "mean" becomes an end in itself, and the individual loses sight of the broader objective. A lower-level manager may become so committed to a particular procedure that following the procedure becomes more important than accomplishing a broader objective. This weakness accounts, at least partially, for excessive bureaucratic "red tape."

Inversion of "ends" and "means" is pathological and hampers realization of broader objectives. Top-level managers should continually do all in their power to direct attention to broader goals and to prevent the development of little "empires" at lower levels.

The service objective discussed previously is one type of social objective. However, we may think of social objectives in a much broader sense. The business corporation must recognize a responsibility to the community or the general public going far beyond the customers of the business. The *social responsibility* of business, as it is often termed, implies a sense of obligation toward the general public. This responsibility takes such forms as environmental protection, educational and philanthropic projects, community planning, equal employment opportunities, government service, and general operation in conformity with the public interest.

The Social Goal of the Firm

The Nature of Social Responsibility

Social responsibility of business has become a matter of evident concern to many business leaders. Business periodicals frequently carry articles regarding the business firm's social responsibility. There are, no doubt, numerous factors contributing to this growing interest in social obligations. The most obvious is the expansion of public regulation that prescribes standards of behavior in many areas—air pollution, minority hiring, honesty in advertising, campaign contributions, product warranties, employee safety, and so on. Encouraged by various spokesmen for the public interest—for example, Ralph Nader, the Sierra Club, and consumer interest groups—public opinion has become more critical and more demanding. The corporation's weakened ties with stockholders and the professionalization of management also contribute to the emphasis on objectives of this type. The corporate manager often finds that the expectations of the public and the employees are presented as forcefully as are the expectations of stockholders.

Growing Concern of Business Leaders

An example of social responsibility in action is the antipollution programs of Dow Chemical Company. Although this company had not eliminated all pollution, it received a *Business Week* Award for Business Citizenship in 1972 because of its great strides in improving the physical environment.

> In Dow's view, pollution is a wasted resource—valuable material dumped into the air and water or fed into costly treatment plants. The company is out to eliminate pollution at the source, by changing production processes and by recycling waste streams for further processing. So far, Dow has recovered enough valuable chemicals and boosted its process efficiencies so much that its abatement program is more than paying its own way.[3]

Justification for a sense of social responsibility on the part of business is grounded in the freedom that society accords to business. We may visualize the existence of a *social contract*. A business organization, like other legitimate organizations, is given freedom to exist and to work toward some legitimate

Justification for Social Responsibility

---

[3] "How Business Tackles Social Problems," *Business Week*, no. 2229 (May 20, 1972): 97.

objective. The payment for that freedom is the firm's contribution to society. Terms of the contract, moreover, are not permanent but change over time in the direction of reduced freedom for the firm and higher expectations regarding performance. Not all societies permit private enterprises to function freely, and society may expect, in return for this consideration, a performance consistent with general social goals.

> Today it is clear that the terms of the contract between society and business are, in fact, changing in substantial and important ways. Business is being asked to assume broader responsibilities to society than ever before and to serve a wider range of human values. Business enterprises, in effect, are being asked to contribute more to the quality of American life than just supplying quantities of goods and services. Inasmuch as business exists to serve society, its future will depend on the quality of management's response to the changing expectations of the public.[5]

There is a price for ignoring social responsibilities. Although business managers are at times tempted to concentrate upon the profit objective to the exclusion of service and social objectives, this path can lead to difficulty. There is always the threat of government control in the background. In a broader sense, the future of business is entwined with the future of society. Decay in society does not lead to health in business. In recognizing social responsibilities, then, management is not disregarding the best interests of business owners. The assumption of at least minimal social responsibilities represents an act of "enlightened self-interest" by corporate management.

Practical Limitations in Corporate Social Responsibility

In the ideal world of perfect competition, profits could be realized only by meticulous regard for the service and social objectives of a business. Dollars of customers would go to the firms that best met the customers' desires for goods and services. As a matter of fact, however, the economy is not that competitive. Business concerns can profit at the expense of the customer. Business organizations may also, at least in the short run, disregard the social consequences of their actions. In the absence of specific statutes, they may pollute streams or manipulate employees. To some degree, then, business management has a choice regarding objectives.

As explained earlier in this chapter, management must see that all inside and outside participants (including the general public and government) realize their minimum expectations. Refusal to shoulder any type of social obligations would produce weaknesses in the coalition of parties involved in the business. Flagrant disregard of customer wishes, for example, would lose business or lead to the emergence of new competition. A callous disregard of social values might prejudice customers and employees against the firm. Some regard for social objectives, therefore, is simply good business.

It would simplify matters greatly if this consistency of goals were always real and evident. Unfortunately, the business firm can be successful with various degrees of social conscience. Management faces a range of alternative be-

---

⁵*Social Responsibilities of Business Corporations* (New York: Committee for Economic Development, 1971), p. 16.

havior and must choose the extent to which various, sometimes conflicting, goals will be recognized.

A realistic view of managerial discretion must recognize the real limitations faced by managers of business firms. These profit-seeking firms operate in a competitive environment and cannot function as philanthropic institutions. If one firm in an industry assumes heavy social costs that are not assumed by its competitors, it may bankrupt itself. Some degree of public regulation is required to eliminate competitive advantages otherwise obtainable by those firms disregarding social obligations.

In summary, management has no simple rule of thumb to follow. Management must meet minimum statutory requirements and normally has the freedom to pursue additional social goals. At the same time, economic realities—competition and costs—impose limits to the firm's social response.

Business activity, as a part of life, poses ethical problems for management. Personal life and business life cannot be neatly compartmentalized with respect to moral judgments. The manager's standards of right and wrong must apply to both areas.

In the wake of Watergate, people questioned the ethical standards and behavior in many areas of society. Business organizations and business managers did not escape such observation and judgment. Unethical behavior of many business leaders was exposed and widely reported in the news media. The significance of these flaws in contemporary business behavior is emphasized in these comments of Max Lerner:

> The predators used to be the swaggering piratical captains of industry; they have now become the managerial heads of impersonal corporations, conglomerates, multinationals. Doubtless, what they do is not so vicious as what the faceless bureaucrats of closed societies do. But the question still lingers, what shall it profit a civilization if it builds its industrial empires but loses its sense of moral direction.[5]

Ethics in Management

Ethics and Business Activity

Problems of ethical behavior are widespread and exist at all levels of our business institutions. The spotlight shifts over time from one sensitive area to another—from conflicts of interest to industrial espionage to tampering with the system of government regulation. From time to time, such issues erupt into national and even international scandals. In the aftermath of Watergate, executives of major corporations admitted illegal contributions of millions of corporate dollars to political campaigns. In July of 1973, for example, American Airlines publicly admitted that $55,000 of the $75,000 in cash that its officials contributed to the Committee to Re-elect the President was actually corporate money. American's chairman was quoted as saying that such sub rosa corporate financing of contributions supposedly orginating from their employees is so common that it "creates a significant national problem." [6] Others that acknowledged illegal contributions included Ashland Oil, Gulf Oil, Phillips

The Pervasive Problem of Business Ethics

---

[5] Max Lerner, "The Shame of the Professions," *Saturday Review,* 3, no. 3 (November 1, 1975): 12.
[6] "The Detectives Hunt for Illegal Givers," *Business Week,* no. 2288 (July 14, 1973): 27–28.

Petroleum, Braniff Airways, Goodyear Tire and Rubber Company, and Minnesota Mining and Manufacturing Company.

In 1975, a number of major corporations disclosed payoffs running into millions of dollars to foreign officials or political parties. United Brands allegedly paid $1.25 million to a high official in Honduras to get its taxes reduced. Gulf Oil, Northrop, and Exxon also made disclosures of overseas payoffs. The identity of these companies makes it clear that ethical issues plague even blue-chip corporations.

Individual scandals are, if anything, even more spectacular. One of the most infamous swindles of modern times was that of Robert Vesco, a "modern buccaneer on the high seas of international finance."[7] His looting of Investors Overseas Services (IOS), an international mutual fund, was described as the "greatest act of piracy of all time."

> Robert Vesco bought politicians, he bought lawyers, he bought accountants, and he bought businessmen. He bought the President's nephew and he tried to buy the President. His largess brought two cabinet officers to a trial at which the Chairman of the Securities and Exchange Commission confessed to having committed perjury five times. Ultimately, he bought the President of Costa Rica, where he now resides.[8]

Ethical issues are by no means limited to the major corporations or their chief executives who make the headlines. Instead, they permeate the entire structure of industry, as they no doubt permeate all human relationships.

We should not allow a review of the tragedies in business morality to obscure the ethical behavior which does exist. Without doubt, much business behavior is commendable and representative of high ethical standards. The purpose of these examples has been to develop an awareness of the serious and pervasive nature of ethical issues. There is obviously great opportunity for improvement in ethical performance generally.

Thorny Nature of Ethical Questions

There is a tendency to oversimplify the nature of ethical problems in business organizations. Frequently, we see decisions as involving simple choices between right and wrong, black and white. As a matter of fact, decisions with ethical overtones are often considerably more complex. The "right" decision from an ethical standpoint may indeed be hazy. Often there are conflicts in values, and the manager perceives different obligations which seem to conflict in their implications.

It has been argued, for example, that investment decisions should consider issues of social responsibility. If a corporation acts in an antisocial manner, institutions holding such stock should presumably bring pressure on its management. However, it is difficult to evaluate issues of this type. Should Xerox be commended for its job training of disadvantaged workers and aid to ghetto business or condemned for doing business in South Africa?[9] Another type of

---

[7] Ray Dirks, "Master Swindlers at Work," *Business and Society Review* (Spring, 1975): 99.

[8] *Ibid.*, p. 98.

[9] For a discussion of the complexity of moral choices in portfolio management, see Burton G. Malkiel and Richard E. Quandt, "Moral Issues in Investment Policy," *Harvard Business Review* 49, no. 2 (March-April, 1971): 37–47.

dilemma confronts the manager who must decide whether to lay off an older, less efficient employee or a younger employee with greater skill and vigor.

In addition, it is difficult for the manager to be free from bias and prejudice and to look at issues objectively. In spite of good intentions, the individual becomes involved in the situation and becomes identified with certain positions or points of view. It becomes difficult to step back and to take a detached point of view in examining the issue from an ethical standpoint.

Guidelines for Ethical Action

The law provides the minimum ethical standard. The question of ethics is often discussed in terms of deviations from the law. Some have urged a shift from a negative to a more positive point of view through the adoption of ethical standards known as *codes of ethics*. Throughout the years, various groups have worked at the task of developing such codes, generally applicable to particular industrial groups. How valuable codes of ethics are in lifting the standards of business conduct is a matter of question. They apparently summarize accepted standards at a given time, but they tend toward generality and are not available for use by most managers.

In the murky areas that present moral dilemmas, the manager may sense a special need for guidelines. The statements in Figure 2–2 have been proposed to guide managers in a number of the "gray" areas of contemporary business.

Guidelines for Eight Gray Areas   **Figure 2–2**

1. THE INCOMPLETE DISCLOSURE.   Provide more information rather than less, even if it goes beyond what the Securities & Exchange Commission and other agencies require. Put yourself in the investor's place and ask, "What do I want to know?" The SEC keeps requiring fuller disclosure, and failure to disclose can bring a suit.
2. THE CORRUPT BOSS.   Many middle managers have gotten into serious trouble—and a few have wound up in jail—by caving in to a boss who cared more about ends than means. Speak up as soon as you are faced with an ethical problem; you may set things straight. "If you can't, get out," says a Xerox director.
3. THE CORRUPT SUBORDINATE.   As a senior man, don't worry about rocking the boat, just get rid of him. A tolerant, "nice guy" attitude can put both of you in trouble. And his misdeeds can infect his co-workers.
4. THE INADVERTENT REMARK.   Think twice about what you tell anyone about your business—at lunch, in the locker room, over the bridge table. A chance remark might get you nailed for leaking company secrets. And the law about passing "inside information" is vague. You could wind up in a courtroom.
5. THE 'PURIFIED' IDEA.   You can usually find a lawyer or a CPA who will endorse a questionable idea or plan—especially if you phrase it just the right way. Just remember, the plan is still questionable and it can get you in trouble.
6. THE PASSIVE DIRECTOR.   Whether you are an inside or an outside director, don't just sit back silent and rubber-stamp management. You can be sued, and the courts take a hard line nowadays on director liability. "Speak up or drop out," says one man who has served on 11 boards.
7. THE EXPENSE-ACCOUNT VACATION.   Go easy on tax deductions

for combination business-pleasure trips. Deduct for your wife only if she is actually involved in your business. . . .

8. THE STOCK OPTION TRAP.   Beware of "fast" option transactions—buying and selling your company's stock within the six-month trading rule period for insiders. More businessmen are getting tripped up on this one.

Source: "Stiffer Rules for Business Ethics," *Business Week,* no. 2324 (March 30, 1974): 88.

Foundation for Business Ethics

Ethical values in the business world reflect the ideals and standards of the society of which it is a part. Each culture has a distinctive system of moral values. It is impossible, therefore, to divorce questions of business ethics from the traditions and standards of the larger culture. It is unlikely that the general level of ethical standards in business conduct will differ in any substantial way from the ethical standards observed in nonbusiness areas of society. In considering business ethics, therefore, we are dealing with only one part of the broader issue of ethical standards in society.

In the United States, there are generally accepted ethical concepts and traditions that are associated, in their origin at least, with our religious life. They are sometimes described as our *Judeo-Christian heritage.* The dignity and importance of the individual are basic elements of this creed. While some people consider religious ideas and theological concepts as the rationalization of accepted practice, it is also possible to see them as the conceptual basis for ethical behavior. In a provocative article, "Can the Businessman Apply Christianity?", Harold L. Johnson has suggested that the historic Christian doctrines can furnish a foundation for business ethics.[10] He holds that these doctrines provide a perspective from which to view modern commercial life and a frame of reference in making decisions.

As an example of Johnson's reasoning, consider the concept of God as a personal, transcendent Being closely associated with human life. The significance of this concept is to place everything human under the rule of God, warning against the idolatry of putting the business firm or career at the center of life. The doctrine of creation holds that material things are not evil and provides a concept for stewardship. In fact, Johnson suggests that this doctrine furnishes a part of the religious foundation for the philosophy of the social responsibility of the businessman. The Christian view of the nature of man reveals his weaknesses, serving as a warning to ambitious executives and against an inflated view of their own abilities. It warns managers at all levels that self-interest and pride may be woven into decisions believed to be objective. It also cautions against excessive optimism that human relations and social responsibility can bring the heavenly city here on earth by teaching that all, including ourselves, have the taint of sin.

Although there is no monolithic code of ethics in society, some of the general cultural values condition the viewpoint of most managers. In view of the diversity in this area of our culture, however, there is still a principle of individual responsibility and choice. An executive may follow ethical standards

---

[10] Harold L. Johnson, "Can the Businessman Apply Christianity?" *Harvard Business Review* 35, no. 5 (September-October, 1957): 68–76.

that are regarded as either more or less acceptable in terms of generally prevailing beliefs. Although the individual manager cannot be completely indifferent to generally accepted standards, managerial choices must also reflect his or her personal code. The individual's personal values and beliefs are thus of prime importance, and they deserve serious study and careful choice.[11]

Summary

Organizational objectives express the purposes or goals of the firm. To some extent, they reflect a *coalition of interests,* a consensus among the various participants, who are all motivated by *personal goals.* Establishing organizational objectives benefits the firm in a number of ways. For example, management provides a basis for decision making and for teamwork among departments and individuals by establishing organizational goals.

The *profit objective* is a basic objective essential for both stockholders and all other participants. The *service objective* specifies the services and products to be provided to customers and, at the most basic level, entails decisions regarding *business strategy.* Overall service objectives are broken down into a *hierarchy of objectives,* and the resultant departmental objectives are sometimes followed so narrowly that they create *interdepartmental conflict.* The *social objective,* which defines the firm's responsibility to the general public, is a matter of growing concern to business leaders.

Business activities involve numerous *ethical* questions. They are frequently complex, involving more than a simple choice between right and wrong. *Codes of ethics* have been established by some groups in an attempt to provide positive statements to serve as a guide for business behavior. The foundation of ethical action is to be found in the spiritual values of our culture and religious life.

Discussion Questions

1. In what sense did the success of foreign automobile manufacturers in gaining a share of the U.S. market depend upon goal-setting errors by U.S. managers?

2. In what way does a clearly stated objective enable all parts of an organization to work effectively together?

3. What is the relationship of the *profit objective* of a business concern to its *social responsibilities?*

4. One well-known business executive said (speaking of his corporation), "We feel strongly that we must support our private colleges and universities and that in so doing we are serving our company's interest." What type of objective is he expressing, and how is it related to other objectives?

5. Why doesn't the corporation whose management exhibits the finest sense of social responsibility always earn the highest profits?

---

[11] The fact that beliefs and values are matters of individual choice and commitment does not make all beliefs equally valid. However, the discussion of personal faith is beyond the scope of this book. For reasoned presentations of the Christian faith, involving a minimum of theological jargon, see the following: C. S. Lewis, *Mere Christianity* (New York: Macmillan Publishing Company, 1960) or Paul Little, *Know Why You Believe* (Downers Grove, Ill.: InterVarsity Press, 1968).

6. Could an insurance sales representative simultaneously have two *goals*—a personal desire for a commission and a concern for the customer's security?

7. In your opinion, what would be the most powerful personal objectives of a corporate executive earning $500,000 annually?

8. Why can't business managers agree as to what is *ethical* or *unethical behavior*?

9. Of what value is a *code of ethics*?

Supplementary Reading

Crawford, C. Merle. "Strategies for New Product Development." *Business Horizons* 15, no. 6 (December, 1972): 49–58.

Hays, Douglas A. "Management Goals in a Crisis Society." *Michigan Business Review* 22, no. 5 (November, 1970): 7–11.

Lodge, George Cabot. "Business and the Changing Society." *Harvard Business Review* 52, no. 2 (March–April, 1974): 59–72.

McGuire, Joseph W., ed. *Contemporary Management: Issues and Viewpoints*, Chapter 7. Englewood Cliffs, N.J.: Prentice-Hall, Inc., 1974.

Purcell, Theodore. "A Practical Guide to Ethics in Business." *Business and Society*, no. 13 (Spring, 1975): 43–50.

"Watergating on Main Street: What is Happening to Ethical Standards in America?" *Saturday Review* 3, no. 3 (November 1, 1975): 10–27.

Case 2

Ashland's Political Contributions

Ashland Oil, Inc., the country's largest independent refiner and marketer of petroleum products, admitted on June 27, 1975, that the company had made almost $500,000 in questionable payments, over an eight-year period, to consultants and government officials in Gabon, Nigeria, the Dominican Republic, Libya, and perhaps other countries. The company said that in some instances the money may have been used for "unlawful political contributions." This disclosure also followed a seven-month study by a special committee of the board of directors.

The company also announced that three officials, including the chairman, Orin E. Atkins, had agreed to pay Ashland $325,000 as reimbursement for illegal political contributions in the United States. Mr. Atkins had earlier pleaded "no contest" to similar charges and paid a fine of $1,000.

Mr. Atkins will be permitted to repay the total of $175,000 over a five-year period. The board also unanimously resolved that no changes be made in company management. Much of the company's recent growth, according to the company's statement, was attributed to the forceful leadership of Mr. Atkins.

Ashland's solution to the case differed from actions taken by some firms in similar situations. In some companies, top management officials have taken early retirement following revelation of illegal political contributions and overseas slush funds. For example, several officials left the Minnesota Mining and Manufacturing Company following a political funding scandal.

The Ashland board also adopted a series of committee recommendations, one of which was a policy against future illegal payments of any kind.

1. A number of oil companies in addition to Ashland admitted making illegal payments ("bribes") in foreign countries. They argued it was the only way they could do business in some countries because of prevailing business standards in those countries. To what extent should a multinational corporation adapt to the "system" in a particular country?

2. How serious do you regard the domestic illegal political contributions? How well did the chairman, Mr. Atkins, understand that Ashland was an open system?

3. What is your evaluation of Ashland's solution to the problem?

4. How do you anticipate that other managers of Ashland will react to the decisions of Ashland's board of directors?

Questions

Objectives

1. Justify the importance attached to the corporate planning function.
2. Explain the relationship of *strategic planning* to business success and point out the relevant factors in determining strategy.
3. Identify the elements of *comprehensive corporate planning* and explain its relationship to the systems concept.
4. Identify the most significant *planning premises* required in current corporate planning and show their implications for planning.
5. Outline the stages in *creative thinking* and point out some approaches to stimulating creativity.

Chapter

Making Operating Plans

Nature and Importance of Planning
Nature of Strategic Planning
Comprehensive Corporate Planning
Planning Premises
Creativity and Business Planning

Case: Strategy in the Soft-Drink Business

Planning begins with decisions about strategy, but it does not end there. Company strategy must be distilled into an interlocking set of long-range and short-range operating plans. In this chapter, we examine the planning process and also the development of creativity—a factor which contributes significantly to the quality of plans.

Nature and Importance of Planning

Growing Emphasis on Planning

The increasing tempo of environmental change—from energy shortage to economic crises—has drawn attention to the need for anticipating developments and planning to meet them. Managers today often face markets and competitive situations that are more turbulent and changeable than ever before. A company and its management must "run fast" just to stay even with competition.

In striving for progress and even survival in such a fast-changing business world, managers try to assess the future and to meet it as rationally as possible. Business planning becomes increasingly attractive with the growing uncertainties and perplexities in the business environment. The major question is not whether to plan but how to plan most effectively.

Nature of Planning

Planning involves thought and decision concerning a proposed course of action. It entails the selection of a given path to the future from the various possible alternatives. It is an intellectual process preceding the activity being planned.

Planning is a continuing activity of management. Managers never reach a point at which they stop planning. This does not mean, however, that they never complete work on specific plans. The budget for a given year may be adopted, but the manager who approves it must immediately turn to other planning and must soon begin consideration of the budget for the following year.

Plans are directed to the accomplishment of some objective or to the solution of some problem confronting the organization. Overall planning is concerned with broad company objectives. Departmental planning is directed to the achievement of subsidiary goals which contribute to realization of the company's more fundamental objectives. At each level of the organization, some planning occurs, and it is concerned with the specific mission of the particular organizational component.

Importance and Neglect of Planning

Many writers and business managers have given lip service, at least, to the importance of planning. In theory, we can see that it has a unique role in the performance of other managerial functions. Of course, the various functions are interrelated in that no one function can exist without the others. Furthermore, operating experience and data collected in connection with the control function are used extensively in subsequent planning. However, planning is necessary before any intelligent consideration can be given to organizational relationships, staffing, direction, or control. Although defective performance in any area is undesirable, planning errors go to the very heart of the organization. Serious mistakes or omissions in planning can hardly be offset by effective organizing or controlling.

The profit advantage of good planning is conceptually appealing, therefore, but it must be taken somewhat on faith. Empirical evidence is limited. One bit of evidence is found in a few local studies of failing small firms which have consistently revealed deficiencies in planning.

In spite of its primacy, planning is perhaps the most easily neglected of all managerial functions. It is a rare manager who does not become too busy. The natural reaction is to devote time to those activities clamoring for attention. March and Simon have suggested a "Gresham's Law" of planning in which daily routine drives out planning.[1] During periods of recession, executives are frequently tempted to divert attention from managing to selling. Although direct participation in selling may be necessary, the neglect of planning is unfortunate. An example is the experience of Samuel B. Casey, Jr., the president and chief executive officer of Pullman, Inc., who described the consequences as follows:

> "Most of my time should be spent on strategic planning," Casey notes. But with sales-related efforts now consuming 50% of his work day, twice as much as three years ago, "Planning has been pushed to the back burner," he says. "It's a tragedy."[2]

The negative effects of neglected planning are not always apparent in the short run. In fact, the business may proceed from month to month and year to year with little outward indication of its weakness in planning. Eventually, however, and often disastrously, management deficiencies in planning are revealed.

As part of its basic planning function, management establishes objectives and policies, which serve as *standing plans* and provide a basic framework within which operational planning occurs. The development of business strategy objectives—which define the basic shape or nature of a firm—is discussed in the following section of this chapter.

Standing Plans

A policy might be defined as *a basic statement serving as a guide for administrative action.* By saying it is a guide, there is an implication that the policy does not usually specify detailed answers to particular problems. The manager has some degree of freedom.[3] As an example, a policy that says "No discrimination in hiring" does not dictate the employment choice. It simply eliminates one factor as an element in the choice. It would still be desirable to analyze the ability of all candidates.

Some policies are particulary concerned with the "how" of administrative action.[4] By establishing an objective, as explained earlier, the organization determines its destination. Many policies are concerned with the route for reaching that destination. In other cases, objectives gain substance as they find ex-

---

[1]James G. March and Herbert A. Simon, *Organizations* (New York: John Wiley & Sons, Inc., 1958), p. 185.

[2]"Executive Suite Salesmanship," *Business Week*, no. 2403 (October 20, 1975): 70.

[3]In contrast, a *rule*—such as "no smoking"—permits no discretion regarding action to be taken.

[4]A policy establishes general guidelines, in contrast to a *procedure*, which specifies the chronological sequence of steps or tasks.

pression in policies. Personnel objectives, for example, are abstract statements until they become embodied in concrete policies.

Nature of Strategic Planning

The Nature of Strategy

The service objective of a firm is expressed in its basic *strategy* or *strategic plan*. In developing business strategy, managers are basically answering the question, "What type of business shall we be?" At the most general level, *strategic decisions* are concerned with such issues as breadth of product line, geographical scope, industry position, extent of vertical integration, and orientation toward growth.

By strategic decision making, top management determines the position of the firm relative to its environment. At any given time, the firm's orientation to the environment may be described as its *strategic posture*. Changes in this posture require redeployment of the firm's assets into new configurations. Strategic decisions express the firm's most basic purposes and the direction it wishes to take in relating to and serving the society of which it is a part.

If such decisions are to be made intelligently, they must be based upon an assessment of trends and changes in the firm's environment. In particular, the corporate strategist is concerned with market trends, competitive strategies, and the implications of these factors for the future of the firm.

Importance of Business Strategy

In a competitive industry, a particular firm positions itself relative to the market and competitors by its basic strategy. In view of this fact, the importance of strategic choices is clear. Good strategy will provide an opportunity for survival and growth. Poor strategy will doom a firm to decline, deterioration, and eventual death.

In the recent history of American business, there are numerous examples of both successful and unsuccessful strategy. The Penn Central bankruptcy case is an example of failure in determining strategy.

> At 5:00 p.m. on a Sunday afternoon, the once mighty Penn Central, with billions in assets, declared bankruptcy. In their short-run rush to become a conglomerate, the management of Penn Central seemed to have forgotten how to run a railroad. The financial drain caused by this departure from *long-run* strategy resulted in collapse.
>
> On the other hand, Union Pacific was able to diversify while maintaining a fundamental strategy committed to the railroad business. The result has been a record of successful operations.[5]

Environmental and Resource Factors

Environmental conditions provide the badckground for strategic decisions. As changes occur in the environment, conditions become more or less favorable for particular strategies.

The other important set of factors is the resources of the firm. Resources—whether they are financial, human, or otherwise—may presumably be used in any of various ways. In choosing a business strategy, the manager decides

---

[5] From the book, *Corporate Management in Crisis: Why the Mighty Fall* by Joel E. Ross and Michael J. Kami. © 1973 by Prentice-Hall, Inc. Published by Prentice-Hall, Inc., Englewood Cliffs, New Jersey.

upon the environmental opportunities to which resources may be most profitably applied.

Of all the types of decisions required in business operation, strategic decisions involve the greatest uncertainty. Their complexity grows out of the possibility of their changing the firm's relationship to the environment. More routine decisions accept the basic framework of the firm as given and thereby reduce the area of uncertainty. The environment with its changing patterns at times almost defies prediction and intelligent forecasting.

Uncertainty and Judgment

This does not mean that the strategist lacks any data whatsoever. It does mean that the issues are typically fuzzy and the best strategy is unclear. As a result, the manager must use more subjective judgment than is required for more routine decisions.

Approaches to long-range planning differ greatly from one corporation to another. In recent years, there has been a shift from informal planning "by reaction" to comprehensive formal planning programs designed to improve profitability and assure future success. This section examines the nature of the modern planning approach used by our leading corporations.

Comprehensive Corporate Planning

Comprehensive long-run planning begins with a consideration of business strategy. As discussed in the preceding section, top management must decide what type of company they aspire to have in the light of existing opportunities and limitations.

Steps in Comprehensive Long-Range Planning

The second step of long-range planning involves the preparation of production, facilities, marketing, manpower, and financial plans on a department-by-department basis. Preparation of these plans requires forecasts of economic conditions and a projection of other probable developments. An evaluation of existing conditions affecting the firm is also basic to this step in planning.

Following formulation of departmental plans, a step of integration must be taken. It is this step that produces a truly comprehensive plan rather than a set of contradictory plans. Each departmental plan must be questioned as to its contribution to established objectives. Each must also be examined to determine its compatibility with other plans of the corporation. If six departments each propose to spend one million dollars and only three million dollars is available, changes are imperative.

The planning cycle is completed as plans are implemented and results analyzed. Results become inputs into the planning process and improve planning for subsequent periods.

A recent example of the introduction of comprehensive corporate planning is provided by Phillips Petroleum Company of Bartlesville, Oklahoma.[6] Although Phillips ranks only tenth in the industry in size, it had, by the late 1960s, become one of the country's most diversified oil companies. In addition

Example: An Introduction of Comprehensive Corporate Planning

---

[6] "Phillips Gets Its Growth Under Control," *Business Week.* no. 2270 (March 10, 1973): 164–66.

to producing oil, the company also produced chemicals, plastic products, and synthetic fibers.

Unfortunately, profits failed to materialize as hoped. As the company entered the 1970s, its earnings were the same as they had been a decade earlier. However, sales and assets had nearly doubled during the same period. The company found that it had too many service stations, too little crude oil, and too many losing ventures.

Although the company engaged in planning, the planning—basically departmental—was inadequate and deficient. Each department submitted annual capital plans, but the plans lacked adequate financial and market analysis. What long-range planning occurred was vague and directionless.

To avoid repetition of earlier mistakes, Phillips created a corporate planning and budgeting committee in 1971. This committee screens and integrates departmental plans. It also oversees a five-year plan designed to keep capital spending focused on long-term objectives. One part of this long-range plan has involved a shift of capital spending from manufacturing and marketing to exploration and production.

The shift in emphasis has started to pay big dividends. By 1976, Phillips was expected to be producing more than double what it produced in 1973—a result of recent discoveries. After three years of decline, earnings turned around in 1971 and were up by 12 percent in 1972. The improved planning introduced by Phillips' management seems to have been a key element in this transformation.

The Systems Concept in Planning

The systems concept in planning highlights the relationships between the corporate system (that is, the business firm) and its environmental systems. In particular, the relationship of the firm with the social, economic, and industrial systems in which it functions becomes important in developing long-range and short-range plans. The fact that the business firm is part of larger systems calls for careful adjustment of plans and strategy to the environmental systems.

The type of comprehensive corporate planning now employed by many modern business corporations, integrating and coordinating departmental plans, uses the systems concept. Departmental plans which individually appear logical may, when considered collectively, exceed the resources of the company or entail other inconsistencies. Comprehensive planning produces an internally consistent hierarchy of plans, starting with the broad plans for the total enterprise and including the supporting specific and detailed operational plans.

The concept of *suboptimization* is pertinent to the practice of planning for the entire system. It is possible for a given department to optimize its output by reducing the efficiency of other departments or other functions. Optimizing credit department operations, for example, would reduce sales by imposing very high credit standards. Simultaneous optimization of all departments may be impossible. The ideal combination of plans calls for optimization of company-wide operations. This often necessitates suboptimization—that is, operating at less than ideal conditions in particular departments—in order that the overall operations of the entire company might be optimized.

The planner is confronted with numerous uncertainties in the business environment. Some of these are external to the firm and beyond the control of its management. The health of the economy represents one such factor. Planning, of necessity, involves some consideration of these factors. What would be good planning based upon one premise becomes unwise if this premise proves to be wrong. Effective planning, thus, requires an awareness and accurate identification of the planning premises.

Classifying these as premises or assumptions does not indicate that they are accepted blindly or picked out of thin air. Premises involve predictions, and the predictions should be made as scientifically as possible. In some cases, of course, they can be little more than educated guesses.

One of the primary assumptions required for business planning concerns the role of government and public policy. The general attitude of government is often viewed by corporate management as "friendly" or "unfriendly" to business. An unfriendly administration may act less favorably toward business in any number of ways. It is possible, of course, that popular thinking may exaggerate the magnitude of political differences as far as their practical effect on business is concerned. Assessment of this attitude is made, explicitly or implicitly, by the reflective business planner.

In 1966, the Pittston Company, a diversified company producing both coal and oil, was described as hesitant to expand its coal mining business. The reason for the hesitancy was not the industry's prospects, which looked good at the time, but rather Pittston Chairman Joseph P. Routh's assessment of the political situation.

> Routh says he is uncertain because of "the political climate." He thinks the coal industry needs higher prices, but he's afraid President Lyndon Johnson's attitude toward business may restrict profits growth. "If President Johnson continues punitive action," he complains, "the outlook is bad for all businesses. I call it 'killing the goose that lays the golden egg.'"
>
> As the unquestioned boss of Pittston, 72-year-old Joe Routh clearly has the power to hold back expansion until the political situation is more to his liking. Whether he is *right* to hold back is very much an open question. "We're shifting emphasis from oil to coal," he insists. But, as things now stand, he seems to be referring to a mood, not a deed.[7]

Business conditions and the business cycle are of interest to almost every businessman. With an upswing in business activity, most firms tend to prosper. A severe recession, on the other hand, can reduce profits or result in financial losses.

Planning must anticipate probable economic conditions in selecting the best course of action for the future. In fact, the planner's interest is not limited to short-run economic conditions. Long-run business prospects and the rate of economic growth for the economy and for specific industries are important to many decisions. Expansion plans involving major commitments, for example, must be based upon predictions of this type. The tremendous error of Sewell

Planning Premises

Nature of Planning Premises

Public Policy

Economic Conditions

---

[7] "I Was Proved Wrong," *Forbes* 97, no. 3 (February 1, 1966): 25.

Avery of Montgomery Ward in financial and expansion policy following World War II is now a legend in the history of American business. While its competitor, Sears, Roebuck and Company, expanded, Montgomery Ward guarded its cash and waited for a depression.

Fashion Trends   Among the many other external factors affecting business planning is that of fashion trends. The seriousness of this factor varies, obviously, from one type of business to another. Its influence often exists, however, in industries that have the appearance of immunity to fashion change. If the product being produced or sold is subject to rapid fashion obsolescence, an error in planning can be critical. The warehouse may quickly be filled with items that are no longer in style.

Fashion trends, then, pose a real challenge to the business planner. Though sometimes difficult to fathom, they can hardly be ignored. Fortunately for the planner, there is a regularity in fashion changes that makes some prediction possible. Although changes in fashion often appear whimsical, studies have shown a remarkable regularity in such changes in various product areas.

> To the businessman who is baffled or frustrated by this problem of rapidly shifting tastes, I would say that product planning does not have to be a guessing game. All of the fashion cycles that have been measured are surprisingly regular and very long.[8]

Other External Factors   Various other external conditions or factors are subject to change and demand assumptions of some type as the basis for planning. Competitors' plans and activities constitute one such factor. If a competitor succeeds in introducing an improved or a revolutionary new product, the market for conventional or unimproved items is clearly reduced. Sales promotion campaigns of one competitor may likewise take business away from other firms. By the same token, weaknesses in competition provide opportunities that may be exploited through planning.

Raw materials and labor markets are also significant in business planning. Anticipated price increases or shortages in raw materials, for example, may lead to planned stockpiling. Provisions being written into major labor contracts and general trends in personnel practices affect expectations of personnel in most companies. If wages in other companies are going up on the average of 5 percent, it may be unrealistic to budget on the basis of stable labor costs.

Population trends and shifts to urban (or suburban) living likewise affect planning by many types of concerns. Many firms find their location planning strongly affected by the shifting residential patterns of the population.

No doubt, numerous other factors having a significant effect on the planning process could be cited. These are merely suggested as some of the basic elements requiring attention by most concerns.

---

[8] Dwight E. Robinson, "Style Changes: Cyclical, Inexorable, and Forseeable," *Harvard Business Review* 53, no. 6 (November-December, 1975): 121.

Effective planning calls for an imaginative approach to the solution of business problems. Traditional thinking can do little more than perpetuate the status quo. Stimulation of creativity within the firm, therefore, should contribute directly to the planning process.

Creativity involves new ideas, new approaches, and new combinations of existing knowledge. It stands in sharp contrast to memorization of facts and learning of detail devised by others. Business and organizational problems may be solved by the process of creative thinking. In doing so, the individual mind is directed to an understanding of the problem and to an imaginative search for a practical solution. Rather than taking an obvious explanation, the creative individual is always questioning, probing for a deeper understanding, and seeking a better way.

It is obvious that the capacity for creative thinking is not uniformly distributed. It is likely, however, that most individuals have greater potential for original and imaginative thinking than is ever exploited. Development and use of the creative talent of ordinary individuals is necessary to avoid the scandalous waste of this resource.

Some individuals have demonstrated great inventiveness and an unusual ability to develop ideas that had never occurred to others. Their combination of an able mind and diligent work has resulted in notable and praiseworthy achievements. We look at such outstanding characters with admiration and a little awe, often failing to realize there is a little of that potential within each of us, and also unaware of the hard work behind many of their achievements. By observing them—Kettering, Steinmetz, Le Tourneau, Salk, and the like—we derive not only inspiration but also some idea of the nature of creative activity.

Some who have studied the process of creative thinking have suggested the existence of steps or stages in the development of a new idea. The "flash of genius" may be preceded by other stages that are less obvious to an observer. Although these stages may be described in various ways, the following will suggest their general nature:

1. Problem discovery
2. Investigation
3. Incubation
4. Insight
5. Verification

In *problem discovery*, the individual becomes aware of some particular difficulty or need. Although it might seem that all should share this ability in common—that of sensing or detecting problems—some are more sensitive to the existence of problems than are others. The possibility for product improvement, as an example, may be visualized as a problem by the unusually perceptive individual. Another may be totally unaware of such a problem. This realization of need for a solution or improvement launches the creative thinker. A production manager, for example, may become concerned with the need for improving some part of the production process.

In the second stage, the individual turns to an *investigation* of the facts. This step may merely entail a mental re-examination of present knowledge about the subject. It may also involve a more systematic search of literature, past experience, and various other sources. This is the fact-gathering part of the process.

In the *incubation* stage, the mind reflects upon the problem and related material. At this point, it is difficult to hurry a solution. If a solution is not immediately apparent, the problem solver may leave the problem and return to it later. Often, the mind considers the matter only subconsciously. While the individual is busy at other pursuits, the mind may return with some new question or thought about the problem at hand.

If the creative process is completed, a moment of illumination occurs. The pieces may suddenly fit together. This stage of "seeing the light" or acquiring *insight* often occurs quickly. The individual may awaken in the middle of the night with a clear understanding of some baffling problem. Sometimes it is difficult to record with sufficient speed the ideas coming with this insight into the problem and its solution.

It is necessary to check out or *verify* the ideas that have occurred in the preceding stage. Merely devising a solution does not guarantee that it will be a good one in all respects. If the plan or idea appears basically sound, it is "debugged" and modified as necessary for effective use. Additional cycles of creative thinking may be required in adapting and applying the original idea. If this stage of verification is neglected, the result may be a fascinating but impractical idea.

Stimulating Creativity

Recruitment of personnel who are unusually creative is the first step in developing creativity in an organization. The employer is interested in the spark that distinguishes the imaginative from the routine employee. Identification of the particularly creative individual is difficult, and recruiters must look for something more than educational degrees and years of experience.

If an organization is to maximize the creative abilities of its members, it must also grant to them a considerable degree of freedom. This clearly rules out an insistence upon more than minimum conformity. Employees cannot be limited to following a set of rules and prescribed procedures. Rather, they may be encouraged to think about the work that is theirs to perform. Through delegation, they may receive freedom and responsibility in devising their own work methods.

It is also possible to grant creative individuals assistance in detailed and routine work. A professor may be given assistance in grading tests and thereby be permitted to engage in research. An engineer may be given assistance in drafting, filing, and typing. The problem is not so much the humble nature of routine work as it is the encroachment of detail upon time that should be devoted to achievement on a higher level.

Stimulation of creative effort may also be attempted through continued recognition of achievement. This recognition includes financial rewards, but it is not limited to them. In fact, the symbolic significance of a financial reward may constitute its greatest value. It is recognition that the contribution itself is important, and this may require some financial reward. The promotional practices of the organization should likewise reflect the understanding and appreciation of management for the creative activities of particular individuals. Whether recognition occurs by financial reward, job title, citation, or in other ways, the important thing is that there actually be recognition. Individuals who know that management is aware of the significance of their contributions have much of their reward.

An openness to criticism and tolerance of uncomfortable questions also contribute to an innovative atmosphere. A willingness to modify traditional organization structures and to change customary procedures is a part of this requirement. Although these characteristics are easy to specify, they are difficult to achieve. The status quo becomes accepted to the point that change is virtually impossible.

This may account for the fact that young organizations often (though not necessarily) display greater flexibility than those which are older. But older, well-established organizations can, with effort, take deliberate steps to encourage critical analysis on the part of their own members.

The role of supervisory management is critical in developing a proper atmosphere for creativity. Supervisors can get into a rut, plodding along with little regard for new ideas. They may know exactly why a new idea *won't* work but care little about developing one that will. It is imperative to have vitality at this level. If a superior's encouragement is evident, the subordinate is much more inclined to devote thought to creative activities.

Summary

Planning has become a function of vital interest and importance to all levels of management, including the top executive group. Planning consists of the activities involved in choosing courses of action to achieve company objectives. To some degree, the planning function has a position of first importance in its relationship to other managerial functions.

Business strategy refers to basic decisions affecting the very nature of the business and its relationship to the environment. Decisions regarding product line *specialization* or *diversification* illustrate strategic planning decisions. Strategy must be based upon the *resources* available in the firm and the changing conditions of the *environment*. Because of the unknowns, particularly in future developments, and the complex nature of these decisions, strategic decision making necessitates much subjective judgment.

Comprehensive corporate planning entails establishment of objectives, preparation of departmental plans, and integration of these plans into a comprehensive corporate plan. This process is based upon the *systems concept*, which stresses the integration of individual plans into a comprehensive plan and also emphasizes the need for careful analysis of the relationship between the business system and the environmental systems of which it is a part.

In planning, it is necessary for management to adopt certain assumptions or *premises*—particularly with regard to external factors—that serve as a background for the planning function. One major premise of this type involves *public policy* and the relationship of government to business. Prospective *economic conditions* constitute another factor of importance in business planning. Still other factors, such as *fashion trends, competitive developments,* and *population trends,* must be taken into consideration in any attempt at intelligent planning.

Creative ability represents a talent that needs to be nurtured and used in the business organization. The creative process involves a number of stages, including *problem discovery, investigation, incubation, insight,* and *verification.* Business organizations may stimulate creativity by recruiting particularly creative individuals, maximizing their freedom, providing assistance in detailed work, granting recognition for their achievements, and providing the proper supervisory atmosphere.

Discussion Questions

1. What is the relationship between *objectives, policies,* and *operational planning?*

2. What accounts for the increasing importance of planning in business organization?

3. Explain the concept of the greater importance of planning as compared with other managerial functions.

4. Define *business strategy* and explain its relationship to the objectives discussed in Chapter 2.

5. Explain the difference between *strategic posture* and *strategic plan.*

6. Why is it that a good strategy, selected carefully with proper consideration of all relevant variables, cannot be continued indefinitely?

7. In what ways are strategic decisions different from administrative, routine decisions?

8. In view of the uncertainties confronting most business organizations, how can you justify attempts at *long-range planning?*

9. In past years, major innovations in various fields occurred every fifteen or twenty years. The intervals are now much shorter—five or ten years—and may shrink even further in the years ahead. What are the planning implications of this change?

10. Identify and explain each of the stages in *creative thinking.*

Supplementary Reading

Ackoff, Russell L. *A Concept of Corporate Planning.* New York: Wiley-Interscience, 1970.

Cleland, David I. and King, William R. "Organizing for Long-Range Planning." *Business Horizons* 17, no. 4 (August, 1974): 25–32.

Cohen, Kalman J. and Cyert, Richard M. "Strategy: Formulation, Implementation, and Monitoring." *The Journal of Business* 46, no. 3 (July, 1973): 349–67.

Gilbert, Xavier and Lorange, Peter. "Five Pillars for Your Planning." *European Business,* no. 42 (Autumn, 1974): 57–63.

Mintzberg, Henry. "Strategy-Making in Three Modes." *California Management Review* 16, no. 2 (Winter, 1973): 44–53.

Sayles, L. R. "The Innovation Process: An Organizational Analysis." *Journal of Management Studies* 2, no. 3 (October, 1974): 190–204.

Uyterhoeven, Hugo E. R.; Ackerman, Robert W.; and Rosenblum, John W. *Strategy and*

Organization: Text and Cases in General Management. Homewood, Ill.: Richard D. Irwin, Inc., 1973.

Vancil, Richard F. and Lorange, Peter. "Strategic Planning in Diversified Companies." *Harvard Business Review* 53, no. 1 (January-February, 1975): 81–90.

Case 3

Strategy in the Soft-Drink Business

By 1975, Dr Pepper had acquired 5 percent of the soft-drink market and completed a nationwide distribution network, following rapid growth during the preceding decade. The cherry-flavored soft drink made its advance largely at the expense of Coke and Pepsi—the "Big Two" of the soft-drink industry. The success of Dr Pepper raises a number of strategy issues.

Independent Bottlers

Independent bottlers operate under franchise from a parent company such as the Coca-Cola Company. The franchise agreement, however, does not prohibit a bottler from selling another product, such as Dr Pepper, in addition to those supplied by the franchisor. In other words, a Coke bottler may sell Dr Pepper even though the Coca-Cola franchise agreement has been signed.

Dr Pepper has generally tried to get the largest bottler in each area, which was often the Coke bottler. In fact, one-fourth of the Coke bottlers distributed Dr Pepper instead of Coke's competitive product, Mr. PiBB. Coke franchisees faced pressure to give up Dr Pepper, however, and the Coca-Cola Company's hometown franchisee in Atlanta "returned to the fold" in 1975.

The decision to drop Dr Pepper is not an easy one for independent bottlers. They realize that Dr Pepper is a good product that has more consumer awareness than Mr. PiBB. By selling Dr Pepper, a Coke bottler can sew up the local cherry-flavored market. The reason is that Coca-Cola is unlikely to sell a Mr. PiBB franchise to a 7-Up or Pepsi bottler.

Dr Pepper's Situation

The management of Dr Pepper realizes that Dr Pepper is reaching the end of domestic growth through expansion into new territories. They plan to emphasize the single-bottle market, which includes vending machines, fountain sales, and spectator events. They believe that the sale of single drinks is important in order to allow consumers on a continuing basis to sample its distinctive taste.

Management expects Dr Pepper's marketing staff to (a) include Dr Pepper in special supermarket promotions that run locally for Coke and Pepsi, (b) press supermarkets to give Dr Pepper more display space, (c) increase cooperative advertising on a local level, and (d) promote free sampling of Dr Pepper.

They expect to spend fewer dollars relative to sales in national advertising because of Coke's and Pepsi's power there. The "Big Two" spend more than $130 million annually for advertising—a sum that exceeds Dr Pepper's total sales volume.

Dr Pepper's management minimizes the thought of open warfare. They assume that they may be an "irritant" to the "Big Two" but believe they are too small to constitute a significant threat.

Coca-Cola's Concern

Dr Pepper's success in signing up Coke bottlers has been a matter of concern to the Coca-Cola Company. They not only persuaded the Atlanta franchisee to "return home," but Coca-Cola also regained their Miami and Rochester bottlers. Of course, they are also pressuring other bottlers to do likewise.

Coca-Cola is not accustomed to being second in any type of competition. They look on local bottlers as the lifeblood of the parent company. If they let Dr Pepper go unchallenged, Coke bottlers may in the future take on Lipton Tea or Hawaiian Punch, further diluting their efforts to sell Coke. As of 1975, in fact, Welch Food, Inc., was contracting with Coke bottlers to sell "Welch's Sparkling Grape Soda" instead of Coke's Fanta brand grape soda.

Questions

1. What strategy should an independent bottler who sells both Coke and Dr Pepper follow?
2. Evaluate Dr Pepper's advertising strategy, particularly its deemphasis of national advertising.
3. What strategic change for Dr Pepper, if any, is called for now that it has attained national distribution?
4. What should be the strategy of the Coca-Cola Company as it sees the inroads being made by Dr Pepper?

Objectives

1. Explain decision making and the types of decisions that managers must make.
2. Identify the steps in decision making and show the contribution of each.
3. Recognize the limitations of the decision-making process, including its limited rationality.
4. Explain the general nature of *operations research* and identify its major values and limitations in solving business problems.

Chapter

Decision Making

The Nature of Managerial Decision Making
Steps in Decision Making
Information for Decision Making
Limitations of the Decision-Making Process
Using Quantitative Methods

Case: The Consulting Client's Complaint

Managers must of necessity be decision makers, because the decision-making process is a part of the fabric of management. Decision making is not always easy or pleasant, however. In the executive suite, in fact, there is a tempting tendency to postpone decisions, to wait for further developments, to engage in additional study. Of course, such a procedure is often logical. There comes a time, however, when choice is necessary. Effective managers distinguish themselves by their ability to reach logical decisions at such times.

The Nature of Managerial Decision Making

What is Decision Making?

Managerial decison making involves a *conscious choice.* By making such a choice, a manager comes to a conclusion and selects a particular course of action from two or more alternatives. Choice, of course, need not always be conscious. A particular behavior pattern may be selected on the basis of habit or rule of thumb. Although some would classify all choices as decision making, our particular concern is with conscious choices made by management.

In defining decision making, there is a tendency to focus upon the final moment in which the manager selects a course of action. A decision is announced, for example, that a new branch plant will be built in a particular city. Management has obviously made a decision. This concentration upon the final choice, however, tends to obscure the fact that decision making is in reality a process in which the choice of a particular solution is only the final step. Deliberation, evaluation, and thought are involved. The various stages of decision making, which are described in another section of this chapter, include steps of investigation and analysis as well as the final choice of alternatives.

Decision making is a much slower process than it seems would be the case. Rather than occurring in a matter of hours or days, decision making often drags on, surprisingly, for weeks, months, and even years! This tendency toward slowness in rendering decisions has been verified through empirical investigations.[1] As one example, a period of almost four years was required for a decision regarding installation of electronic data processing. In another case, the question of replacing overhead cranes with magnetically controlled cranes, for safety reasons, required two years for decision.

Behavioral scientists have stressed the numerous organizational influences at work in reaching a given decision. Many managers and even nonmanagerial personnel often influence the final choice. Herbert A. Simon refers to the *composite* decision and suggests that almost no decision made in an organization is the task of a single individual.[2]

Figure 4–1 shows the series of key business decisions involved in the development of "Surlyn" ionomer resin by the DuPont Company. It is clear from this figure that a series of decisions was involved in developing this product. It is also apparent that the management levels at which these decisions were made varied with the nature and importance of the decision. Of necessity, any such diagram oversimplifies the actual process of decision making. No doubt,

---

[1] Robert Dubin, "Business Behavior *Behaviorally* Viewed," in *Social Science Approaches to Business Behavior,* ed. George B. Strother (Homewood, Ill.: Richard D. Irwin, Inc., and The Dorsey Press, Inc., 1962), pp. 30–32.

[2] Herbert A. Simon, *Administrative Behavior,* 3rd ed. (New York: The Free Press, 1976), pp. 221–28.

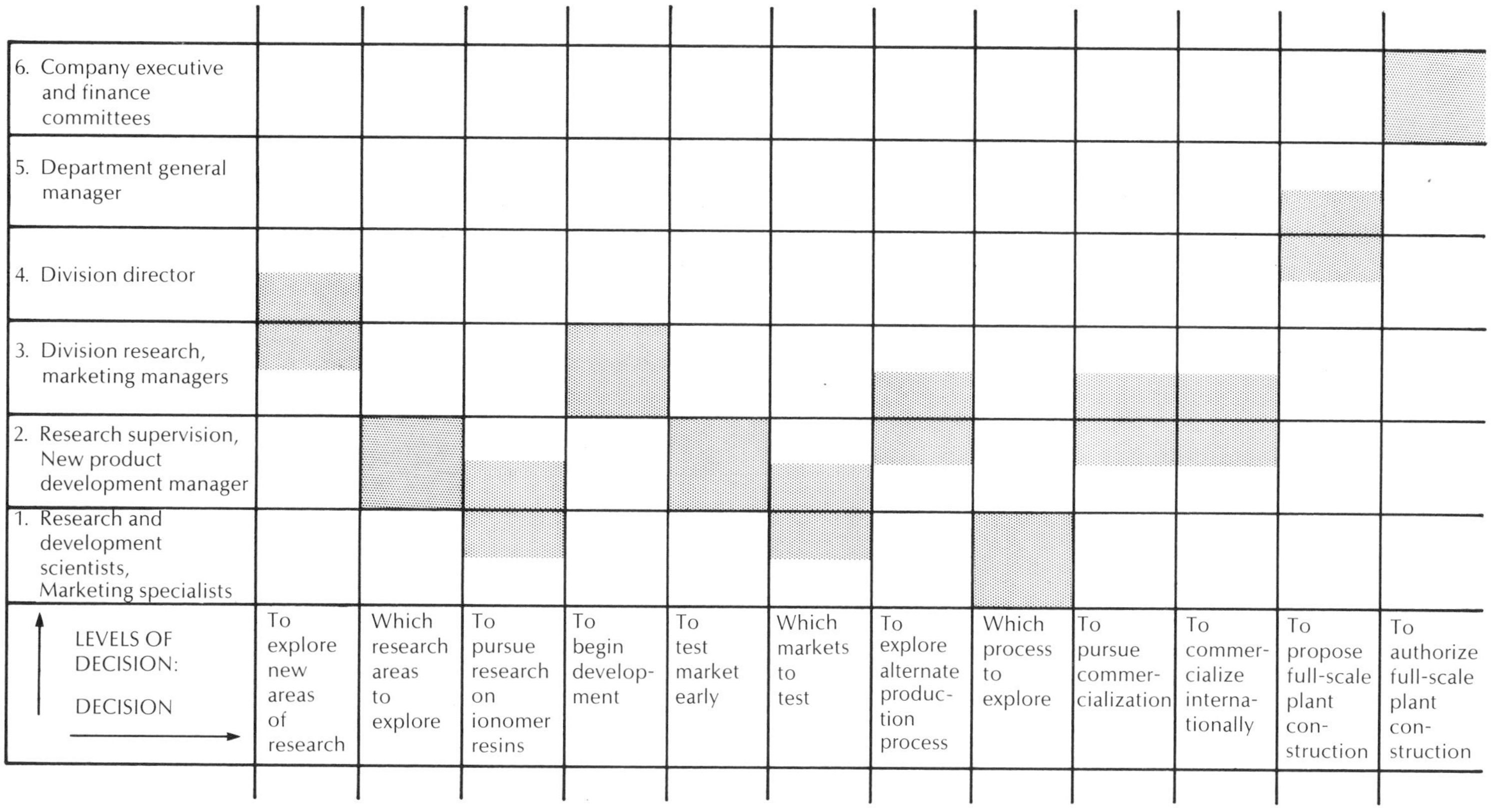

Figure 4-1 — Who Decides What: Key Business Decisions in the Development of "Surlyn" Ionomer Resin

LEVELS OF DECISION	To explore new areas of research	Which research areas to explore	To pursue research on ionomer resins	To begin development	To test market early	Which markets to test	To explore alternate production process	Which process to explore	To pursue commercialization	To commercialize internationally	To propose full-scale plant construction	To authorize full-scale plant construction
6. Company executive and finance committees												■
5. Department general manager											■	
4. Division director	■											
3. Division research, marketing managers				■			■		■	■		
2. Research supervision, New product development manager		■	■		■	■						
1. Research and development scientists, Marketing specialists								■				

Source: *The D of Research and Development* (Wilmington: E. I. DuPont de Nemours and Company, 1966), pp. 28–29.

Figure 4-1 *Who Decides What: Key Business Decisions in the Development of "Surlyn" Ionomer Resin*

some decisions that are portrayed as the responsibility of one individual were in reality composite decisions. And it is obvious that there were numerous additional decisions supplementing the key decisions indicated in the figure.

Types of Decisions

Managers at the various organizational levels make many different types of decisions. Some are simple—such as approving a vacation leave—whereas others are difficult—such as approving an experimental product for production and marketing. At top levels, decisions are broad and establish company strategy. At lower levels, decisions involve limited actions that implement company strategy.

A simple classification of decisions into those which are *routine* and those which are *nonroutine* provides a useful distinction for study of managerial decision making. *Routine decisions* include those which recur frequently, involve standard decision procedures, and entail a minimum of uncertainty. The decision maker can usually rely upon policies, rules, past precedents, standardized methods of processing, or computational techniques. Probably 90 percent of management decisions are routine, although any manager's experience is significant in determining whether a specific decision is routine.

Nonroutine decisions include those which are difficult because they are novel, nonrecurring, and unstructured. Their complexity is compounded by incomplete knowledge and the absence of accepted methods of resolution. Nonroutine decisions include not only major corporate decisions, such as merger or acquisition, but also more restricted ones, such as adoption of a new advertising theme or purchase of a new labor-saving piece of equipment. A much higher degree of subjective judgment and even intuition are involved in nonroutine decisions. It is this type, nonroutine decisions, that is of primary concern in this chapter.

How Decisions Are Made

Effective administrators find it difficult to dissect the mental processes they employ in reaching decisions. Attempts to probe the decision-making process have encountered such reactions as the following:

> I don't think we businessmen know how we make decisions.
> I don't know how I do it; I just do it.
> There's no formula for effective decision making.
> Thinking only causes mistakes.

Such remarks indicate that decision making involves more than a strictly rational analysis of cold facts. Judgment or intuition is apparently used in the process. Behind this, undoubtedly, is the fact that many of the significant elements in decisions are intangible. Even those considerations that are more tangible may require judgment in assessing their importance. It is not easy to analyze the psychological processes involved in reaching a business decision.

Ideally, managers should stress logical or fact-based methods of decision making. In most decisions at present, this can only be approximated. Attention to the question, however, can improve the process even though certain intangibles and imponderables remain.

When decision making is examined in the light of systems theory, its complexity becomes apparent. Problems do not exist in isolation. The manager discovers that there are many "angles" or facets involved in individual decisions. An adjustment to one part of the system may throw another part of the system out of adjustment. Objectives are often conflicting. Minimizing inventory costs, for example, requires minimum inventory levels which may, in turn, interfere with speedy response to dealer orders. Decisions of this type may, therefore, require *suboptimization* of parts of the organization—a concept discussed in Chapter 3.

Not only must executives analyze the effect their decisions may have on the internal subsystems of the firm, but they must also be aware of the external consequences of their decision making. The trend toward "consumerism" from a more observant public, for instance, has caused management to become more aware of its responsibility to provide better and safer products at reasonable prices to its customers.

The Systems View of Decision Making

We can view decision making as involving the series of steps shown in Figure 4-2.

A problem may take various forms; it may, for example, be a condition of inefficiency, a breakdown in operations, or an opportunity to be exploited. The first step consists of problem identification. Problems requiring analysis and decision making are brought to the surface in various ways.[3] As a result, one can never be sure that the most important problems are known or recognized at any one time.

Steps in Decision Making

Identification of Problem

Steps in Decision Making   **Figure 4-2**

Problems sometimes explode in the face of management. A foreman resigns, or a government contract is canceled. Some of the most important problems arise out of new objectives set by top management. In other cases, imagination and perception are needed to detect the problem. In any study of the organization and its activities, a manager may sense problems or needs of which others are completely unaware.

The principle of the Polaroid Land camera resulted from a chance conversation between the inventor, Edwin H. Land, and his daughter, who asked about having some pictures developed which they had just taken. In a flash, he saw here an opportunity to revolutionize photography with a process which would

[3] Chester I. Barnard has suggested the following origins of occasions for decision: (1) authoritative communications from superiors, (2) cases referred for decision by subordinates, and (3) cases originating in the initiative of the executive concerned. Used with permission of the publishers from Chester I. Barnard, *The Function of the Executive*, Cambridge, Mass.: Harvard University Press, Copyright 1938, by the President and Fellows of Harvard College, 1966, by Grace F. Noera Barnard, p. 190.

yield a finished print within moments after exposure. This set off the train of events which led finally to the picture-in-a-minute camera.[4]

Occasionally, managers waste time developing solutions to the wrong problems. Superficial disturbances can be misleading and fail to reveal underlying difficulties. What appears to be a problem may not be the problem at all. Management must constantly strive, then, to sift from the superficial difficulties the true problems that require investigation and solution.

Search for Alternatives   Consideration of the various possible solutions or alternative courses of action constitutes the second stage of decision making. Ordinarily, a business problem may be solved in any number of ways. If there were only one possible solution, of course, management would be powerless to devise alternatives and no decision would be required. If one is to take an objective or scientific approach to problem solving, however, he or she must consider alternatives rather than jumping to a conclusion concerning a single proposal.

Imagination and creative thinking are often required to devise possible solutions to a given problem. The entire range of alternatives is not immediately apparent.

Just what the alternatives might be depends upon the situation. Various courses of action may suggest themselves as a result of problem analysis. Overt action, furthermore, is not the only possibility. No action at all is frequently a possibility, and the best decision may be to let things stand as they are.

In searching for solutions, the decision maker faces certain constraints that limit his or her sphere of discretion. The following have been suggested as establishing limits to managerial discretion:[5]

1. Authoritative constraints
2. Biological constraints
3. Physical constraints
4. Technological constraints
5. Economic constraints

Authoritative constraints can be illustrated by the action of a superior in limiting the range of discretion for a salesperson in quoting prices. The other constraints are concerned with biological limitations, physical laws and factors, extent of technological development and knowledge, and the existence of economic conditions or limitations.

Evaluation of Alternatives   The scientific approach requires selection of the best solution on the basis of a careful evaluation of alternatives. The probable consequences of each course of action must be determined and weighed in choosing the solution. Unfortunately, the consequences are not always clear. The future is uncertain, and factual knowledge is never complete.

Compilation of pertinent facts is necessary to assure a decision that does

---

[4] Joseph D. Cooper, *The Art of Decision-Making* (Garden City, N.Y.: Doubleday & Company, Inc., 1961), p. 16.

[5] Robert Tannenbaum, Irving R. Weschler, and Fred Massarik, *Leadership and Organization: A Behavioral Science Approach* (New York: McGraw-Hill Book Company, 1961), pp. 277–78.

more than reflect the bias or feelings of the decision maker. A problem exists as to the extent one should go in gathering such information. Economic and time factors preclude an unlimited search, and, try as one may, some facts are elusive and can never be established. As a result, subjective judgment is invariably required.

After factual information is gathered, it must be classified in some meaningful way. It must also be weighed. Both pros and cons must be considered. Some apparently conflicting evidence is often present. The decision maker must distinguish between significant and trivial facts.

The climax of the decision-making process arrives when the manager exercises the final judgment. The manager may have gone step by step through an analysis of the problem and the proposed solutions, but the moment arrives when choice is necessary.

Choice of Alternative

Assuming the choice is based upon a thorough analysis, a decisive manager is to be admired. Indecision often indicates an unwillingness to face the situation. By choosing, one commits oneself to a given position. In some decisions, a reputation is at stake, and the decision maker may risk disagreement and misunderstanding. Decision making can thus be an agonizing process to some managers. The "loneliness" of decision making has been noted by Clarence B. Randall, who described the decision maker's feeling of individual responsibility as follows:

> It is human to wish to share the risk of error and to feel the comforting strength of outside support, like the flying buttresses, along the wall of a medieval cathedral. But the strong man, the one who gives free enterprise its vitality, is the man who weighs thoughtfully the entire range of available opinion and then determines policy by relying solely on his own judgment.[6]

Forthright expression of the decision once it is made can help clear the air of uncertainty. Explanations to those affected may be desirable if the reasoning supporting the particular course of action is not clear. This step is often necessary to gain the requisite understanding and support.

"It is a capital mistake to theorize before one has data," wrote Sir Arthur Conan Doyle in his *Adventures of Sherlock Holmes.* His statement could easily apply today to the manager who faces a multitude of decisions. The importance of pertinent, timely information for decision making cannot be overlooked.

Information for Decision Making

The Need for Information

Information has been called "the raw material of which decisions are made." And, just as in manufacturing, there is a direct correlation between the quality of the raw material and the quality of the resultant product.

One of the most common complaints a manager has is the lack of adequate information for decision making. As a business grows and becomes more complex, the manager's need for relevant information increases even more. In today's world of giant conglomerates and far-flung overseas operations, a manager without adequate information is completely lost.

---

[6] Joseph D. Cooper, *The Art of Decision-Making,* p. 120.

**Management
Information
Systems**

A manager receives the information needed for decision making through the firm's *management information system.* A management information system is just what the name implies—a system which collects factual information related to internal operations and to the environment and which provides that information to managers in usable form.

Management information systems require planning if they are to be effective. If such planning is neglected, the result can be a dangerous ignorance about business operations. In 1974, Thomas R. Wilcox was elected chairman and chief executive officer of San Francisco's Crocker National Corporation, the nation's twelfth largest bank.[7] He found that the bank's information system was so primitive that he could not get answers to basic questions of costs, profitability, and management responsibilities. The directors were receiving old-fashioned financial reports that were "not particularly germane to this century." Not surprisingly, the first key outsider Wilcox brought in was a specialist in management information systems.

**Computerized
Information
Systems**

Management information systems have existed, formally and informally, for centuries. Due to the development of the electronic computer, however, such systems have undergone a complete revolution during the past 25 years. The contribution of the computer to management information has been, and will continue to be, very great.

Initially, the computer was used primarily for record-keeping and accounting functions and, in many companies, computer usage has never gone beyond that initial stage. But more progressive firms have recognized that the computer is indeed the heart of the total management information system, as shown in Figure 4–3. These firms realize that information is as important a resource as employees, money, materials, machines, and facilities.

The computer aids the manager by providing accurate, up-to-date information. Such information should be instrumental in improving the quality of managerial decision making. A superior management information system provides an advantage just as real as an advantage based on lower costs of production or raw materials. This information can also greatly reduce the manager's decision-making time. Such an advantage should not be overlooked for, in many instances, time may be the most scarce of all corporate resources.

**Limitations of
Management
Information
Systems**

Computer-based management information systems are not without their limitations. One problem is that management, in many cases, expects more from a computer system than the system can realistically provide. "Essentially, computers cannot think or make decisions. Rather, they can only process decision data and implement decisions according to rules supplied by the computer user."[8]

Secondly, although one of the primary functions of the computer is to overcome the problem of too little information, the result in some instances has

---

[7] "Crocker's Tom Wilcox: Tough Management for a Stodgy Bank," *Business Week*, no. 2393 (August 11, 1975): p. 41.

[8] William C. House, ed., *The Impact of Information Technology on Management Operation* (Princeton, N.J.: Auerbach Publishers, 1971), p. 231.

Simplified View of a Management Information System   **Figure 4-3**

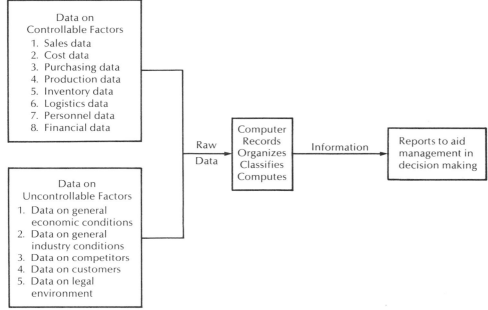

been too much information. Managers become deluged with reports containing more detail than they need and more information than they have time to consider.

A third problem is that many companies have allowed computer costs to run out of control. The more information a company wants, the higher the cost will be. Many computers have been put to trivial uses, turning out information not worth its costs.

None of these problems is insurmountable, however. The intelligent manager will clearly understand what the computer can and cannot do and will neither overestimate nor underuse its capabilities.

Limitations of the Decision-Making Process

Implementation of Decisions

It is easy to think of the effective manager as one who can lean back and think through a difficult problem. No doubt, such an ability is an excellent quality of a manager.

The practical administrator, however, spends a great deal of time in *implementing* decisions—in seeing that they are carried out. This requires an ability to secure the cooperation of others in seeing that plans are followed. The success or failure of a decision is largely determined by how well it is implemented. Although implementation itself entails a type of decision making, the decisions are different from those contemplated in most of the discussion of this chapter.

In terms of percentage of time, decision making as a part of the planning process may require only a minor portion of the manager's work day. In other words, a manager is an organizer and motivator in addition to being a decision maker.

**Limited
Rationality in
Decision Making**

In most discussions of decision making, the value and practice of rationality is assumed. Decision makers presumably investigate and then decide logically on the basis of their investigation. Empirical studies of decision making, however, have revealed a process involving competition and even conflict.[9] Special interests of specific departments and individuals tend to interfere with the rational process by which facts are investigated and decisions reached.

From the standpoint of a particular department, a rational decision—that is, a rational decision for the firm as a whole—may be favorable or unfavorable. It may strengthen or weaken the position of a given department. To protect and enhance their various positions, therefore, rival managers often compete with one another, bargain, build alliances with others, and in sometimes devious ways attempt to influence outcomes. Such tactics diminish and occasionally demolish rationality.

The personality and values of decision makers likewise affect and tend to limit rationality in decision making. Some individuals, for example, have a greater aversion to risk than others. Their decisions will naturally differ from those of decision makers having a greater preference for risk, even with the same set of factual information. The significance of values in decision making may be illustrated by the dilemma of multinational managers whose ethical codes regulate the extent to which they will pay off foreign politicians to obtain business favors.

Unfortunately, rationality is also limited by the fact that many business decisions must be made in the absence of complete knowledge. The process of decision making has not yet reached the point that the manager can dispense with subjective judgment.

Simon has stressed the limited rationality of the decision-making process.[10] Because businessmen never have all the facts and cannot know the consequences of every alternative in every situation, it is impossible for them to maximize. Their minds cannot even conceive of all possible alternatives. Instead of achieving maximum profits in every situation, therefore, managers must settle for satisfactory profits. In other words, they cannot maximize; they must of necessity *satisfice.*

> Whereas economic man maximizes—selects the best alternative from among all those available to him, his cousin, administrative man, satisfices—looks for a course of action that is satisfactory or "good enough." Examples of satisficing criteria, familiar enough to businessmen if unfamiliar to most economists, are "share of market," "adequate profit," "fair price." [11]

The attention directed at decision making, and particularly the emphasis upon quantitative analysis, tends to reduce the use of intuitive judgment and to make possible greater rationality in solutions to problems. However, the current state of knowledge is not such as to eliminate extensive use of subjective judgment.

[9] See, for example, Andrew M. Pettigrew, *The Politics of Organizational Decision-Making* (London: Tavistock Publications Limited, 1973).

[10] Herbert A. Simon, *Administrative Behavior*, Chapter 4.

[11] *Ibid.*, p. xxix.

The use of quantitative techniques in the process of business management is not a recent development. Such factors as the rate of inventory turnover, quality control limits, and return on investment involve quantitative concepts for use in decision making, and all have been used for many years. However, the modern emphasis on quantitative methods involves a much different concept known as *operations research* (OR).

Although these modern techniques are, in some cases, based on mathematical principles dating back as far as the eighteenth century, the specific body of knowledge known today as OR did not emerge until World War II. During the war, both British and American military leaders enlisted teams of scientists and mathematicians to aid them in solving complex military problems, such as assigning targets and scheduling bomb strikes or determining the safest method of transporting men and supplies across the oceans. The value of such systematic, mathematical analysis quickly became evident and, following the war, those who had served on, and worked with, OR teams began to realize that the same basic concepts could be applied to other areas, such as business decision making.

Perhaps the major impetus to the growth of OR, however, was the invention of the electronic computer. Since OR is designed to deal with a complex set of interrelated factors, a tremendous amount of data is necessary for maximum effectiveness. Such large volumes of data can only be processed practicably by computer. Otherwise, some OR problems would take several individuals with desk calculators years to solve.

Using Quantitative Methods

The Development of Operations Research

Basically, OR is a mathematical application of the scientific method to the solution of business problems. It has also been called "management science," or, less accurately, "quantitative common sense." Its primary distinguishing characteristics have been described as the following:

1. A systems view of the problem—a company-wide viewpoint is taken which includes all of the significant interrelated variables contained in the problem.
2. The team approach—personnel with heterogeneous backgrounds and training work together on specific problems.
3. An emphasis upon the use of formal mathematical models and statistical and quantitative techniques.

Definition of Operations Research

Although OR is quite often applied to company-wide problems, such as determining the best allocation of a firm's resources, it is also useful in more restricted areas, such as inventory control and distribution problems. The following list of practical applications of OR, while not in any sense exhaustive, indicates its widespread usefulness:

1. Long-range planning and forecasting
2. Production scheduling
3. Warehouse and retail outlet location selection
4. Portfolio management
5. New product development
6. Product and marketing mix selection
7. Air and highway traffic control

Uses of Operations Research

Such a list implies that companies using OR in their daily operations are found in many different industries. A complete listing of such firms is impossible, but some of the better-known companies using OR techniques are: American Airlines; American Telephone and Telegraph; Chase Manhattan Bank; DuPont; Eastman Kodak; General Electric; General Motors; Gulf Oil; Metropolitan Life Insurance; PPG Industries; Procter and Gamble; Sears, Roebuck; United States Steel; and Xerox.

The Use of Models   The essence of the OR approach to decision making is *model building.* A model is basically a simplified representation of an actual situation or object. Some types of models are quite common—model airplanes or automobiles built to scale are physical models; a road map is a geographic model; and the diagrams used in elementary economics textbooks to describe the concept of supply and demand are graphic models.

A model contains only the most important and basic features of the real system it represents. It is not necessary, for example, that a road map show houses, buildings, and trees. Such a map would be so large as to be completely unwieldy. However, a model can also be too abstract. A map showing only interstate highways would be of little use to a traveler going to a town located 50 miles from such a highway.

Mathematical Models   The models used in OR analysis are mathematical, but their fundamental concept is not different from that of the road map—a simplified representation of a real system. The operations of any company, for instance, can be represented by a basic equation:

$$\text{Net Income} = \text{Revenue} - (\text{Expenses} + \text{Taxes})$$

The components of the equation can then be subdivided. Expenses, for example, can be broken down into manufacturing cost, selling cost, and administrative cost, and each could be further subdivided.[12]

OR models are constructed by devising a set of equations which represent those significant variables that must be considered and the relationships among those variables. Any important variable which would affect the decision must be included. Some models are highly complex and are, therefore, very difficult to construct. But underlying this complexity is always the basic OR equation that a measure of the system's overall performance (P) equals the relationship (f) between a set of significant controllable aspects of the system (C_i) and a set of uncontrollable aspects (U_j). Expressed symbolically, it would appear as

$$P = f(C_i, U_j).[13]$$

Operations Research Techniques   One of the most widely used OR tools is *linear programming,* a mathematical technique for determining the optimal allocation of a firm's limited resources,

[12]K. W. Bennett, "Company Plan Models—a Must," *Iron Age* 206, no. 18 (October 29, 1970): 35.

[13]Russell L. Ackoff and Patrick Rivett, *A Manager's Guide to Operations Research* (New York: John Wiley & Sons, Inc., 1963), pp. 24–25.

including money, capital equipment, raw materials, and personnel. A company may wish, for example, to find the lowest-cost method of distributing products from five or six manufacturing plants to a large number of warehouses scattered all over the country.

Other OR techniques include *queuing theory* (or waiting line theory), *decision tree analysis, simulation,* and *heuristic programming.* These and other quantitative methods are discussed in standard works in this field.[14]

Although our discussion has emphasized the applicability of OR to decision making, it should be apparent that it is not a panacea for all business problems. Perhaps its chief limitation is that some variables in business decisions are simply not quantifiable. Yet, to use OR properly, all variables must be assigned quantitative weights.

Limitations of Operations Research

Some variables, such as changes in general business conditions or customer reaction to style changes, can only be estimated in quantitative terms. If unrealistic estimates are used in solving the problem, the results will be undependable. A model must accurately reflect existing conditions if misleading results are to be avoided.

But estimates need not be perfect to improve the quality of decision making. Even a fair estimate may be better than a vague feeling in the decision maker's mind. Even so, the difficulty in deriving accurate quantitative data and in determining relationships carefully is a limiting factor in quantitative analysis. Some factors are extremely difficult to quantify. If quantification cannot be done intelligently, the approach is questionable.

There is also a spurious accuracy that may be associated with quantitative analysis. The use of numbers and equations gives an appearance of scientific accuracy. The resulting willingness to place too much confidence in quantitative methods may be dangerous.

A further limitation in OR usage is the gap that exists between the manager and the OR specialist. The manager may have little knowledge or appreciation of sophisticated mathematical techniques, while the OR specialist has little knowledge of the problems the manager faces. This limitation, however, is being gradually overcome by training business school students in quantitative techniques and by assigning line managers to OR teams.

Finally, the more sophisticated forms of quantitative analysis are both elaborate and costly. Large, complex problems can be economically subjected to analysis in this way, but many smaller problems and minor decisions cannot justify such refinements in their solution. Management cannot afford to shoot every sparrow with a cannon.

We should also note that the use of quantitative tools is concerned with only one phase of the decision-making process. Quantitative analysis is not ordinarily used to identify the problem or to develop the alternative possibilities that are open. It does not, therefore, constitute a substitute for the entire decision-making process according to traditional methods.

---

[14]See, for example, Harvey M. Wagner, *Principles of Operations Research with Applications to Managerial Decisions,* 2nd ed. (Englewood Cliffs, N.J.: Prentice-Hall, Inc., 1975).

Summary   The decision-making process is an important, integral part of the management process. It involves a *conscious choice* of a particular course of action in the solution of a business problem. The nature of the decision-making process is not completely understood, and managers themselves often admit that they do not know how they make decisions.

The decision-making process begins with the *identification of a problem* and proceeds to a search for possible solutions or *alternative courses of action.* These alternatives have practical limitations in that they must be chosen within the constraints that prescribe the boundaries for the solution. Alternatives must be carefully *evaluated,* and the evaluation should lead logically to the *choice of a particular alternative.*

Decision making can be greatly improved by the intelligent use of pertinent, timely information available to the manager through a computer-based *management information system.* The wise manager recognizes that, although such systems have certain limitations, they can be of tremendous value in helping to make decisions.

The manager is an organizer, motivator, and controller as well as a decision maker. It is possible to develop a distorted view of the managerial process by extreme emphasis upon the decision-making function. It is also important to recognize that *nonrational factors* enter into some business decision making and that many decisions must still be made without adequate objective information for completely rational choices.

The application of quantitative techniques to managerial decision making can aid greatly in reducing the risk and uncertainty the manager must confront daily. Although some quantitative tools have been used by managers for decades, the emphasis in recent years has been on *operations research*—a concept which emerged during World War II. Used in conjunction with the computer, OR is the *mathematical application of the scientific method* to the solution of business problems.

At the center of the OR approach is the *mathematical model*—a set of equations representing the actual problem situation. The specific technique used to construct and solve the model depends upon the nature of the problem. OR does have definite limitations, the major one being that some aspects of business decisions are simply not quantifiable. But the field is still relatively new and its practical applications are already numerous.

Discussion Questions

1. What is the difference, if any, between *decision making* and *choosing a course of action?*

2. Why should decision making be such a slow process?

3. "Problems, problems—all I have is problems!" These words of one manager indicate a sharp awareness of problems. In what way, then, could *problem identification* be difficult?

4. What are the principal difficulties that hamper the development of *alternatives* in decision making?

5. If the previous steps in decision making are taken, why is the final step of *choosing an alternative* difficult?

6. Assume that your manufacturing company is faced with the decision of adding a new product line. You have been asked for your recommendation. What information would you need to make such a decision? How would a modern *management information system* help you?

7. If a manager is effective as a decision maker, does this indicate that he or she is a good manager?

8. What is the concept of *rationality* in decision making, and how do conflicting departmental interests affect it?

9. Explain how the concept of *satisficing* might apply in the decision to purchase an electronic computer for use in a large business corporation.

10. Is *OR* simply "quantitative common sense"?

11. What are some advantages of the *team approach* to OR?

12. In your opinion, why is OR not being more widely used in business decision making today?

Broom, H. N. *Production Management*, Rev. ed., Chapter 3. Homewood, Ill.: Richard D. Irwin, Inc., 1967.

Drucker, Peter F. *Management: Tasks, Responsibilities, Practices*, Chapter 37. New York: Harper and Row, Publishers, 1974.

Fredericks, Ward A. "A Manager's Perspective of Management Information Systems." *MSU Business Topics* 19, no. 2 (Spring, 1971): 7–12.

Grayson, C. Jackson, Jr. "Management Science and Business Practice." *Harvard Business Review* 51, no. 4 (July-August, 1973): 41–48.

Harrison, E. Frank. *The Managerial Decision-Making Process.* Boston: Houghton Mifflin Company, 1975.

Leavitt, Harold J. "Beyond the Analytic Manager." *California Management Review* 17, no. 3 (Spring, 1975): 5–12.

Mockler, Robert J. *Information Systems for Management.* Columbus, Ohio: Charles E. Merrill Publishing Company, 1974.

Patchen, Martin. "The Locus and Basis of Influence on Organizational Decisions." *Organizational Behavior and Human Behavior* 11, no. 2 (April, 1974): 195–221.

Thierauf, Robert J. and Klekamp, Robert C. *Decision Making Through Operations Research*, 2nd ed. New York: John Wiley & Sons, Inc., 1975.

Supplementary Reading

Case 4

The Consulting Client's Complaint*

You are regional manager of an international management consulting company. You have a staff of six consultants reporting to you, each of whom enjoys a considerable amount of autonomy with clients in the field.

*Taken from Victor H. Vroom and Arthur G. Jago, "Decision Making As a Social Process: Normative and Descriptive Models of Leader Behavior," *Decision Sciences* 5, (December, 1974): 168.

Yesterday you received a complaint from one of your major clients to the effect that the consultant whom you assigned to work on the contract with them was not doing his job effectively. They were not very explicit as to the nature of the problem, but it was clear that they were dissatisfied and that something would have to be done if you were to restore the client's faith in your company.

The consultant assigned to work on that contract has been with the company for six years. He is a systems analyst and is one of the best in that profession. For the first four or five years his performance was superb, and he was a model for the other more junior consultants. However, recently he has seemed to have a "chip on his shoulder," and his previous identification with the company and its objectives has been replaced with indifference. His negative attitude has been noticed by other consultants, as well as by clients. This is not the first such complaint that you have had from a client this year about his performance. A previous client even reported to you that the consultant reported to work several times obviously suffering from a hangover and that he had been seen around town in the company of "fast" women.

It is important to get to the root of this problem quickly if that client is to be retained. The consultant obviously has the skill necessary to work with the clients effectively. If only he were willing to use it!

Questions   1. State the problem and outline at least three possible alternatives.

2. In what ways will "values" enter into your decision in this situation?

3. To what extent should you bring your subordinate (or subordinates) into the decision-making process?

4. What are likely to be the major difficulties in reaching a totally rational decision in this case?

3

Establishing Organizational Relationships

Objectives

1. Explain the types of decisions entailed in organizing and the values associated with "good" organization.
2. Identify the underlying forces influencing the shape of organizations.
3. Recognize the reasons for job specialization and the possible contribution of job enrichment.
4. Identify various organizational patterns and provide a rationale for choosing a pattern.

Chapter

The Basic Organization Structure

The manager's organizing function begins with job designing and goes on to the formal structuring of relationships among jobs, people, and activities. This chapter examines *structural* aspects of organizational life—specifically, the nature of a manager's organizing function, determination of job content, underlying forces which shape formal organizations, and patterns of grouping jobs and activities.

Nature and Importance of Organizing

The manager's first organizing step is that of role determination. It is analogous to a playwright's creation of roles in a drama. In business organization, the roles take such forms as truck driver, accountant, junior scientist, and department manager. After these roles or jobs are established, a manager must devise a framework to specify lines of coordination and authority.

Formal Organization

The framework of relationships that ties together the specialized roles is the chain of command or management hierarchy. Each employee reports to some manager, and each manager, in turn, to some higher-level executive. Through this network, all roles are presumably brought under the control of one top-level administrative official.

Social scientists developed a theory of *formal organization* that stressed the rational nature of this formal organization and applied the name *bureaucracy* to it. According to this theory, the formal organization is visualized as a pyramid of officials who direct and coordinate the work of specialists by use of formal procedures. It is considered important that roles be carefully defined and rules for interaction clearly delineated.

The formal organization, or bureaucracy, therefore, consists of the management-specified framework of relationships. This formal organization is the skeleton for the social system and is supplemented by informal relationships that develop spontaneously among organization members without explicit definition by management. The formal organization is also modified as members of the organization introduce variations in prescribed relationships. These supplements and modifications introduced spontaneously by organizational members are known as the *informal organization* and are discussed at greater length in Chapter 9.

Organization Charting

Creation of an organization structure is often considered synonymous with the preparation of organization charts. The chart is a device used to portray formal organizational relationships, but we must recognize that the chart is only a picture. The chart is no more the organization itself than any symbol is the thing that it represents. The real organization structure is the total pattern of human relationships that exists. Informal relationships always supplement the formal structure.

An organization chart has limited value, then, in creating an effective organization. It may be used in reasoning about the organization and possibly in communicating the existing or desired organization structure. The chart will not assure action that conforms to the pictured pattern. Existing patterns of behavior may prevail in spite of new charts that are issued. In spite of these limitations, however, organization charts do perform a practical, useful function in many companies.

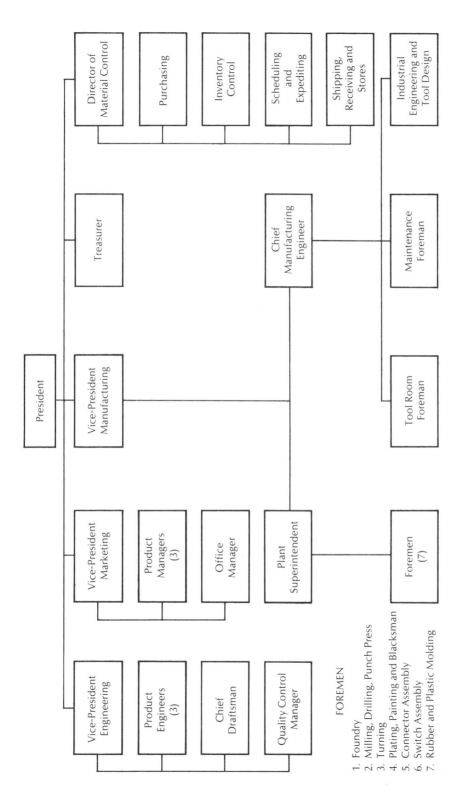

Figure 5–1 *Organization Chart of Anderson Power Products, Inc.*

Source: Reprinted by permission of the publisher from *Organization Planning Manual* by Joseph J. Famularo, p. 69, © 1971 by American Management Association, Inc.

Benefits of Proper Organization

The benefits arising from good organizing are those related to what a theorist calls *sound organization*. Charting an organization, for example, brings to light and helps eliminate weaknesses, including gaps in responsibility, overlapping of functions, duplicating effort, and working at cross purposes. The organizer attempts to create a highly rationalized structure—that is, a structure logically designed to work efficiently through careful work specialization, a well-defined hierarchy, and a set of rules and procedures.

In addition, study of organization is desirable in that it provides the incumbent of a position with a clearer understanding of management expectations. It also stresses unity of command, thus eliminating confusion and clearly identifying the line of responsibility of each individual. The planned organization also specifies the authority assigned to each position, so that the incumbent will be aware of the scope and limits of authority in the position.

Critical Views of Detailed Organization Planning

Administrators and scholars do not agree as to the desirability of extensive organization planning. The general argument of its critics holds that some flexibility in organizational relationships and procedures is desirable. They feel that excessive detail in specifying functions and responsibilities tends to be stifling and that firms can operate efficiently without extensive organization planning and without its paraphernalia, including charts and manuals.

In general, critics of the carefully planned organization object to rigid chains of command and organization charts that become ends in themselves. Bureaucracy is replaced by *bureaupathology* in which red tape triumphs and means become ends.[1] In the eyes of critics, some companies simply become over-organized. These critics or skeptics believe formal organization should be flexible.

Both advocates and critics of organization planning have a point. It *is* desirable to devote at least some study to the specification of organizational relationships. In fact, it is likely that the conflict between organization planners and the "don't-fence-me-in" school appears greater on the surface than it really is in practice. This is not to deny a significant difference in viewpoint but simply to note that organization-planning critics do reach some understanding among executives as to major responsibilities and that planners do admit the need for some flexibility.

The Challenge of Parkinson's Law

A few years ago, C. Northcote Parkinson wrote satirically on organization and administration. In his famous "law," he stated that "work expands so as to fill the time available for its completion."[2] Parkinson's suggestion is that organizations do not grow logically merely to care for increased work loads. In other words, one can draw no conclusion about the magnitude of the work performed on the basis of the size of the organization. "The rise in the total of those employed," said Parkinson, "is governed by Parkinson's Law and would be much the same whether the volume of the work were to increase, diminish, or even disappear."[3]

---

[1] See Victor A. Thompson, *Modern Organization* (New York: Alfred A. Knopf, 1961), Chapter 8, for an excellent discussion of this topic.

[2] C. Northcote Parkinson, *Parkinson's Law* (Boston: Houghton Mifflin Company, 1957), p. 2.

[3] *Ibid.*, p. 4.

If there is a measure of truth in the writing of Parkinson (and as a satirist, of course, Parkinson overstates his case), then it would appear that personal considerations are influential in the determination of organization design. Those in a position to influence decisions regarding organization may act on the basis of "what's best for me" rather than "what's best for the company." The term *empire building* has been applied to situations of this kind, and those thought to be building organizations for the primary purpose of increasing personal prestige have been denounced as *empire builders.*

Underlying Forces that Shape Organizations

The Dynamic Nature of Business Organizations

The dynamic nature of business enterprise produces repercussions in organizational relationships. As a concern adds new and different products, it may be necessary to modify the organization in order to produce and sell the new products efficiently. Decentralization may similarly be justified by changes of this type.

Our conclusion, therefore, is that organization structures reflect the functions and purposes of organizations. As the nature of the business changes, its organization structure must likewise change. Three significant factors in this process of change are the technology of the firm, the environment of the firm, and the strategy of the firm. Each helps to shape and to change organization structure.

Technology and Structure

A few decades ago, writers generally assumed that organizational concepts were universally applicable. More recently, this assumption has been questioned by observers who emphasize the drastic differences in industrial technology. (Technology, in this case, refers to methods of operation—including both the machinery and related techniques or methods of production.)

Perhaps the best-known research in this area was the study of about 100 British manufacturing plants conducted by a university research team and reported by Joan Woodward.[4] The researchers gathered extensive data about the features of formal organization of each plant but experienced difficulty in discerning a logical pattern. In other words, the type of organization structure did not initially appear to be significant in explaining differences in degrees of success.

Organization differences became sharp, however, when the plants were grouped according to type of production technology. Eleven classes of technology were established, involving various kinds of unit production, batch production, mass production, and process production.

When the plants were divided into the eleven categories, organization patterns were immediately apparent. The patterns included such traditional features as span of control and use of line and staff.

> Among the organizational characteristics showing a direct relationship with technical advance were: the length of the line of command; the span of control of the chief executive; the percentage of total turnover allocated to the payment of wages and salaries, and the ratios of managers to total per-

[4] Joan Woodward, *Industrial Organization: Theory and Practice* (London: Oxford University Press, 1965).

sonnel, of clerical and administrative staff to manual workers, of direct to indirect labor, and of graduate to non-graduate supervision in production departments.[5]

Within technological groupings, the study also revealed a connection between type of structure and successful performance. Thus, it appeared that given types of structures were more appropriate for given technologies. In other words, there tended to be an optimal type of organization.

The Woodward study has been extended and its results corroborated in other settings. In spite of the investigations to date, however, knowledge about the nature of the technology-organization relationship and its implications is limited. We know that a relationship exists, but it is difficult to state confidently what features of organization go with what forms of technology.

Environment and Structure

There are substantial differences in business environments. We recognize, for example, that steel producers, residential builders, food retailers, and public utilities face substantially different external situations. Some business environments are stable and predictable, whereas others are characterized by shifting conditions, uncertainty, and difficulty in predicting a future course of events.

As one example of environment-organization research, Lorsch and Morse examined differences in the environments of selected manufacturing plants and research laboratories.[6] They found the environments of manufacturing plants to be relatively stable and certain. Once production was scheduled, the automated nature of plant facilities took over. Rate of change in knowledge was slow. New types of products required only minimal changes in manufacturing and assembly operations. Feedback was immediate, with regular inspection of product quality during the manufacturing process and prompt reports of customer dissatisfaction. Strategic concerns centered on cost, quality, and delivery.

Managers of the industrial research laboratories, on the other hand, faced uncertain and rapidly changing environments. Problems could be approached in a variety of ways with various possible solutions. Information necessary to work out research problems was ambiguous, open to varied interpretations, and apt to become obsolete. Knowledge was changing rapidly, and feedback was long term—for example, five years from laboratory idea to manufacturing success.

The research of Lorsch and Morse indicated that the more successful manufacturing organizations emphasized formal structure, using formal job descriptions, rules, procedures, detailed control systems, and greater centralization of decision making. The high-performing laboratories, on the other hand, displayed greater flexibility in management with only general job descriptions, a minimum of rules, reliance on self-discipline, and greater participative decision making.

---

[5] *Ibid.*, p. 51.

[6] Jay W. Lorsch and John J. Morse, *Organizations and Their Members* (New York: Harper and Row, Publishers, 1974). The research project described here also examined the significance of personal characteristics of organization members as related to environment and internal organization.

As markets change, businesses devise new strategies and organize to pursue those strategies. To discover the possible influence of strategy on organization, therefore, one must analyze the organization changes that accompany or follow strategy changes. A major study by Alfred D. Chandler, Jr., demonstrated this connection between business strategy and organization structure.[7]

Strategy and Structure

Chandler defines strategy as the determination of basic long-term goals and the adoption of courses of action and allocation of resources to carry out these goals. Decisions to diversify or to set up distant plants are examples of strategic decisions. Chandler examined the administrative histories of close to 100 large industrial enterprises, and he analyzed in detail the organizational development of DuPont, General Motors, Standard Oil (New Jersey), and Sears Roebuck. His general thesis may be stated as follows:

> Strategic growth resulted from an awareness of the opportunities and needs—created by changing population, income, and technology—to employ existing or expanding resources more profitably. A new strategy required a new or at least refashioned structure if the enlarged enterprise was to be operated efficiently. The failure to develop a new internal structure, like the failure to respond to new external opportunities and needs, was a consequence of overconcentration on operational activities by the executives responsible for the destiny of their enterprises, or from their inability, because of past training and education and present position, to develop an entrepreneurial outlook.[8]

By deciding the array of duties to be included in a specific job, the manager specifies the *role* of the person selected to fill that job. A *role* may be defined as the behavior or set of activities expected of a particular individual, the *focal* person—in this case, the job incumbent. In other words, managers express their intentions when they create a job. A typist, for example, may be expected to type letters, answer the telephone, obtain supplies for the office, and perform other specified duties. Of course, the technology of the organization and its overall structure and policies have much to do with the nature of individual jobs.

Establishing Individual Jobs

Specifying Job Content

As a matter of fact, there are expectations of many groups and individuals, the *role set,* concerning the behavior of any one person. Figure 5–2 illustrates these relationships. Fellow employees and subordinates, for example, also expect the focal individual to behave in particular ways. Many of their expectations, of course, result from their knowledge of job requirements.

Management's definition of job requirements, then, establishes the formal organizational expectations concerning the incumbent. This expectation becomes critical as far as the employee's relationship with the employer is concerned. The employee must presumably fulfill these role requirements in some reasonable degree in order to continue employment and receive the normal rewards for satisfactory performance.

---

[7] Alfred D. Chandler, Jr., *Strategy and Structure* (Cambridge: The MIT Press, 1962).

[8] *Ibid.*, pp. 15–16.

Figure 5-2   *Role Set and Role Expectations*

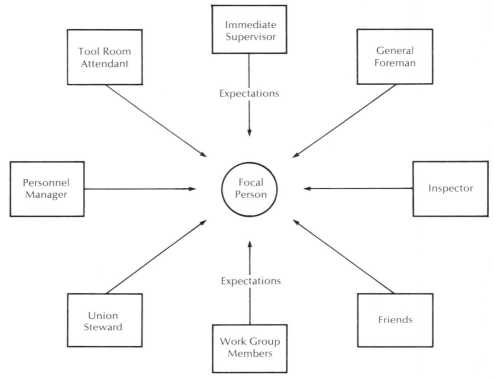

Technological Imperatives and Job Design

As a small organization grows, some division of duties and specialization of work occur spontaneously. This is necessary in order to achieve efficiency in production—a fact recognized by both classical economic theory and the scientific management philosophy.

There was a strong emphasis in the scientific management movement upon work standardization. The employee was expected to perform the task in precisely the same way each time, using the method considered most efficient by a methods analyst.

The continued use of the principle of division of labor is common knowledge. The modern assembly line provides an excellent example. Each employee has only one or a few minor functions in the assembly process to perform. This type of specialization in modern industry has made possible its impressive growth in productivity.

Meaningful Work

Much concern has been expressed in recent years about the nature of work. Work is viewed as something more than earning a livelihood. Work affects the employee's life in many ways, including not only the standard of living, but also the employee's physical condition, leisure time, mental health, and family life. According to some, management should assume a responsibility for providing suitably challenging work for all members of the organization.

While work specialization and standardization greatly increased productivity, a number of negative results were also experienced.[9] From the standpoint of the individual worker, jobs frequently became less attractive. Performing only a very specialized part of a total job gave employees less feeling of accomplishment than they had enjoyed previously.

The extent of work dissatisfaction in America is not entirely clear and may be exaggerated in popular thinking. Some individuals apparently adjust to boring work. Most employed people seem to be reasonably contented with their work. Nevertheless, much dissatisfaction does exist, particularly in such cases as the highly routinized assembly line.

Automobile assembly work has long been recognized as a prime example of extreme specialization—what some critics call "dehumanized work." In general, most automobile assembly jobs lack challenge, diversity, or opportunity for significant decision making. At the General Motors' plant in Lordstown, Ohio, one worker was quoted as follows:

> My former job at a steel mill was hot and dirty, but I felt like a man there. Here I feel like nothing.[10]

How far can job specialization profitably be carried? Even from an engineering approach, there is a principle of diminishing returns. Continued subdivision of jobs may reach the point beyond which little or no gain can be realized from further subdivision.

Job Enrichment

Operational inefficiencies may actually result from excessive specialization. As work becomes extremely specialized, for example, it becomes difficult to divide work evenly among all employees. As a result, those with shorter work assignments have some idle time. Quality control responsibility may also be difficult to establish in the case of specialized work.

As an offset to any realized technical gains in work efficiency, we have seen that workers find the monotony and reduction of skill unpleasant. From the standpoint of administration, these are undesirable consequences. In deciding upon the extent to which specialization should be carried, then, the manager must consider the matter from the standpoint of both engineering and human relations. It is possible that a minor gain in technical efficiency may be more than offset by lower morale.

Considerations of this type have led to questions concerning the proper extent of job specialization. The shape or size of the organization building block has been scrutinized. Some organizers have concluded that it is often too small—that some jobs have become overspecialized. This has led to efforts to restore variety and, more importantly, responsibility and self-determination to specialized jobs—in short, to despecialize them. This process became known as *job enlargement* or *job enrichment*. The latter term is preferable in emphasizing an increase in difficulty and responsibility in contrast to an increase in variety only.

---

[9] For a stimulating discussion of the seriousness of the problem and the extent to which employees *need* involvement in their work, see Robert Dubin, *Human Relations in Administration,* 4th ed. (Englewood Cliffs, N.J.: Prentice-Hall, Inc., 1974), pp. 125–29.

[10] "The Spreading Lordstown Syndrome," *Business Week,* no. 2218 (March 4, 1972): 69.

Patterns of Organization

Choosing a Pattern

After determining job content, the organizer must consider the way that jobs and groups of jobs should be related to each other. In grouping activities into organizational components, some integrating pattern or principle is required.

The organizer frequently has a choice of patterns, several of which are widely used and recognized. Perhaps the best known is the *functional* pattern in which the type of activity or function serves as the organizing principle. Sales, for example, constitutes one department, while manufacturing activities are grouped in a separate department. In contrast to the functional pattern, a *product* pattern groups both manufacturing and sales activities related to one product into the same department. Other possible patterns are based on the *location* of the activity, the *customer*, and the *process*. The list is not exhaustive, however, and various other patterns can be found in addition to these that are rather commonly used.

The Nature of Divisionalization

The large industrial corporation has three patterns available to it as the basis for its overall organization. In the small manufacturing enterprise, the functional pattern is customarily used. At the top level, the functions of sales, manufacturing, and finance serve as the basis for the company's major departments. Large industrial concerns, however, have two other patterns as possibilities. One of these is based upon the product, and the other upon geography (also called *territory* or *location*).

Companies that use either the product or geographical format at the top level have been described as *divisionalized* organizations.[11] Divisionalization frequently goes hand in hand with decentralization of authority. The General Motors Corporation, for example, is divisionalized on the basis of products (Buick Motor Division, Oldsmobile Division, Allison Division, Frigidaire Division, etc.). Each operating division functions autonomously under the broad or general direction of the corporation.

Function as the Pattern

As noted, small manufacturing enterprises find the functional pattern particularly appropriate. This pattern is not limited to the top level of the organization, however. Within the manufacturing department—a functional department—work may be further subdivided on the basis of function. Organizational components at this level may include drilling, grinding, painting, and so on. Different office units similarly may perform typing, filing, and messenger service.

An example of the functional pattern is the organization of the Raymond Corporation, whose structure is shown in Figure 5–3.

Efficiency and economy are among the more important advantages of functional organization, especially for relatively small companies. All selling, for example, is concentrated in one department. A potential weakness in the functional pattern is its tendency to encourage a narrowness of viewpoint. It is easy for functional executives and personnel to look at problems from the standpoint of selling or manufacturing or some other functional specialty rather than seeing them from the standpoint of the company as a whole.

---

[11] Louis A. Allen, *The Management Profession* (New York: McGraw-Hill Book Company, 1964), pp. 190–96. See also Peter F. Drucker, *The Practice of Management* (New York: Harper & Row, Publishers, 1954), p. 205. Drucker's distinction between *federal decentralization* and *functional decentralization* is quite similar to Allen's distinction between divisionalized and nondivisionalized structures.

The Raymond Corporation   **Figure 5-3**

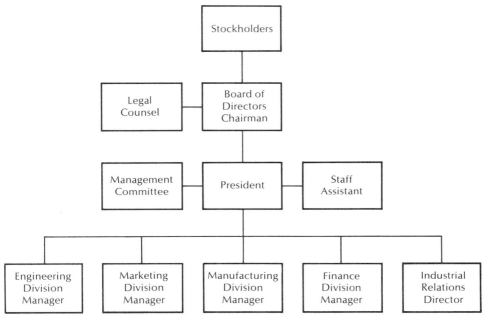

Source: Reprinted by permission of the publisher from *Organization Planning Manual* by Joseph J. Famularo, p. 113, © 1971 by American Management Association, Inc.

Product as the Pattern

The possibility of a product pattern exists not only at the top level (divisionalization) but also at lower levels. In a functional sales department, for example, sales personnel may be specialized on the basis of product lines. Or the manufacturing department may include plants specialized in the manufacturing of different products. An example of the product pattern is presented in Figure 5-4.

The advantages of product divisionalization are particularly significant in the case of a highly diversified product line. The work and requirements of manufacturing or sales personnel in a consumer products division, for example, are drastically different from those in an atomic power division.

Executive development is another attractive feature of product organization. In the functional organization, executives are trained in functional areas and imbued with a functional viewpoint. In contrast, the general manager of a product department and his or her assistant have the responsibility for dealing with problems in various functional areas—including production, sales, and research and development.

Location as the Pattern

Location of work provides another possible pattern for organization. For the most part, this is a matter of geography—for example, establishing various regional offices—but it may also be necessary to use location in grouping activities in a given plant or office. Maintenance personnel, for example, may be combined into administrative units on the basis of particular buildings or plant areas.

Figure 5-4   *Westinghouse Electric Corporation*

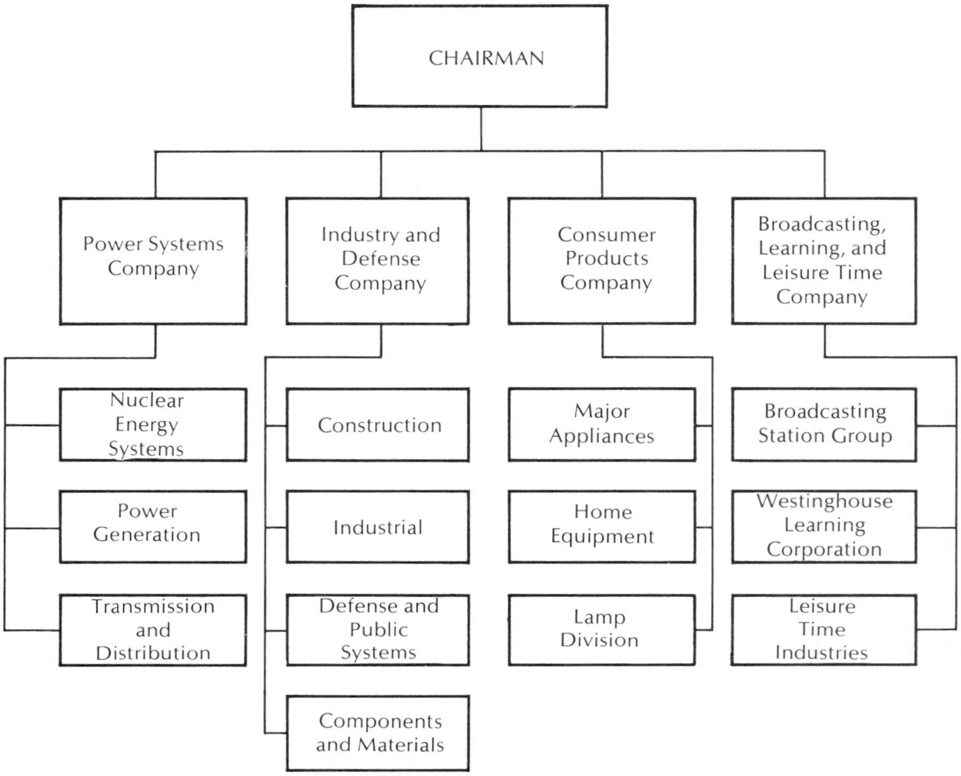

Source: Company Records (1972). This simplified chart does not show all the staff offices and associated activities of the corporation.

An example of territorial divisionalization is the organization structure of a major insurance company (Figure 5–5).

Organization on the basis of location has certain advantages in common with the product pattern. Breadth of managerial experience is secured in the administration of regional areas. Financial control of operations is also facilitated by permitting separate accounting for the financial results of each territorial unit.

Customers as the Pattern

In sales organizations, differences in the needs of customers often lead to an organization plan based upon certain customer classifications. Distinctions are often made, for example, in selling to industrial users and in selling to wholesalers or retailers. If customer differences are substantial, an argument for some customer pattern becomes strong.

As an example of the reasoning involved in adopting a customer pattern, consider a change in the organization of the sales force of the International Business Machines Corporation. The Manhattan sales offices of IBM had used the traditional geographical arrangement, but four sales offices were created in

Regional Office Organization of a Major Insurance Company   **Figure 5-5**

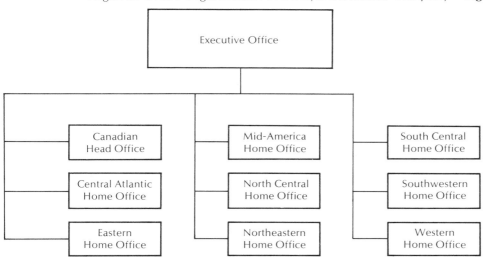

Source: Company Records (1972).

1959 to serve one or more industries that constituted IBM customers.[12] The reasoning was that sales representatives must become specialists in the business of their customers and in the adaptation of IBM equipment to those particular industries. The new offices included a financial office to deal with banks and brokers; an office to sell to insurance companies; an office dealing with textiles, retail trade, and associated business; and an office catering to petroleum, industrial, and transportation industries. The new pattern proved effective, and 80 percent of the IBM sales force was reported to be specialized on an industry basis in 1962.[13]

Summary

The process of *organizing* involves the grouping of jobs into a *framework* for coordination and direction. This organizational framework, the *formal organization,* may be portrayed by use of an *organization chart.* Although careful structuring of the organization is thought to be beneficial in terms of clarifying lines of command and eliminating gaps and overlaps, some critics argue that extremely detailed organization structures may be dysfunctional.

According to the argument of *Parkinson's Law,* personal considerations directly affect the design of organizations. Following this reasoning, individual managers *(empire builders)* are believed to manipulate the structure in order to maximize results for themselves.

Underlying forces that shape organizations include the firm's *technology, environment,* and *strategy.* Changes in these factors lead to changes in structure.

---

[12] "IBM Shift in New York Sales Setup May Set Pattern for Wider Change," *Business Week,* no. 1577 (November 21, 1959): 133.

[13] "The Switch to Specialized Sales," *Dun's Review and Modern Industry* 80, no. 2 (August, 1962): 44.

By creating jobs and specifying job content, management creates organizational *roles*. These are the sets of behaviors or activities expected of individual members of the organization. The underlying technology and quest for efficiency tend to force an oversimplification of jobs, a reduction in the range of duties, and a lowering of skill demands.

One often dysfunctional result of management's attempt to simplify jobs for reasons of efficiency has been to reduce the employee's sense of accomplishment and to increase monotony of work. Dissatisfaction with this situation has directed concern in recent years to the *quality of working life* and the desire of many individuals for *meaningful work*. *Job enrichment* represents one approach to the restoration of meaning and pride in work.

Once job content is determined, it is necessary to group jobs and activities in devising an overall structure. *Patterns* that may be used in grouping include, among others, *function, product, location,* and *customers*. Companies using either product or locational patterns for their overall organization are referred to as *divisionalized* organizations. In such companies, this pattern of organization is normally associated with the organizational philosophy of *decentralization*.

Discussion Questions

1. What specific factors might account for the greater effectiveness that results from good organization?

2. In what sense is an organization chart symbolic?

3. Is it true, speaking of formal organization planning, that if you "put a person in a square" you limit him? What would be the nature of this limitation, and how serious would it be?

4. Give several examples, including some based upon your own observations, of organization changes caused by the dynamic nature of business enterprise.

5. Explain the meaning of the following terms: *role, focal person, role set*.

6. What explains the historic trend toward narrowing the scope of industrial jobs?

7. Evaluate the impact of work specialization upon employees.

8. What is meant by the *pattern* of organization? Why is a mixture of patterns customary?

9. What is the meaning of *divisionalization*?

Supplementary Reading

Drucker, Peter F. "New Templates for Today's Organizations." *Harvard Business Review* 52, no. 1 (January–February, 1974): 45–53.

Ford, Robert N. "Job Enrichment Lessons from AT & T." *Harvard Business Review* 51, no. 1 (January–February, 1973): 96–106.

Hackman, J. Richard. "Is Job Enrichment Just a Fad?" *Harvard Business Review* 53, no. 5 (September–October, 1975): 129–38.

Levitan, Sar and Johnston, William B. *Work Is Here To Stay, Alas*. Salt Lake City: Olympus Publishing Company, 1973.

O'Toole, James, ed. *Work and the Quality of Life: Resource Papers for Work in America.* Cambridge, Mass.: The MIT Press, 1974.

Tsaklanganos, Angelos A. "The Organization Chart: A Managerial Myth." *Advanced Management Journal* 38, no. 2 (April, 1973): 53–57.

Case 5

Job Enlargement*

The manufacturing operations at Plant Y of the Crestline Corporation consist of fabricating and assembling a major consumer durable product. Traditionally, the manufacturing systems have been designed and built around the typical high-speed assembly-line operation.

As general production superintendent of Plant Y, Mr. Brown, who has developed through the management ranks largely by following traditional management principles, must give final approval to all systems changes that will affect his operations.

A new design of one of the major components for the ultimate product has been completed by product engineering. In turn, it has been released to manufacturing engineering for implementation into the assembly line system.

The manufacturing engineering group recently studied the available research relative to the advantages of the job-enlargement principle versus the paced-conveyor system—in terms of providing relief from monotony and boredom. Realizing that job dissatisfaction has been and continues to be an apparent problem, a system which includes job enlargement was developed to assemble the new component along with the traditional paced-conveyor system. Each system was then presented to Mr. Brown for his approval, with the recommendation from the manufacturing engineering group that he adopt the job enlargement systems design.

Mr. Brown, being aware of the perceived monotony and boredom of the assembly line, decided to accept the recommendation and adopt the job-enlargement principle.

As the production date arrived, the facilities were completed and a number of operators moved from the assembly conveyor to a new job. They, in turn, were told to assemble the component completely and to stamp their work with a personalized identification stamp which had been provided.

Output and quality during the first week was below that which was anticipated and showed very little improvement during the next several weeks. In fact, the output was significantly below that of similar work at an adjacent paced-conveyor operation.

---

*From John V. Murray and Thomas J. Von der Embse, *Organizational Behavior: Critical Incidents and Analysis* (Columbus, Ohio: Charles E. Merrill Publishing Company, 1973), pp. 214–15.

Mr. Brown's boss is upset, to say the least, since efficiency is low and excessive overtime is necessary to meet schedules. Mr. Brown, realizing that he is responsible for production, is trying to determine what happened and what course of action to take.

Questions

1. What are the possible reasons that job enlargement has failed to increase or even maintain productivity?

2. Evaluate Mr. Brown's approach in adopting and installing the new system.

3. What effect might the compensation system have on the job enlargement plan?

4. In view of the present problem, what should be Mr. Brown's next move?

Objectives

1. Define *authority* and explain limitations imposed by subordinates.
2. Justify adherence to the chain of command by citing problems resulting from multiple supervision.
3. Explain variables determining optimum span-of-control size.
4. Enumerate benefits of, and barriers to, delegation of authority.
5. Describe conditions leading to decentralization and its organizational advantages.

Chapter

Lines of Authority and Delegation

The Nature and Use of Authority
The Chain of Command
The Span of Control
Delegation of Authority

Case: The Scoutmaster

The heart of the organization structure is the chain of command. Through the chain, managers use authority to provide direction and coordination of organized endeavor. This chapter examines authoritative relationships in organizations, focusing specifically on the nature of authority, the chain of command, the span of control, and the delegation of authority.

The Nature and Use of Authority

What Is Authority?

Authority may be defined as a superior's capacity, on the basis of formal position, to make decisions affecting the behavior of subordinates. Authority is evident in the various areas of society. In the family, the parent makes decisions for minor children. In football, the quarterback calls plays. In the business world, the manager acts as the decision maker on issues affecting the business. When authority is recognized, the subordinate relinquishes an individual right of decision and accepts the decision of a superior.

The concept of authority employed here incorporates the idea of power or ability to secure compliance with a superior's orders. Authority might be called *institutionalized power* to emphasize its connection with the formal organization and to distinguish it from other types of power. Members of organizations recognize the power of managers because of their acceptance of the formal organization and its managerial positions. This does not imply that it is absolute power, having no limitations, but authority must have some degree of effectiveness to be recognized as authority. Otherwise, it is a hollow, meaningless, "paper" right of command.

In contrast to the concept of authority, *power* requires no formal position to be recognized as power. It refers to capacity or ability to make things happen, to get results. Only a part of the total power is institutionalized. This means that others beside managers have power. In the informal organization, for example, output quotas may be established and enforced.

Limits to the Exercise of Formal Authority

Citizens of a country do not always obey its statutes, even though they recognize the statutes as the law of the land. If violation is sufficiently serious, we classify offenders as criminals. Frequently, however, the offense is viewed less seriously. Motorists, for example, often ignore traffic ordinances. Even good citizens are thus in a position of conflict with established civil authority.

In a challenge to traditional views, Chester I. Barnard drew attention to the possibility of a subordinate's rejection of direction by higher authority. In fact, Barnard felt that disobedience of subordinates was commonplace. "It is surprising," said Barnard, "how much that in theory is authoritative, in the best of organizations in practice lacks authority—or, in plain language, how generally orders are disobeyed." [1] Acceptance of the order, then, becomes an important step or part of making the authority of the order giver effective.

This reasoning does not mean that subordinates automatically resent and resist all authority or that they have a generally rebellious attitude. The point of this reasoning is simply that the authority (or institutionalized power) represented by a superior's order is seldom so absolute, unequivocal, or in-

---

[1] Chester I. Barnard, *The Functions of the Executive* (Cambridge, Mass.: Harvard University Press, 1938), p. 162.

escapable that the subordinate has no choice whatever. As Herbert A. Simon has expressed it, "the leader, or the superior, is merely a bus driver whose passengers will leave him unless he takes them in the direction they wish to go."[2]

The fact that subordinates possess power does not eliminate authority as a management right. If managers become overly concerned with their own lack of power and fearful of using authority, they will appear weaker than they are. Managers do have power and must use it as necessary for the good of the organization. An understanding of subordinate power should not render managers impotent but rather contribute to good judgment in their decisions and to avoiding the type of orders that might be difficult to enforce.

On rare occasions, subordinates openly defy official orders, and a condition of mutiny exists. Such insubordination represents an urgent problem of serious proportions to an administrator. Management must either back down—often difficult to do gracefully—or take disciplinary action. In other words, an open, direct challenge by a subordinate forces an immediate showdown.

Forms of Resistance to Authority

In most cases, however, resistance is less direct or formal, occurring subtly. Subordinates manage to resist without forcing a showdown. They may go through the motions of compliance but fail to follow through with the behavior desired by the superior. This type of challenge to authority is often most baffling and troublesome for administrators.

When a demand comes from a superior, for example, there is a possibility the superior may have expressed it on the spur of the moment and will later forget about it. Therefore, the subordinate may also proceed to "forget" about the request and await results. If the superior checks again, another type of strategy is called for. It may be necessary for the subordinate in this case to enlist the support of colleagues, report numerous unfavorable consequences after initiating the requested action, or carry out the request half-heartedly.

Rules that presumably control subordinates are also a potential weapon in the hands of subordinates. An overly zealous observance of rules may actually be dysfunctional. The following incident illustrates the limitation that rule-keeping may impose upon management power:

> Train crews in a marshaling yard were handling 150 trains a day. Through short cuts (often violating safety rules) they were able to finish their work in six hours. The rest of the time they could sleep or read.
>
> Then management decided that since the men had so much free time they could handle 200 trains. Immediately the men began to follow all the rules. They would never move a train even a few feet without having someone to go to the rear and wave a red flag. As a result, the men put in a full day's work, but productivity fell to 50 trains a day. Soon management gave up its demands for 200.[3]

The ability of subordinates to thwart executive authority varies greatly with the social context. In most military organizations, for example, compliance

---

[2] Herbert A. Simon, *Administrative Behavior*, 3rd ed. (New York: The Free Press, 1976), p. 134.

[3] George Strauss and Leonard R. Sayles, *Personnel: The Human Problems of Management*, 2nd ed. (Englewood Cliffs, N.J.: Prentice-Hall, Inc., 1967), p. 189.

with official orders is more nearly automatic than is customary with business organizations. Business organizations also differ among themselves as to the amount of power residing in the official structure.

The Chain of Command

What Is the Chain of Command?

In its simplest form, a chain of command is the relationship between a superior and a subordinate. Starting at the top with the chief executive, we may visualize a series of lines connecting the executive with the next layer of management. These subordinate managers, in turn, are connected with their subordinates. An organization chart diagrams these organizational relationships with lines fanning out from the chief executive and increasing in number at lower levels of the organization. In fact, it has the familiar shape of a pyramid. The total network of relationships constitutes the organization's chain (or, more technically, chains) of command.

Each position is connected to the chain of command at some point, which means that each individual reports, either directly or indirectly, to the chief executive.

Aspects of the Chain of Command

The phrase "chain of command" implies an authoritative relationship, but the chain has at least three distinguishable characteristics—namely, *authority, responsibility,* and *communication.*

As an authoritative chain, the manager's status is that of order-giver. The chain is an *official* channel, and the superior's communications are authoritative. The chain of command is also a line of responsibility which holds subordinates accountable for their performance. Subordinates are conscious of the superior's surveillance and recognize their own obligation, even though their responsibility may be enforced informally.

It is often said that authority should be commensurate with responsibility. This means that there is a basic unfairness involved in attempting to hold an individual responsible for that which he or she lacks the necessary authority to accomplish. Unfortunately, there are occasional instances of this type in which higher management fails to see the limitations confronting a subordinate or neglects to confer upon him or her the necessary authority.

The communication between a manager and subordinates gives substance to the relationship. In other words, superiors and subordinates experience their relationships through discussion and other contacts with each other. Although these communications are official, they are by no means limited to orders or commands. Discussions regularly treat such subjects as the progress of work, problems that are encountered, personal matters, and other information of mutual interest.

Difficulties in Adhering to the Chain of Command

In practice, adherence to the chain of command can never be complete. The different strata of management cannot be rigidly compartmentalized. A president deals directly with vice-presidents but also communicates with their subordinates. In all likelihood, these contacts involve not only casual personal conversations but also serious discussions of business matters. Almost any manager is known personally and evaluated by two or three levels of supervision. Associations of this type are not confined to *joint conferences* in which

Features of the Chain of Command **Figure 6-1**

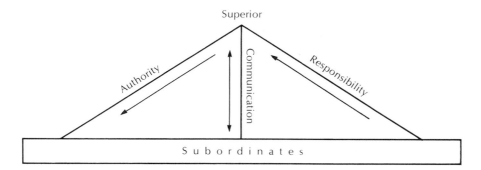

several layers of management are present but also include "leapfrogging" that runs counter to the chain-of-command concept.

Several forces contribute to this flexibility of the chain of command. One is the need for speed in communications. Communications through channels necessarily go rather slowly, as suggested by Figure 6–2.

Communication Through the Chain of Command **Figure 6-2**

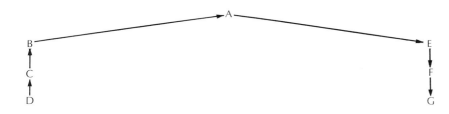

Need for accuracy in communication also encourages short-circuiting of the official chain of command. Mere transmission of information through a number of individuals tends to introduce inaccuracies and distortions. The president may get, through official channels, reports of progress and problems. To insure an accurate picture of conditions at any level, however, the president may need to see or discuss these matters personally.

Some short-circuiting by subordinates is also justified as a protection against unfairness in supervision. Even though managers may be reasonable in considering subordinate needs and fair in discipline most of the time, there are occasional instances of arbitrary and harsh administrative action. In such cases, the subordinate has little recourse except to "go over the head" of the superior. In the early days of IBM, Thomas J. Watson encouraged employees to bring their problems, such as unfair managerial treatment, to him personally. An invitation of this type, if taken seriously, could conceivably lead to serious administrative problems by playing one level of the organization against another. But if used with discretion, it can also provide a relief valve in case of unjust managerial decisions.

Some modification of the strict chain of command thus seems a prime necessity to many administrators. Yet, though some relaxation of the chain is necessary, it is not without its hazards, as noted in the following section.

Dangers in Short-Circuiting the Chain of Command

Short-circuiting the official chain of command quickly undermines the position of a bypassed manager. The mere practice of bypassing may indicate to the short-circuited manager a lack of confidence by the superior. The natural effect is a weakening of morale. In contacts between the bypassed manager and that manager's subordinates, the effectiveness of leadership is impaired. Subordinates may well reason, "If the boss does not take our supervisor seriously, why should we?"

Short-circuiting is often confusing to subordinates of a bypassed manager. In effect, such subordinates are subjected to multiple supervision and to the probable unpleasantness involved in such an arrangement. The immediate supervisor's orders may be countermanded by a higher level of management. General confusion is a distinct possibility.

Short-circuiting is more or less serious depending upon a number of specific circumstances. Emergency situations, for example, lead to greater tolerance of contacts outside the chain of command. No one considers it necessary to shout "Fire" through channels! In the absence of emergencies, the willingness of intermediate management levels to tolerate leapfrogging depends upon such other factors as the importance of subject discussed, the nature of the contact (whether it is confined to discussion or involves decisions), and the extent to which intermediate levels are kept fully informed.

Administrative finesse is required in keeping out-of-channels contacts harmless to the organization structure and positive in their contribution to organizational purposes. There is a fine line, for example, between informational discussions and discussions in which advice is given or implied.

Unity of Command

The concept of unity of command holds that no person should be subject to the direct command of more than one superior at any given time. In practice, this precept is often violated. In some cases, a subordinate reports to two or more superiors of approximately equal status. In other situations, one manager exercises *administrative* control, while another manager provides *technical* control over work. Sometimes organizational relationships are vague, and the subordinate finds that two or more superiors are behaving as though the subordinate reports to each of them. While it may look as though the subordinate should take action in such a case to clear the air, he or she may be in a weak position to question the company's organization. Any number of situations may thus result in deviation from unity of command.

The reasoning supporting the desirability of unity of command maintains that two or more superiors are unlikely to agree perfectly in their instructions to the same subordinate. The subordinate must then choose the instructions to follow. The subordinate may also need to assign priorities to projects originating with various supervisors—and of necessity to disappoint one or more of them. Different managers are likewise inclined to have different expectations regarding employee performance.

It also becomes difficult, if not impossible, to hold the subordinate accountable. The subordinate may tell Superior X, "I couldn't do it because I was tied up on a project for Superior Y." The subordinate is also in a strategic position to play off one supervisor against another, inasmuch as neither supervisor has complete knowledge of the total assignment.

Business experience has shown that completely unified command is not an absolute requirement for success. Any manager is subjected to influences and pressures from others. Even though outside influence is sometimes described as "advice," the manager may feel obliged to follow the suggestions. A practical view of the unity-of-command concept must recognize the logic of some of these apparent conflicts that occur.

The Span of Control

In the chapter thus far, we have looked at authority and its exercise through the chain of command. A related question concerns the breadth of a manager's reach—that is, the number of subordinates that he or she can effectively manage.

What Is the Span of Control?

The *span of control* refers to the number of immediate subordinates reporting to a given manager. If the president gives orders to only one executive vice-president, the president's span of control is one, even though the executive vice-president may have a number of subordinate managers who, in turn, direct operations. If the president has six vice-presidents reporting, however, the span of control is six.

Span of control is the phrase that has been traditionally used in describing this relationship. This phrase itself emphasizes the manager's function of controlling, but the concept is considerably broader. It might also be termed *span of management.*

Relationship to Echelons

The size of the span of control is inversely related to the number of echelons, or layers, in an organization. As the span is broadened, there is a tendency to flatten the structure.

In Figure 6–3 we can see that a span of two would require four echelons to direct eight operative employees, whereas a span of four would require only three echelons.

The cure for an excessively large span is the insertion of additional layers. Suppose that a small business grows to the point that eight production workers are employed, in addition to salespeople and other personnel. All of them report to the president. The usual solution is the appointment of a shop supervisor, thereby reducing the president's span of control and creating a third level in the business.

Limiting the Span of Control

It is clear that there need to be limits on the size of the span of control. The strength and time of any manager are limited. One manager, for example, could not personally direct the work of a thousand employees. In an extreme case, then, there can be little argument about the need for reducing the span.

As subordinates are added and organizations grow, the size of managerial spans tends to grow. However, the increasing demands on managers eventually create pressures for reducing the span.

Figure 6-3 *Spans of Different Sizes*

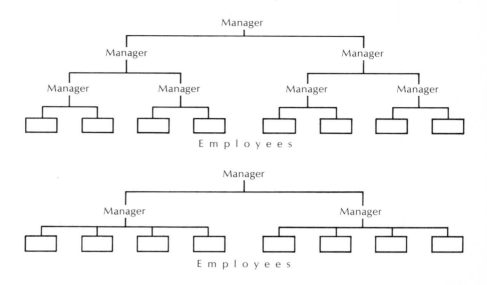

In the past, it was popular to specify rather precise limits to the desirable size of the span of control. One well-known approach of this type is identified with V. A. Graicunas, a French management consultant, who made a mathematical analysis of the span of control.[4] In general, Graicunas suggested that the number of management relationships in a span of control expands at a faster rate than the span of control itself. In other words, the addition of one position to the span of control provides a proportionately greater increase in the number of significant relationships, thereby increasing the complexity of the manager's task.

On the basis of these definitions of significant relationships, Graicunas discovered that, with expansion of the span of control, the number of relationships grew at an astounding rate and quickly reached astronomical proportions. With 4 subordinates, he discovered a total of 44 relationships, but with 8 subordinates, the total number was 1,080. With 12 subordinates, the number of relationships rose to 24,708. On the basis of this reasoning, Graicunas recommended a maximum span of four or five for most management positions. Beyond this point, the management task seemed to become hopelessly complex.

A National Industrial Conference Board survey of 274 company heads reported spans ranging from one to more than twenty.[5] In about 80 percent of the cases, however, the spans varied between four and ten.

In surveys of practice, we must be careful to avoid hasty generalization. Executives differ in their definition of "direct reporting." Furthermore, the pre-

[4] V. A. Graicunas, "Relationship in Organization," in *Papers on the Science of Administration,* eds. Luther Gulick and L. Urwick (New York: Institute of Public Administration, 1937), pp. 181 ff.

[5] Harold Stieglitz, *The Chief Executive—and His Job* (New York: National Industrial Conference Board, Inc., 1969), pp. 15–17.

ceding surveys were quite restricted. However, these and other surveys tend to confirm our general observations of widely varying span size.

Enlarging the span, as noted earlier, produces a flatter organization by reducing the number of echelons. This facilitates vertical communications by eliminating organizational levels that can become communication bottlenecks. It seems likely that the communications network as a whole benefits more from the flatter organization with its broader spans of control, even though managers have less time available for communicating with individual subordinates.

Values in Expanding the Span of Control

By broadening the span of control, organizations may also experience an increase in morale. As a result of the larger number of subordinates, an executive is forced to use different management methods from those possible with a small span. It is difficult to supervise subordinates in detail, to look over their shoulders while they are working. There is some evidence that this boosts both morale and productivity, although the evidence is far from conclusive.

Another advantage of the larger span of control is the reduction of administrative overhead cost. By having each manager direct a larger number of subordinates, the necessary number of management officials is substantially reduced in any sizable organization. Supervisory salaries may constitute a significant part of the total operating costs. If this reduction can be accomplished without a marked decrease in efficiency, the organization clearly benefits, from a cost and profit standpoint, by the use of a larger span of control.

The diversity in existing sizes of spans can be explained, at least partially, by variations in the managerial situation. A number of possible variables can be easily identified. Unfortunately, most of these variables are merely hypotheses, and more extensive research is required to be sure of their validity.[6]

Variables Affecting Optimum Size of Span

The type of work, for example, seems to have some bearing in determining the appropriate span. The similarity of functions supervised affects the nature of problems coming to the manager's attention. If the work of subordinates is similar in nature and involves few new problems or unusual situations, the pattern of work becomes well established and requires only minor attention from the manager. The importance of the work, its inherent difficulty, and its geographical spread likewise affect the difficulty of management.

In analyzing the optimum span of control, we should not overlook the executive as an individual. Managers differ in their physical, mental, and emotional characteristics. Some individuals are tougher physically and more resilient in reacting to the demands of their offices. Some might be described as "easy-going," while others are "ulcer-prone." The mental ability of some people also equips them to size up situations and reach decisions more quickly than is possible for others. Such individual differences are recognized among college students in that, to achieve the same grade, some students spend long hours of study while others barely "crack a book."

---

[6] One carefully designed research study, using a small sample, is reported in Jon G. Udell, "An Empirical Test of Hypotheses Relating to Span of Control," *Administrative Science Quarterly* 12, no. 3 (December, 1967),: 420–39.

A number of management practices facilitate direction by managers and thus contribute to their capacity for adjusting to a larger span of control. One of these is the delegation of authority. If managers delegate substantial amounts of authority to subordinates and use relatively little detailed supervision, they free themselves from burdensome, time-consuming work. Executives are also able to broaden their span of control by the use of staff assistants. A staff specialist can provide another set of legs, eyes, and ears for the executive.

The executive who is sufficiently fortunate to have talented, competent subordinates is in a position to minimize time spent in control of their activities. Competent, well-trained personnel are less prone to make errors, requiring less correction and counseling from their superiors. In addition, the ability of subordinates may manifest itself in readily identifying problem areas and in devising solutions to these problems. Their creative thinking can also save the time of their superiors.

Delegation of Authority

Definition of Delegation

Delegation of authority involves an assignment of responsibility and authority by a superior to a subordinate. Through delegation, a manager is given the right to plan the activities of a unit, direct the work of subordinate personnel, and make other decisions pertinent to the operations of the organization. If authority is delegated to an operative employee, the right is that of deciding various details of the work and using property and supplies belonging to the employer.

Granting authority need not involve a "blank check" to be classified as delegation. Even in similar lines of work, managers differ in the degree of freedom extended to subordinates. It is less a matter of *delegation versus nondelegation* than it is a matter of *more or less* delegation. At one end of the scale is the autocrat who clings tenaciously to power, while at the other end is the leader who places almost the total burden on subordinates. Most managers operate somewhere between these two extremes.

There is a significant distinction between delegation of authority that is real and that which is nominal. Many managers go through the motions of delegating authority, subscribe to the principle in theory, and believe they are delegating, but fail to delegate significantly. In discussion, a superior may easily tip off a subordinate as to the superior's point of view. It is possible, therefore, for a subordinate who is presumably operating independently to receive detailed control from the superior.

Responsibility of Delegator and Delegatee

When authority is delegated, an obligation is thereby placed upon the subordinate. For example, a department manager in a retail store who is granted authority to purchase goods sold in the department is expected to exercise authority in such a way as to bring profit to the company.

Delegation of authority is a two-sided coin—a fact that any management employee clearly recognizes. A manager is well aware of personal obligation toward the employing organization in exercising authority.

Although an executive may delegate authority to a subordinate and thereby create an obligation on the subordinate's part, the executive doing the delegating does not escape responsibility to higher management. Instead, delegation creates an additional relationship of obligation between subordinate and superior. The executive who delegates is still held accountable for the overall mission for which he or she is responsible. See Figure 6–4.

Authority and Responsibility   **Figure 6–4**

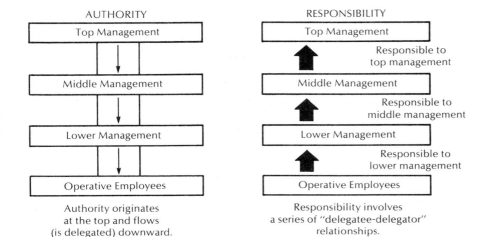

AUTHORITY

Authority originates at the top and flows (is delegated) downward.

RESPONSIBILITY

Responsibility involves a series of "delegatee-delegator" relationships.

Psychological Barriers to Delegation

Some of the most persistent problems in delegation are psychological. Many managers experience difficulty in adopting an approach to management that relies upon delegation of authority. Frequently, the manager has developed a practice of supervision that makes little use of delegation and that keeps the manager in personal contact with all phases of the work. This approach may have been developed over a period of many years and involve a deeply ingrained habit pattern.

One factor accounting for the existence of a psychological barrier is the feeling of importance attached to the exercise of power. The egos of managers are involved, and they can sense their own importance as subordinates come to them with questions and refer problems to them for decision.

A manager's feeling of insecurity may make it difficult to be a good delegator. Unfortunately, many managers do find themselves insecure in their own positions. Surveys of supervisory and managerial attitudes have shown that a substantial percentage of management personnel, even in well-managed organizations, are quite unsure where they stand with their immediate superiors and the company which employs them. In one of the best-managed companies in the United States, 18 percent of its management personnel reported, in response to a survey question, that they did not feel reasonably confident of their standing with respect to job performance.

This feeling of insecurity may affect delegation in different ways. On the one hand, the insecure manager feels it necessary to keep in close touch with work for which he or she is responsible. The manager fears the consequences if all responsibilities are not carefully discharged. It is difficult, with this attitude, to allow a subordinate to take part of the work and perform it without careful scrutiny.

Not all barriers to delegation are found in the delegator. Frequently, we visualize all subordinates as eagerly reaching out to grasp any decision-making authority proffered them. Unfortunately, the real-life situation reveals many subordinates to be somewhat apprehensive about accepting authority.

Advantages of Delegation

A major advantage of delegating authority is that it relieves the delegator of certain time-consuming work. Any manager can be more effective by delegating minor duties. A manager who is constantly immersed in the details of work that could be accomplished by subordinates is unable to care for the major responsibilities of the position.

A manager also learns to manage by working and by making decisions as a manager. The implications for delegation of authority are clear. By forcing a subordinate to assume responsibility and to make decisions, the superior is insisting upon the subordinate's "practicing management." If the superior were to make most decisions personally, the subordinate would be deprived of practice.

It is widely believed that personnel respond to delegated authority favorably, that they enjoy the greater responsibilities. Obviously, this generalization could not apply to all operative employees or even to all managers. Some individuals—and they can be found in any sizable organization—like the security associated with detailed supervision.

It seems likely, however, that most employees, particularly those in management positions, respond positively toward delegated authority.

Decentralization in Business Organizations

As business organizations grow, they become more difficult to manage. When they become huge—with tens of thousands or hundreds of thousands of employees—they become unwieldy. Their management becomes virtually impossible unless organizational and management practices evolve to permit a different type of control.

Over fifty years ago, General Motors pioneered an approach to management of large organizations that was to become famous. Introduced by Alfred P. Sloan, Jr., about 1920, this management approach become known as *decentralized management.* Decentralization facilitated, or at least permitted, the tremendous growth that made General Motors the leading industrial concern in the world, with almost three-quarters of a million employees and sales of more than $30 billion.[7]

Decentralized management basically involves the subdivision of a large organization into components of more manageable size. The key to decentralization, however, was the autonomy accorded to separate divisions. They were directed by divisional heads who functioned much like chief executives. To be sure, decentralization did not grant total freedom to operating divisions. At General Motors, the phrase "centralized policies and decentralized operations" described the balance of control and freedom sought in this company.

---

[7] In terms of sales volume alone, Exxon is the leading industrial corporation, with more than $40 billion sales in 1974.

Any manager may delegate authority to a subordinate or subordinates. Delegation may thus be a highly individualized relationship. When delegation is used systematically and extensively throughout an organization, the arrangement may be described as decentralization. In a decentralized organization, authority and decision making have been pushed downward throughout the organization. Decentralization thus necessitates delegation, but delegation, on the other hand, might be used by a particular manager without being part of a decentralization program.

The advantages cited earlier for delegation of authority apply to decentralization as well. Another significant advantage of decentralized management that functions along divisional lines is the *profit-center* principle. The division manager who is given freedom in management can be held responsible for the profitable operations of the division. Decentralization also facilitates product diversification. It is difficult, if not impossible, for a company having a highly diversified line of products to operate with tightly centralized management.

Summary

Authority is the capacity to make decisions affecting the behavior of subordinates. It may also be described as *institutionalized power.* Limitations exist in the extent to which formal authority is accepted by subordinate members of an organization. Forms of resistance include not only open defiance but also subtle disobedience in which there is an appearance of compliance.

There are significant values realized through adherence to the *chain of command*—notably, the preservation of the status of management officials and the avoidance of confusion to subordinate personnel. Subordinates often find it distressing to receive multiple supervision, whether it results from short-circuiting the chain of command or from conflict with the concept of *unity of command.*

In considering the *span of control,* it appears that the determination of precise, quantitative limits that are generally applicable to many organizations is difficult, if not impossible. There are also difficulties in extending the size of the span of control, but some have found advantages, particularly in terms of communication, productivity, and morale, in the use of a broader span of control that results in a flatter organization. Some of the variables affecting the desirable size of the span of control include the nature of work being performed, the qualities of the manager as an individual, managerial methods and procedures, and the capacity and training of subordinates.

By *delegation of authority,* a manager conveys to a subordinate the right to make decisions that would otherwise be made by the delegator. Although the recipient of delegation, the delegatee, is responsible to the delegating manager for the proper exercise of authority, the delegator still has the same responsibility as before to higher levels of management.

Probably the most serious type of barrier to delegation of authority is the *psychological barrier.* Failure to delegate authority, when caused by such a barrier, stems from such factors as deeply ingrained habit patterns, sense of individual importance, and feeling of insecurity. Among the advantages of delegation are the relief of the delegator from time-consuming work, development of subordinate personnel, and improvement of morale.

Decentralization occurs when delegation is used systematically and extensively throughout an organization. Growth of organizations and increasing diversity in operations provide extreme pressure for this type of management. In addition to the advantages cited for delegation of authority, decentralization aids control through use of the *profit-center* principle and facilitates product diversification.

Discussion Questions

1. How does the concept of *authority* differ from that of *power*?

2. If subordinates are inclined to resist authority, what forms may their resistance take?

3. Explain the three aspects or characteristics of the *chain of command*.

4. What pressures encourage short-circuiting of the chain of command? Do these factors constitute valid reasons or merely excuses for short-circuiting?

5. Suppose a top-level executive feels it is necessary to go outside channels in contacting a manager two or three levels below. How can adverse effects be minimized?

6. Does the concept of *unity of command* appear to be merely a textbook principle or does it appear to have practical significance in administrative situations?

7. How is the span of control related to the number of echelons in an organization?

8. What weaknesses or limitations exist in the *Graicunas approach* to the establishment of quantitative limits to the span of control?

9. What seems to be the greatest advantage resulting from expanding the span of control?

10. If we assume that the most capable managers occupy top management positions, should they have broader spans of control than managers at lower levels?

11. Distinguish between *delegation* and *decentralization*.

12. If responsibility and authority are supposed to be equal, as one "principle" of management suggests, why can't a manager delegate *responsibility* in the same way that the manager delegates authority?

13. How can a feeling of insecurity act as a barrier to delegation?

14. Discuss the relationship of delegation of authority and morale of employees. Do subordinates really want authority and its accompanying responsibility?

15. What is the relationship of business size to decentralization?

Supplementary Reading

Albanese, Robert. "Criteria for Evaluating Authority Patterns." *Academy of Management Journal* 16, no. 1 (March, 1973): 102–11.

Carlisle, Howard M. "A Contingency Approach to Decentralization." *Advanced Management Journal* 39, no. 3 (July, 1974): 9–18.

McConkey, Dale D. *No-Nonsense Delegation*. New York: American Management Association, 1974.

Oncken, William, Jr., and Wass, Donald L. "Management Time: Who's Got the Monkey?" *Harvard Business Review* 52, no. 6 (November–December, 1974): 75–80.

Udell, Jon G. "An Empirical Test of Hypotheses Relating to Span of Control." *Administrative Science Quarterly* 12, no. 3 (December, 1967): 420–39.

Webber, Ross A. *Management*, Chapter 17. Homewood, Ill.: Richard D. Irwin, Inc., 1975.

Case 6

The Scoutmaster*

Tom Daniels was one of several foremen working for Robert McGraw, the equipment manager of an independent telephone company. As shown in Exhibit 1, he had a number of two-men work crews under his supervision.

Yesterday morning, Daniels called in Jack Worley, a workcrew leader whose helper was off for the day, and gave him his assignment. He was to complete the hookup of a new automobile agency's switchboard. The cut-over time was 5 p.m., but Daniels emphasized that the job was to be completed today even if it took longer. The point didn't seem very important at that time since both men agreed that the job was one that should be completed well before five.

At 5 p.m. Worley called the office and asked for Daniels. He did this although he knew—as did all workcrew members—that at 5 p.m. Daniels customarily was at another company location where he could be reached by telephone. When informed that Daniels was out of the office, Worley asked to speak to McGraw.

As soon as he had the equipment manager on the line, Worley explained that he was on a job that was going to take longer than expected because of some complications that had arisen. He then asked for permission to complete the job the next day so that he could get home in time to meet the Boy Scout troop of which he was the scoutmaster. McGraw—not knowing, of course, anything about the details of the assignment—agreed to his request to leave and finish the next day.

At 5:30 Daniels returned to the office and tried to contact Worley's location. Getting no answer, he went out to the site. He found that the job had not been completed and that Worley had left. He was unable to get the job finished that night because of the press of work and the lack of available crews.

The next morning, seething because of the customer complaint he had just answered, Daniels went in to McGraw's office to explain the situation. McGraw then told him that it was he who had given Worley permission to leave.

*Case prepared by Professor A. Ranger Curran of Youngstown State University.

Questions   1. What is the *organizational* problem in this case?

2. Justify or criticize Worley's decision not to finish the work.

3. Justify or criticize Worley's method of implementing his decision.

4. Evaluate McGraw's handling of the situation.

5. What should Daniels do about his problem?

Exhibit 1   *Organization Chart*

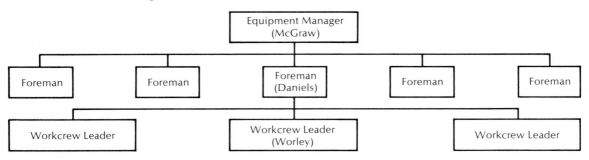

Objectives

1. Recognize basic distinctions between line and staff functions and between personal staff and specialized staff functions.
2. Outline and defend the proper authority relationships between line and staff functions.
3. Explain interdepartmental conflict and its causes.
4. Present the strengths and weaknesses of various conflict resolution methods.

Chapter

7

Interdepartmental Relationships and Conflict

The Nature of Interdepartmental Relationships
Authority Relationships of Line and Staff
Interdepartmental Conflict

Case: The Staff Man

Departments as well as individuals must work together if organizations are to achieve their goals. In place of cooperation, however, we often see conflict. This chapter examines interdepartmental relationships, particularly those between line and staff units. The discussion also considers the causes of interdepartmental conflict and methods of conflict resolution.

The Nature of Interdepartmental Relationships

The basic objective in analyzing formal relationships among individuals and departments is the achievement of teamwork. Harmony is essential if an organization is to achieve its objectives most effectively. The interdependency of individuals and departments in business operations results in numerous opportunities for cooperation or conflict.

The Need for Teamwork

In examining the organization structure—and line-staff relationships in particular—the objective of well-coordinated team effort must be emphasized. There is no virtue in proving the superiority of some specified definition of "staff" or in arguing that a certain activity is a "line" function unless these distinctions contribute to better teamwork. Regardless of the labels we attach to organization functions, it is important that we understand the factors that build constructive relationships and the practices that generate hostility and conflict.

Primary Activities and Departments

In most organizations, a simple distinction can be made between activities that accomplish the basic purposes of the organization and activities that are indirectly helpful. In a college, for example, the teaching faculty provides educational services, whereas the student financial aid office contributes indirectly by helping students to finance their education. In manufacturing plants, production departments make products for customers, whereas personnel offices recruit employees for production and other departments. In department stores, selling departments sell merchandise to customers, whereas credit departments evaluate the financial quality of customers.

Building strong cooperative relationships among departments begins with recognizing these distinctions between primary and secondary activities. From this *functional* point of view, *line activities are those that contribute directly to accomplishment of the organization's primary objective.* The primary or line functions of a manufacturing concern, for example, include producing and selling some product. The firm exists to make and sell products, and customers pay for this service. Employees in production and sales, accordingly, are line personnel, and the manufacturing and sales departments are line departments of the enterprise. In basic economic terms, line departments produce "time, place, and form" utility for customers.

Supporting Activities and Departments

Having defined line functions as those contributing directly to accomplishment of major objectives, we have thereby relegated other activities to the category of staff. In a more positive fashion, *staff functions* should be visualized as *supporting functions.* Their performance in some way facilitates the accomplishment of primary objectives by line departments. Customers have little direct concern with staff functions, because they produce no direct values. They would never pay for staff services, although such services contribute indirectly to the design, production, and sale of the product.

Staff work is often described as advisory to other departments. In addition, the staff may be used for investigation, fact gathering, and service. In fact, the service contributed by some departments is sufficiently great that some writers make a distinction between service functions and staff functions. There is often a close interrelationship between advice and service, however, and many nonline departments provide a combination of both.

Even with a definition of the type outlined here, it is not easy to classify all activities. There are always borderline functions. Many functions, however, are obviously line or obviously staff.

Significance of Line-Staff Distinction

The significance of the distinction is not classification per se. Regardless of what terms are used—and some would prefer to call them *operating* and *auxiliary* departments—the value lies in the emphasis placed upon line functions. They are revealed as the core of the organization. Their failure is equivalent to organization failure, and their success is essential for survival. Understanding the crucial role of line functions enables management to insist that all departments and personnel make a positive contribution to the line functions.

One useful distinction as to types of staff is that of *personal staff* and *specialized staff*.[1] The personal staff is an individual who serves one particular superior. Personal staff assignments may be specialized or involve a sort of generalized troubleshooting which ranges across a broad subject area. The assistant to the president of a firm is an example of this type of staff position.

Types of Staff Functions

In contrast to the service of a personal staff officer, the specialized staff serves an entire organization. It also has a special area of competence in which it is expected to be particularly proficient. Such activities as personnel or labor relations, public relations, and legal counsel are examples of specialized staff functions.

Much of the line and staff problem in a typical organization centers about the question of authority between line and staff departments or personnel. Who decides questions of mutual interest to both line and staff departments? In considering this question, it is best to begin by observing the need for maintaining line authority. Subsequently, it will be possible to note desirable or necessary modifications and exceptions.

Authority Relationships of Line and Staff

In using a staff to support the line organization, it is important to avoid the evil of multiple supervision. To preserve unity of command, staff must be denied command authority. Only in this way can line authority be preserved and the line manager be held responsible for results.

Maintaining Line Authority

The staff position often sounds romantic and less demanding in its requirements upon the incumbent. It is a difficult assignment to fill effectively, however, because of the denial of the right to command. The staff official lacks the tool of authority that is built into line positions.

[2] Louis A. Allen, *The Management Profession* (New York: McGraw-Hill Book Company, 1964), p. 222.

The Basis of Staff Influence

How then can staff managers exert influence and effectively perform the functions for which they are responsible? Lacking authority, they must achieve their objectives in some other way. Since they cannot force their departments and activities or personal advice "down the throat" of line departments, they must, in effect, sell their staff service. Effective salesmanship in this area demands a good product to sell. At any rate, it is much easier for staff to gain acceptance by the line if the staff has something of high quality to offer. To achieve this objective, staff must possess competence and expert knowledge. Theirs is the "authority of ideas."

At the same time, staff is not accepted if it appears unrealistic and "ivory towerish." If staff advice seems impractical, line officials quickly adopt the attitude, "You just don't understand the way we operate." This is the reason that many organizations insist that some staff personnel have previous line operating experience.

Staff Infringement on Line Authority

Organizational myopia seems to be an occupational disease of staff personnel. It is difficult for staff officials to see the organization as the chief executive sees it. Rather, the staff sees line problems in terms of a specialized viewpoint.

This natural tendency toward preoccupation with one staff department is a natural result of a number of factors. The staff, particularly the specialized staff, has expert knowledge in a given area. This situation generates self-confidence in the thinking of staff.

The staff also lacks a familiarity with other aspects of the line administrator's functions. Staff may have difficulty in grasping or fully comprehending the pressures and frustrations confronting the line and the complex social arrangements that exist. There may be little or no awareness of dangers involved in pressuring for a "good" solution or program.

When the sense of perspective that sees staff as an adjunct of the line is lost, any attitude in the direction of self-effacement and sublimation disappears. The staff official begins to think in terms of group effort in which the contribution of each individual is equally essential. The final stage in this progression is usurpation of line authority.

Staff Responsibility for Avoiding Infringement

As noted, it takes courage (if not foolhardiness) for a lowly line supervisor to defy a high-ranking staff officer. Of course, line managers theoretically have this right, but it is not realistic to think that they will always exercise it as aggressively as might be desirable. Expecting the defense of line authority to come from the line, then, is optimistic unless the offices are at the same level in the organization structure.

Staff must tread softly to avoid threats to line authority. It needs to lean over backwards to avoid making decisions for line managers. The following situation graphically portrays the possible range of behavior open to a staff official as a line manager comes to him for advice:

> To give this the added emphasis that it deserves, how shall the personnel manager respond when the foreman says, "What shall I do about John Doe's seniority?"
>
> To be asked any question for information is, of course, subtly flattering because knowledge is implied. The personnel manager, therefore, is natu-

rally inclined to reply, "Give Doe seniority above Smith." When he does, he will be guilty of encroachment. If he is just a bit wiser than this, he may use the subjunctive mood and say, "I would give Doe seniority above Smith." This carries a connotation of advice, to be sure, but the foreman still will be very likely to return to Doe and say, "The personnel manager says to give you seniority above Smith." This is not much better on the part of the personnel manager and is no better at all for the foreman-Doe relationship.

But now suppose the foreman says to the personnel manager, "What shall I do about John Doe's seniority?" and the personnel manager replies, "What do you think should be done?" This obviously puts the colloquy on an entirely different basis. If the foreman then says, "I'd put him below Smith on the seniority list," the personnel manager can find out why the foreman would so decide and can give his own reasons for a different view. If, in addition, the personnel manager emphasizes that the final decision is the foreman's, an altogether different organization result is achieved. Instead of an order, advice and information have been exchanged.[2]

To be effective, this type of approach by staff must be consistent. As Roy has noted, "Good executives and sound relationships do not result from single incidents but accrue from a multitude of them."[3] Staff must take the leadership in fighting its natural tendency toward domination.

Functional Authority of Staff

The organizational world is not simple. Unfortunately, it is difficult in some cases to observe the supposedly ideal authority relationships between line and staff. Situations arise in which it appears desirable from the standpoint of the organization as a whole to delegate to staff some degree of decision-making authority. A deliberate decision may place certain issues or decisions in the hands of staff. Such power is often referred to as *functional authority*, which differs from usurpation of line authority in which staff merely moves in and takes over.

One of the most common forms of functional authority is the assignment to specialized staff of controls pertaining to their own areas. Often these controls are routine or procedural—"how to do it" rather than "what to do." The accounting office polices accounting procedures, and the personnel department checks certain personnel transactions. In effect, this grants to the staff some measure of authority.

> The difference between functional and staff authority is often hard to distinguish, for in some cases it is more nearly a difference in degree than a difference in kind. Functional authority, as often differentiated, is that degree of authority standing somewhere between the so-called full or command authority of the line officer and the advisory or informational authority of the staff officer. It is frequently called "instructional authority" since the relationship between supervisor and subordinate resembles more nearly that between instructor and pupil than that between master and servant.[4]

---

[2] Robert H. Roy, *The Administrative Process* (Baltimore: The Johns Hopkins Press, 1958), pp. 66–67, copyright, 1958, the Johns Hopkins Press.

[3] *Ibid.*, p. 67.

[4] E. H. Anderson, "The Functional Concept in Organization," *Advanced Management* 25, no. 10 (October, 1960): 18.

Following is a specific example of the need for functional authority. Suppose that industrial production processes involve great hazard to life and property. The need for safety in such a case may be so great as to require line authority for safety inspectors. Although safety is normally regarded as a staff function, it may be desirable to grant the safety inspector authority to shut down an operation in order to insure adequate safety for personnel and equipment.

To minimize the dangers involved in functional authority, certain precautions must be observed. There should be a clear specification of the types of questions and the particular staff groups in which functional authority is recognized. The scope of the authority of staff should be carefully prescribed to avoid granting blanket authority over broad areas. If the need for functional authority is not permanent or continuing, its time limit should also be clearly stipulated so that the date of expiration may be known.

The Project Manager

The complex activities and relationships required in high-technology industries have required new approaches in coordination and control. One approach is the use of the project manager position—a type of staff having functional authority.[5] In practice, this position is hybrid rather than pure line or pure staff. Although it has the appearance of a staff office, it often possesses greater authority than is customary in staff functions.

The typical project manager coordinates a development and production project that constitutes a major undertaking for a manufacturer and that involves work in a number of departments. It could be used to manage such undertakings as the introduction of a new consumer product, but to date it has been used primarily in the aerospace industry.

The project manager is responsible for completion of the end product in accordance with performance requirements, budgeted costs, and projected time schedules. A diagram of project management relationships is shown in Figure 7–1. The project manager integrates sales, engineering, manufacturing, and accounting activities by giving directions to personnel in those departments—even though these personnel report on a line basis to their respective functional heads. The project manager does more than offer advice or service, although there are variations in the amount of authority invested in such positions. However, authority and responsibility are often unequal in a practical sense. Top management tends to hold project managers responsible for achieving results that exceed their formal authority. It is clear that serious problems may be involved in an organizational arrangement of this type. Even though the arrangement is not problem free, the device is significant as an innovative response to an operational problem that was not solved by conventional organization theory.

Interdepartmental Conflict

Even though organization structures are designed to promote collaboration, most organizations experience internal conflicts which hamper their perfor-

[5] A somewhat similar position is the *product manager* who serves as marketing manager of one product in a multiproduct consumer company. See Robert M. Fulmer, "Product Management: Panacea or Pandora's Box?" *California Management Review* 7, no. 4, (Summer, 1965): 63–74.

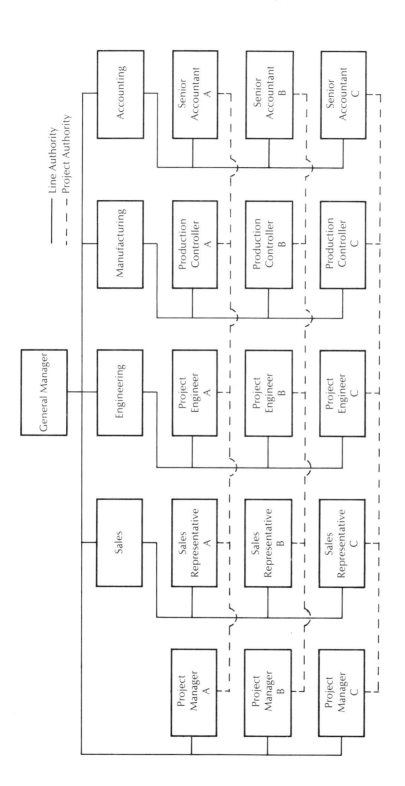

Figure 7-1 *Project Organization in General Industry*

Source: John M. Stewart, "Making Project Management Work," *Business Horizons* 8, no. 3 (Fall, 1965): 58.

mance. Many conflicts involve segments of the organization—group against group or department against department.

Interdepartmental conflict is a major weakness in the functioning of business organizations.[6] Although the existence of such conflict is obvious to those experienced in modern organizational life, two examples will be cited.

In a manufacturing concern, conflict occurred between a small research and development group and first-line production foremen. The four managers in the R and D group held college degrees, but foremen complained that they lacked practical experience. Foremen charged that the engineers did not provide enough detailed information in their drawings, that they lacked an adequate understanding of equipment capacity, that they specified impractical materials based on some salesperson's suggestion, and that they created unnecessary production interruptions to try out new techniques. On the other hand, the engineers felt that line foremen were unwilling to change production methods and that they lacked an adequate education to comprehend broader responsibilities and to understand explanations of engineers. The result was a running battle between the engineering and production functions.

In a retail establishment, the department managers experienced constant tension and occasional conflict with two auxiliary departments—credit and auditing. These managers felt the credit department was inflexible in approving credit, rejecting credit applications of worthy customers because of "red tape." The audit department served as the control arm of higher management and, in the eyes of department managers, displayed an amazing lack of understanding in their "snooping." The fact that a department manager had aggressively sought to obtain an item for the past six months was no excuse for being sold out. Also, department managers were required to document completely any error charged to auditing, but auditors simply conveyed a "we-don't-make-mistakes" attitude. One department head described her view of staff personnel as follows:

> I would classify staff men in one of three ways—(1) those I never saw, (2) those who put their own interests above mine, and (3) those who genuinely wanted to help. It seldom took more than one encounter to decide how to classify a particular man. Once I decided he belonged to group 2, I took evasionary tactics to keep him in the dark.

Even though much conflict is disruptive and harmful to the organization, we cannot categorically denounce all conflict as destructive. Some social scientists, indeed, speak positively of "conflict management" as an opportunity for benefitting the corporation.

One potential benefit from conflict is the improved thinking that may emerge from competition among departments. Unfortunately, there is often a "fallout" of hostility and ill will from conflict situations. Negative feelings may

---

[6] For a more extensive treatment of line-staff conflict, see E. Rhenman, L. Stromberg, and G. Westerlund, *Conflict and Cooperation in Business Organizations* (New York: John Wiley & Sons, Ltd., 1970) and Melville Dalton, "Conflicts Between Staff and Line Managerial Officers," *American Sociological Review* 15, no. 3 (June, 1950): 342–51.

offset or even cancel the benefits that might otherwise result from such conflict. This suggests the importance of controlling conflict situations sufficiently to avoid dysfunctional consequences. As Webber summarized it, "The emerging thesis is that too little expressed conflict leads to stagnancy, but uncontrolled conflict threatens chaos." [7]

Causes of Interdepartmental Conflict

Although managers should adopt a systems view of the total organization, they often limit their view to their immediate departments. From the standpoint of the corporation as a whole, of course, such narrowness of interests is irrational. Nevertheless, it happens. Departmental managers, either consciously or subconsciously, come to think of their departments as their territory or their "turf."

Territorial encroachment is a threat to narrowly focused department managers. These managers remain alert for intruders or "poachers" in their territorial preserves. In complex organizations, however, the required interactions among departments send personnel from one department across their own boundaries and sometimes deep into the heart of other departmental territories. Line managers, for example, may fear that personnel specialists are infringing on their jobs. Managers of one department can easily see representatives of other departments as "meddling" or interfering with internal department operations.

Conflicts between departments may easily involve more substantial issues, however. Departmental interests may simply be incompatible. One cannot win without the other losing. Two departments, for example, may compete for their own shares of a limited capital budget. Funds allocated to one department are not available for another one.

As another example, time-study engineers are rewarded for analyzing production methods, devising improvements, and installing new procedures. Managers of production departments, on the other hand, are concerned with short-run production costs and a smooth flow of production. Time-study engineers interrupt production schedules without changing the current expense budget. Furthermore, production managers are less than eager to be "shown up" in their areas of experience by the innovations of educated but inexperienced outsiders. [8]

Conflicts among departments are also encouraged by differences between the types of personnel assigned to two different departments. Dalton's well-known study of line and staff relationships discovered that staff personnel in the plants he examined were younger, better educated, and better dressed than line managers. The latter were experienced in the practical aspects of work and followed a different life style than the staff specialists. [9] The heterogeneity seemed to exacerbate problems between the two groups.

---

[7] Ross A. Webber, *Management: Basic Elements of Managing Organizations* (Homewood, Ill.: Richard D. Irwin, Inc., 1975), p. 583.

[8] For a classic study of organizational aspects of industrial engineering, see Ross A. Webber, "Innovation and Conflict in Industrial Engineering," *The Journal of Industrial Engineering* (May, 1967).

[9] Melville Dalton, "Conflicts Between Staff and Line Managerial Officers," *American Sociological Review* 15, no. 3 (June, 1950): 342–51.

In summary, interdepartmental conflicts have both rational and emotional bases. Conflicts in interest and territorial encroachments may create a situation in which both parties cannot win. In addition, these conflicts may also be stimulated by differences in personal characteristics and perceptual differences as well as by other factors.

Methods of Conflict Resolution

To avoid an impasse, organizational conflicts must somehow be resolved. There are a number of approaches to settlement of disputes, some of which are discussed below.

Appeal to the Chain of Command

The organizational system is so designed that all individuals, groups, and departments have some common superior. One obvious method of resolving a point of contention, therefore, is to take it to the appropriate manager.

Appeal to the chain of command has its limitations, however. The most knowledgeable decision makers may be the disputants themselves. Higher-level managers, moreover, cannot possibly be involved in all details of operations at lower levels.

Dominance of the Stronger Party

Conflicts may also be settled as one party or the other gains the upper hand and wins. If a dispute is permitted to continue and if disputants have unequal power, the stronger will win. Unfortunately, there is no more reason here than elsewhere to believe that "might makes right."

Allowing settlement of disputes by dominance produces the problem of defeated or wounded managers. If the defeat is severe, the vanquished manager may permanently withdraw by resignation or transfer. In other cases, the defeated party may accept the defeat, stay on, and wait for a more opportune time to fight again.

Bargaining Between Competitors

The bargaining method has been widely used in resolving labor disputes. However, this approach also applies to other types of conflict, as department heads, for example, attempt to resolve any dispute through the give-and-take of negotiations.

One of the difficulties involved in bargaining through representatives is the representative's standing in the group represented.

> Any signs shown by this leader of his willingness to compromise demonstrates weakness in the constituency's view and threatens his power position. Should he be in a position to resolve the issue so as to make his group a clear winner, at the expense of the other, he returns a hero. Should the compromise be made at his group's expense, the leader returns a loser and finds his leadership position deteriorated.[10]

Modifying Organizational Relationships

In some cases, organizational arrangements may be dysfunctional and lead to conflict. Established work patterns may impose a strain on relationships. A well-known example of this problem is the case of the secretary or secretarial

---

[10] Stephen P. Robbins, *Managing Organizational Conflict: A Nontraditional Approach* (Englewood Cliffs. N. J.: Prentice-Hall, Inc., 1974), p. 71.

pool that provides service for a number of administrators or professionals. The difficulty of pleasing a number of supervisors bothers the subordinate, and the need to compete for the time of the subordinate bothers the supervisors. If changes can be made in faulty organization structure, however, conflict may be dissipated.

The *problem solving*, or *integrative decision-making*, approach to conflict resolution directs attention to the controversy itself and away from the parties in conflict. To the extent that the controversy has been created by poor communication, it can be resolved by discussion. By concentrating upon the issue, furthermore, instead of personalities, the interchange can avoid emotional overtones that make communication difficult. Both sides are committed to the same goal—finding a solution for the mutual problem.

Problem-Solving Approach to Conflict Resolution

A person using the problem-solving approach is, according to Filley, saying the following three things to other involved parties:

(1) "I want a solution which achieves your goals and is acceptable to both of us."
(2) "It is our collective responsibility to be open and honest about facts, opinions, and feelings."
(3) "I will control the process by which we arrive at agreement but will not dictate content." [11]

The problem-solving approach has been described as a *win-win* method, in contrast to *win-lose* and *lose-lose* methods. Both parties, in other words, can be winners by imaginatively working out a mutually satisfactory solution. This method contrasts with a *lose-lose* compromise situation in which both parties give up something for a settlement.

Much undesirable conflict may be avoided by building strong interdepartmental relationships, particularly between line and staff departments. In a sense, positive action to encourage cooperation is "preventive maintenance," eliminating disputes before they can arise.

Developing Strong Line-Staff Relationships

The effective use of staff demands relationships that are clearly understood by both line and staff officials. The administrator, in creating a staff office or position, should clearly identify it as such. It may be difficult for subordinates to distinguish easily between line and staff. Anyone from headquarters may be viewed as having authority. Improper clarification that allows staff personnel to exercise line authority may lead to the problems of confusion and irresponsibility noted earlier or to retaliation by line departments and their refusal to work cooperatively with staff.

Following is an example of the problems and confusion arising in the case of line-staff relationships. A personal staff assistant was given a nebulous assignment and permitted to spy on subordinates:

[11] Alan C. Filley, *Interpersonal Conflict Resolution* (Glenview, Ill.: Scott, Foresman and Company, 1975), pp. 27, 29, 30.

Bill Beaty had had engineering training at college and after graduation had joined a medium-sized food company, working first on the shop floor, then for a number of years as a foreman. Later he became a draftsman and was eventually appointed assistant superintendent. He built up a good production record, attracted the president's attention, and was appointed his assistant.

Neither Beaty nor the president's immediate subordinates were informed of the assistant's duties, relationships, or authority. In fact, the president's subordinates heard about the new position for the first time when they received an "order" from the assistant to change their budget proposals. Beaty was unable to shake loose his past experience of command; in fact, he had not been told he should do so. From then on, the subordinates received one command after another from him.

The president devoted less time to his subordinates than before, and they, in turn, became increasingly resentful. They gave the assistant the minimum cooperation they could get away with, and boycotted him whenever possible. Finally, in desperation, they made one of the vice-presidents their spokesman and began to make suggestions aimed at curtailment of the assistant's direct authority.

Some of these suggestions were accepted, and Beaty felt bitter at what he wrongly conceived to be a demotion. He sought vengeance by finding out what was wrong with his chief's subordinates, with their performance and their relationships with each other, and he reported to the president anything adverse he could pick up. In this way he played the "grey eminence behind the throne." Since he could not issue orders directly, he would command through others.

Finally, the embittered subordinates laid a number of well-concealed traps. They withheld information from the assistant, then showed the president that the assistant was not doing his job. Eventually Beaty was fired.[12]

Effective functioning of the organization demands an informed staff. The industrial engineering staff, for example, must be aware of the processing problems encountered in the manufacturing operations of the business. To be informed, staff must be accepted as a vital working partner in the business. The chief executive, for example, must see that vital staff offices are represented in discussions and meetings with which they have a legitimate concern.

Summary   The objective in examining interdepartmental relationships is *teamwork* in the accomplishment of organizational objectives. *Line functions*, those directly concerned with the accomplishment of an organization's primary objectives, are aided by *staff functions* and staff personnel. The staff may be visualized as providing *support* for line activities in the form of service and advice. One classification of staff functions distinguishes between *personal* staff and *specialized* staff.

Staff should generally occupy an *advisory* rather than a command relationship to line. Infringements on line authority can create serious organization problems by causing a deterioration of line morale and making it difficult to

---

[12] Ernest Dale and Lyndall F. Urwick, *Staff in Organization* (New York: McGraw-Hill Book Company, 1960), pp. 172–73.

hold line officials responsible. As a practical matter, however, the needs of a business organization often require staff to be granted *funstaional authority* in certain areas. To avoid confusion, this authority must be properly limited.

Conflicts among groups and departments often disrupt organizational relationships and operations. Although some conflicts are beneficial to the organization, many are dysfunctional. Causes of such conflicts include the *territorial encroachments* of one department on another and *conflicts in interest* between two or more departments. *Conflict resolution* may be achieved in a number of ways, including *appeal to the chain of command, dominance* of the stronger party, *bargaining* between competitors, *structural modifications,* and *problem solving.* Steps to avoid conflict by developing strong interdepartmental relationships are desirable, particularly among key line and staff departments.

Discussion Questions

1. Formulate the best possible definitions of *line* and *staff* in terms of authority relationships. What weaknesses, if any, do you see in these definitions?

2. In view of the confusion and disagreement concerning line and staff terminology, would it appear desirable to drop the terms that have been used traditionally?

3. What limitation or inaccuracy may be involved in viewing staff offices as having merely an *advisory* relationship to line functions?

4. Suppose the chief executive of a growing company employs an attorney who is designated as the "legal department." Is this an example of a *personal* staff or *specialized* staff?

5. If the staff lacks authority, how can it provide any guidance or control? Won't line managers disregard its suggestions? Should it, therefore, be given some degree of authority?

6. What accounts for the tendency of staff officials to become authoritative in their relationships with other parts of the organization?

7. Explain the concept of *functional authority.* What are its weaknesses?

8. What is the difference between beneficial and destructive interdepartmental conflicts?

9. Give an example of an interdepartmental conflict based on a real *conflict of interest,* if there are such.

10. A lack of clarity in line-staff relationships is rather common. What are the probable reasons for this condition?

11. Who bears the primary responsibility for keeping the staff informed?

Supplementary Reading

Browne, Philip J. and Cotton, Chester C. "The Topdog/Underdog Syndrome in Line-Staff Relations." *Personnel Journal* 54, no. 8 (August, 1975): 443–44.

Coleman, Charles and Rich, Joseph. "Line, Staff and the Systems Perspective." *Human Resource Management* 12, no. 3 (Fall, 1973): 20–27.

Filley, Alan C. *Interpersonal Conflict Resolution.* Glenview, Ill.: Scott, Foresman and Company, 1975.

Kelly, Joe. "Make Conflict Work for You." *Harvard Business Review* 48, no. 4 (July–August, 1970): 103–13.

Robbins, Stephen P. *Managing Organizational Conflict: a Nontraditional Approach.* Englewood Cliffs, N.J.: Prentice-Hall, Inc., 1974.

Case 7

The Staff Man*

Tom Peterson is manager of the technical publications department of a medium-sized manufacturing firm. He has been with the company twenty years and has worked himself "up through the ranks."

Bob Hanna occupies the newly established position of systems analyst, a staff position within the department, reporting directly to Peterson. Hanna is responsible for improving and developing systems for the distribution of the publications. The nature of his job requires that he have several meetings with Peterson each week. Hanna has a good personality and is well liked. He is also well-educated and holds several degrees.

The department is divided into three sections with approximately eight employees in each section. However, all three sections are located in one large office area with no partitions separating the three sections. Bob Hanna is located near the center of the office at a desk vacated by a recent retiree.

More and more of the employees were going to Hanna for advice, even though it was not his job. At first the advice was minor, but eventually the situation developed to the point where Hanna began not only to advise but to direct the work of the employees as an assistant department head would do. When Peterson became aware of the situation, he became enraged and recommended to his own boss that Hanna be fired and the position abolished.

Questions

1. Is Hanna's position that of a "staff man" or an assistant line manager? What is the difference?

2. Who is responsible for Hanna's assumption of an order-giving role?

3. Evaluate Peterson's reaction to the situation.

4. What action would you take if you were Peterson? If you were Hanna?

---

*From John V. Murray and Thomas J. Von der Embse, *Organizational Behavior: Critical Incidents and Analysis* (Columbus, Ohio: Charles E. Merrill Publishing Company, 1973), p. 167.

Objectives

1. Recognize uses of committees, reasons for their use, and difficulties involved in committee management.
2. Outline structure and procedures contributing to, and detracting from, committee effectiveness.

Chapter

8

Using Committees

Someone has facetiously suggested that a camel is a horse that was put together by a committee. As the tone of the comment suggests, committees have their critics. In spite of their weaknesses, however, the general consensus among administrators is that committees are essential in managing large organizations and often useful in managing smaller groups.

Business Use of Committees

Nature and Importance of Committees

Committees have multiplied as organizations have grown in size and complexity. In large governmental, educational, charitable, and business institutions, committees have become an integral part of the administrative structure. In the business field, they are not limited to large corporations but are also found in relatively small concerns. Nor are they limited to top management levels, but they function at middle and lower levels of the organization as well.

Committees are almost infinite in their variety. In duration, for example, there are standing committees maintained permanently, and *ad hoc* (or special purpose) committees appointed to serve only temporarily. In their time requirements, they range from those that meet rarely to those that meet regularly on a weekly and, in some cases, even a daily basis.

With respect to purpose, committees may be policy making, administrative, executive, innovative, informational, and so on. The subjects they consider are as varied as the business enterprise itself, including general management, engineering, product design, research, safety, capital spending, advertising, collective bargaining, public relations, and many others.

The highest-level committee within a business enterprise is its board of directors. This group acts as a policy-making committee, working through appointed officers, but it may also overlap the top administrative levels of the concern through the use of an executive committee. That is, the membership of an executive committee may include individuals who serve as both directors and officers of the corporation.

Extent of Use

Studies have shown that most companies use various types of standing, or regular, committees to supplement their line and staff organizations. A survey sponsored by the *Harvard Business Review* confirmed this use of standing committees. According to their survey results, which are given in greater detail in Figure 8–1, 81.5 percent of the executives responding reported the presence of standing committees in their firms.[1]

These results pertained only to standing committees and revealed nothing concerning the existence of *ad hoc* committees. It is probable that many companies reporting no regular standing committees use special purpose committees from time to time. It is also likely that companies using and reporting upon standing committees supplement them with temporary or special purpose committees.

---

[1] "Problems in Review: Committees on Trial," *Harvard Business Review* 38, no. 3 (May-June, 1960): 7.

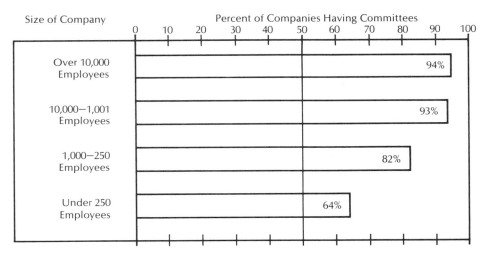

Extent of Company Use of Regular Committees   **Figure 8-1**

Source: "Problems in Review: Committees on Trial," *Harvard Business Review* 38, no. 3 (May-June, 1960): 8.

When confronted with a complex problem or the need for a serious decision, a person often seeks the counsel of others. Almost intuitively, he or she turns to a trusted friend or relative to talk it over, trading ideas and getting reactions and possibly advice from the counselor. The committee system provides an arrangement for systematizing and formalizing group deliberation on organizational problems.

Committee analysis or review of a business problem represents a kind of insurance against a decision based upon faulty reasoning or personal bias. This implies, of course, that the committee is more than a rubber stamp and that members can speak out on issues under consideration. (A cartoon has depicted the chairman putting the question to vote with "All who object, say 'I resign.'") It also implies that the committee chairperson is sufficiently honest and alert to recognize personal bias when a challenge is voiced in the committee and is willing to act accordingly.

The committee can be used to pull together the different abilities and knowledge of its members. No two individuals approach solution of a complex problem in precisely the same way, and varied analytical abilities may, through committee deliberation, be brought to bear upon the same problem. The various departments and functional areas of the organization also involve different points of view, which may be discovered and applied to the question at hand.

The extent to which a committee can be genuinely creative is controversial. Some critics contend that the creative contributions would be fully as great if individual participants were to concentrate their thinking on the problem at hand. For example, Ralph J. Cordiner, former chairman of General Electric, has said, "If you can name for me one great discovery or decision that was made by a committee, I will find you the one man in that committee who had the

Reasons for Use of Committees

Better Decisions Through Group Deliberation

lonely insight—while he was shaving or on his way to work, or maybe while the rest of the committee was chattering away—the lonely insight which solved the problem and was the basis for the decision." [2]

Coordination of Work

Specialization of work, both operative and managerial, makes synchronization of activities difficult. Functions of one department are intertwined with those of other departments. As an example, a decision in the area of research and development may have repercussions affecting sales, production, finance, personnel, public relations, the legal department, and even other activities.

In the organization that has become too large for personal observation by its members, the left hand does not always know what the right hand is doing unless active steps are taken to achieve this objective. The committee provides one way to achieve coordination of effort.

Occasionally, comments are heard that the use of committees for coordination is carried to excess. One executive, for example, remarked, "We spend so much time hearing about the problems of other departments that we have no time to solve our own." However, experienced committee members generally concede the value of committees in coordinating activities.

Securing Cooperation in Execution

In the execution or application of plans and policies, there are certain barriers that interfere with effective administration. Among them are misunderstanding of a given plan or policy and also the feeling that one must follow a policy or plan without an opportunity to express opinions about it. The difficulties, then, may occur in terms of both knowledge and desire.

A committee may be used as a means of attacking both problems. For example, discussion in a committee meeting can bring to light mistaken ideas and answer questions concerning the matter under consideration. A committee member who has objections may be given the opportunity to voice them. Even if some members disagree with the final decision of the chairperson or group, it is difficult for them to oppose the decision as violently as they might if it were simply handed to them without explanation or opportunity for comments.

It is possible, of course, that an administrator may use a committee as a tactical weapon to minimize opposition to intended action. To the extent that the executive simply uses a committee to approve a preconceived plan with no intention of seriously considering committee reactions, however, the committee method loses its effectiveness in securing cooperation in execution.

Training of Participants

Development of personnel for all levels of management is one of the important responsibilities of administrators. By serving as committee members, participants are exposed to ideas and knowledge that may lie outside their usual areas of responsibility. In addition, committee members may engage in study in the process of preparing for committee participation, particularly if they are given some special responsibilities in connection with committee projects and performance.

---

[2] M. R. Lohmann, *Top Management Committees*, AMA Research Study 48 (New York: American Management Association, 1961), pp. 8–9.

Perhaps the greatest training value comes from the give-and-take of committee sessions. In this atmosphere, committee members gain experience in speaking before a group, expressing ideas, and defending points of view.

Dangers and Difficulties in Use of Committees

Committees have their detractors. After Lindbergh's historic solo flight to Europe, Mrs. Charles F. Kettering is reputed to have exclaimed to her husband "Isn't it wonderful! And to think he did it all alone!" "Well," replied Kettering, "it would have been still more wonderful if he had done it with a committee."

Waste of Time and Money

One criticism of committees is that they waste managerial time and thus dollars. An analysis by McKinsey and Company, Inc., of committee assignments in an insurance firm, disclosed that five vice-presidents were each spending 26 hours per month—exclusive of preparation time—in meetings.[3] In an electronics manufacturing concern, vice-presidents reported that committee meetings accounted for half their time. Committee action may be wasteful because there are too many committees in existence, because a committee is too large in its membership, because a committee meets too frequently, or because a committee is inefficient in its methods of operation.

Committees often waste time on subjects of negligible importance or subjects that could be disposed of by one person without difficulty. C. Northcote Parkinson has formulated what he calls the *law of triviality*, which holds that "the time spent on any item of the agenda will be in inverse proportion to the sum involved."[4] His discussion suggests that committees are prone to engage in interminable discussion of items having only passing significance.

Danger of Compromise

One of the greatest potential weaknesses of committees is their tendency toward compromise decisions. One hears such statements as "All a committee ever comes up with is some middle-of-the-road plan which no one completely opposes but which no one really believes," or "Committee solutions simply represent the lowest common denominator of the thinking of the members on that committee." The general thought is that the group lacks the will or forcefulness to reach the same sound conclusion that might be achieved by one person acting alone. Not all compromise is undesirable, of course, but there is no guarantee that the middle of the road is always the best part of the road.

One pressure that contributes to a spirit of compromise is the personal work load of committee members. Because these executives typically have full schedules, it is natural for them to attempt to reach a committee decision quickly in order to resume their regular responsibilities. Also, most committee members do not wish to embarrass other members of the same committee. To save face for all participants, the group may accept a conclusion or solution that is not violently opposed by any of the members.

---

[3] J. Alan Ofner, "Are Committees Worth While?" *Commerce Magazine* 56, no. 2 (March, 1959): 64–65.

[4] C. Northcote Parkinson, *Parkinson's Law* (Boston: Houghton Mifflin Company, 1957), p. 24.

Difficulty in Placing Responsibility

Committee activity may constitute a type of shield behind which an individual manager can take refuge. The fact of committee deliberation may be taken as evidence that an executive has been reasonably prudent in exercising administrative responsibility. A question is implicitly raised as to how a manager can be criticized for a decision on which most people agree. Even though a committee is advisory, its action provides a stamp of approval for the decision of the individual executive.

Holding an individual manager responsible, then, becomes difficult. The higher-level executive seeking to enforce responsibility on a subordinate may appear to be unfair and unreasonable in expectations. This difficulty may be alleviated by insisting upon acceptance of full responsibility by individual managers. The advisory nature of committees may be forcefully emphasized in the statements and attitude of higher-level management.

Delay and Indecision

Committee action takes time. Individual committee members must assemble, and this requires a reconciliation of time demands of the committee with the various personal schedules and other official responsibilities of the members. Committee activity typically is an extra function for the manager. The more important the committee, of course, the more the other work demands must yield to committee activities. In any case, however, some delay is experienced in getting the members of the committee together and in reaching a decision. Subsequent meetings may even be necessary to reach a conclusion.

Early in his career as Secretary of Defense, Robert S. McNamara became perturbed with the slowness of decision making in his department.[5] "The Defense establishment," said McNamara, "could do everything twice as fast as presently." One of two major evils which he felt slowed the decision-making process was the tendency to appoint committees and to "coordinate." Acting upon this evaluation of committees, the Secretary of Defense eliminated 424 committees and scheduled 129 more for deactivation.

Domination by One Individual

Occasionally, a committee operates under the thumb or domination of one person. This individual's reaction provides the key to action by the group. An expression of disapproval, for example, whether verbal or by facial expression, may start the entire group on a negative approach or evaluation. In its most extreme form, such domination results in a committee that constitutes a form of window dressing to approve some pet idea of the dominant individual.

This deterioration of the committee function contrasts sharply with the values that are believed to exist in committees. Committees are presumably characterized by the give-and-take of equals. Committee deliberation represents a pooling of ideas in an atmosphere of mutual respect and tolerance. One member builds upon suggestions of another member. All participants sense a freedom to correct, to question, and to suggest modifications to the ideas and purposes of others.

The dominant individual is ordinarily the chairperson of the committee. Frequently, this person is also the superior of other members of the com-

---

[5] "Committees Are of Value Only for Exchanging Ideas," *Armed Forces Management* 8, no. 2 (November, 1961): 22–24.

mittee. The committee may, therefore, be inclined to show deference for this reason alone. If the chairperson is a driving, dominant leader, it is difficult to change the atmosphere when the scene shifts to a committee room.

In achieving efficiency in committee operation, one of the first and basic steps is to make explicit the objectives and authority of each committee. This step is desirable both to provide for the effective functioning of the committee and also to secure the proper cooperation of outsiders in their relationships with the committee. Figure 8–2 presents a formal statement of committee responsibilities as defined by a machine tool manufacturer.

A periodic review of committees and their objectives is valuable. Committees have a way of starting without extensive study and sometimes without

Effective Operating Procedures for Committees

Committee Objectives

Figure 8–2

Objective and Functions of Finance Committee (Machine Tool Manufacturer)

The purpose of the finance committee is to carry out fiscal policies which will maintain the sound financial condition of the company and provide earnings for the stockholders, commensurate with our contribution to the economy of the country as a whole.

The finance committee has the following responsibilities:

Budget
Approve division and department budgets, and review against actual performance a minimum of once each quarter.

Establish a yearly budget, and review against actual performance a minimum of once each quarter.

Product Price Policies
Establish a flexible price policy which will return to the company all essential costs plus an adequate profit.

Anticipate increasing costs and adjust proposal prices with sufficient lead time to recover increases as they occur.

Expenditures
Establish appropriation procedure setting forth signature requirements for various amounts.

Review over-all appropriation expenditure totals at least once each quarter.

Review all appropriation requests in excess of $5,000, and survey effects on pricing and profit structure. All such appropriations must bear the approval of a quorum of the committee, then follow the regular procedure as set forth in . . . executive standard practice.

Cash Position
Review cash position and cash forecasts following each monthly financial report, and make recommendations as to the timing of expenditures in order to avoid any undue strain on the company's credit.

Review provisions for establishment of credit and borrowings against these credits.

Each member of the committee is to be provided with a copy of the minutes of each meeting.

Reprinted by permission of the publisher from M. R. Lohmann, *Top Management Committees*, AMA Research Study 48, p. 37, © 1961 by American Management Association, Inc.

real justification. A critical review both in establishing and continuing committees helps to avoid those that are vestigial or totally unnecessary.

Membership of Committees

Attendance at committee meetings in which an individual has little interest can be monotonous. The objectives established for a committee help to determine the individuals who should serve on it. Membership should be limited to those who are directly involved or who have an important interest in the function of the committee.

In selecting committee members, a number of points should be considered. For example, the personal knowledge or experience that is useful to the committee is one important factor. The effectiveness of the individual in working with other members of a group is another point in selection. In addition, the need for training of various individuals may be given some consideration in their selection for committee assignments.

There is a tendency for committees to grow too large and to become unduly cumbersome. The average size of business committees is about eight individuals, but committee members often express a preference for a smaller number, particularly about five members. Interestingly enough, some cynical committee members suggest a preference for committees with a membership of one!

Agenda for Committee Meetings

A committee *agenda* is an outline or schedule of subjects to be considered at a committee session. It is normally prepared by the chairperson or the secretary of the committee and may be circulated in advance of the meeting.

Use of an agenda, such as the one shown in Figure 8–3, has the advantage of assuring consideration of all topics that, in the opinion of the chairperson, justify the time and attention of the committee. It has the advantage also of providing a structure for discussion and enables the committee to proceed logically to consider one topic after another. Distribution of the agenda in advance of the committee meeting makes the session less of a "surprise party" and enables members to come better prepared to take up a particular topic.

The Committee Chairperson

The committee chairperson is quite likely the most important single factor in determining the efficiency with which a committee operates. Use of effective committee techniques is, to a great extent, a reflection of the personal ability and insights of the chairperson.

Selection of the chairperson is, therefore, a most important step in assuring an effective committee. This person is sometimes selected on the basis of position, and, in this case, one can only hope that the individual is properly qualified for the role.

In making the selection, knowledge of the subject and experience with the particular problem are important considerations with respect to the chairperson's qualifications. Mere knowledge of subject matter, however, does not qualify the individual for effective committee leadership. The knowledge and experience background must be supplemented with personal traits necessary to function smoothly as a group leader.

The chairperson does not force personal ideas through the committee without adequate consideration by its members. Leadership must be provided in

Agenda for Wednesday Meeting of DuPont's Executive Committee   **Figure 8-3**

Chart Room
1. Fabrics and Finishes Department regular report for January.
2. Grasselli Chemicals Department regular report for January.
3. Photo Products Department regular report for January.
4. Pigments Department regular report for January.
5. Foreign Relations Department—annual report and operating budget.

Committee Room
Unfinished business
6. Engineering Department—operating budget.
7. Motion picture program based on the Company's programs re: "How Our Business System Operates." Joint report from Advertising, Employee Relations, and Public Relations Departments.

New business
8. Organic Chemicals Department regular report for January.
9. Appropriation project covering partial design, procurement of long delivery equipment, and preparation of construction cost estimate New River Pump House, ash and waste retention facilities, Old Hickory Rayon and Cellophane Plants.
10. Appropriation project—replacement of worn-out pirns, Waynesboro Plant.
11. Credit appropriation—additional power facilities, Spruance Rayon Plant.
12. Appropriation—project for synthesis gas via coal partial combustion—Step #I, Belle Works.
13. Adjustment of permanent investment—QY catalyst facilities, Arlington Works.
14. Supplemental report on accomplishment—second year's operation—continuous polyvinyl alcohol and monomer process, Niagara Falls Plant.
15. History, present status, and future prospects of the "Elvanol" polyvinyl alcohol business. Report from Electrochemicals Department.
16. Miscellaneous items.

Source: William H. Mylander, "Management by Executive Committee," *Harvard Business Review* 33, no. 3 (May–June 1955): 54.

committee discussion without becoming dictatorial. This means that the leader must keep the discussion moving, properly recording and noting progress as it is achieved.

The chairperson should have at least minimal human relations skills. Inasmuch as the committee process is a group process involving interpersonal relations, it is desirable that he or she be particularly adept in seeing that good human relations are maintained in the committee room. It is the chairperson's task to draw out the reticent individual and to secure from such a person ideas and contributions regarding proposals under consideration. At the same time, the leader must hold down the loquacious individual who is inclined to voice any idea without sufficient thought. It is also important to sense potential disputes, to handle them so that they involve issues rather than personalities, and to direct the discussions so that differences of opinion do not erupt into personal clashes between individual committee members.

The chairperson may require or allow the discussion of certain items to be carried primarily by the individual most directly involved. When the topic requires a decision, the leader may conclude the discussion at an appropriate point and may announce a decision at that time. To give the committee a more powerful role, the leader may take a vote or state what seems to be the general sentiment or consensus of the group. After the meeting, some follow-up is usually required, and the circulation of the minutes of the committee session can be one part of the follow-up activity.

Summary

Committees have become an integral part of the administrative structure of most modern business organizations. They are almost infinite in variety, differing in terms of their permanency, time required for committee work, purpose, subject matter, power, and in other ways.

Advantages resulting from the use of committees include the improvement of decisions through group deliberation, coordination of work, facilitation of cooperation in the execution or application of plans and policies, and training of participants. Among the offsetting dangers and limitations are the waste of time and money, danger of undesirable compromise in decision making, difficulty in placing responsibility for decisions, delays and indecision in administrative action, and domination of the committee by one individual.

Effective committee action requires efficient organization and operating procedures. These include clearly stipulated committee objectives, properly qualified committee members, carefully prepared agendas for committee meetings, and a competent committee chairperson.

Discussion Questions

1. Should a decision of a committee be better than the decision of its most capable and thoughtful member? Why?

2. In what ways does committee activity provide better coordination of specialized departments or activities than that achieved by other administrative techniques?

3. If committee members are selected on the basis of their ability to make an effective contribution rather than their need for training, how can committees develop managerial personnel?

4. Which of the suggested dangers or difficulties in the use of committees appears most serious? What is the basis for your answer?

5. Is it possible for a manager to chair a committee containing his or her subordinates without dominating the sessions?

6. What is the value of preparing written objectives for committees?

7. Is it likely that a committee agenda has any practical value if committee members are the usual busy executives?

8. What criteria should be used in selecting a committee chairperson?

Filley, A. C. "Committee Management: Guidelines from Social Science Research." *California Management Review* 13, no. 1 (Fall, 1970): 13–21.

Golde, Roger A. "Are Your Meetings Like This One?" *Harvard Business Review* 50, no. 1 (January-February, 1972): 68–77.

Grote, Richard C. "Hidden Saboteurs of Group Meetings." *Personnel* 47, no. 5 (September-October, 1970): 42–48.

Tasklanganos, Angelos A. "The Committee in Business: Asset or Liability?" *Personnel Journal* 54, no. 2 (February, 1975): 90–93.

Supplementary Reading

Case 8

The Monthly Committee Meeting

Brenda, a young business manager, served as a member of the executive committee of a local civic organization. Although this position meant nothing financially, it provided experience in committee work, permitted association with individuals on a professional level, and gave an outlet for service to the community. As a result of these considerations, Brenda had welcomed the opportunity to serve in this way. The chairperson of the committee was also executive director and a salaried member of the organization.

During the eight months she had served on the committee, Brenda's enthusiasm had gradually declined, but she had never tried to pinpoint the reason. In any event, the meetings were less fun than she had anticipated.

Brenda was now at her eighth committee meeting. Fifteen minutes had elapsed, and that meant about one hour and 45 minutes remained. Sessions always lasted two hours. An agenda lay on the table in front of her. It was a typed list of twelve numbered items. Most of them were self-explanatory, except for two that seemed meaningless. The agenda had been passed out at the beginning of the session, and Brenda was sure that items 7 and 10 would be clear enough when the committee got to them and the chairperson explained the meaning of the secret code words.

The chairperson's leadership behavior had surprised Brenda, although the surprise and newness had worn off in the eight months. As an executive in a business organization, Brenda was accustomed to forthright leadership by a "take charge" manager. In this committee, however, the chairperson always acted in a thoroughly democratic manner. On almost every issue, the chairperson introduced the item in a cautious voice and then asked, "I wonder how we would feel about this?" Brenda thought the chairperson might explain the "angles," perhaps say how he felt about it, and then suggest a course of action. But, she reasoned, that might reflect her own business background and authoritative inclinations. Could a chairperson express an opinion without stifling committee thought?

Would that lead to domination by the chairperson? These questions kept coming to mind.

Brenda was even surprised by the chairperson's chair. Rather than positioning himself at one end of the table, the seemingly natural leadership position, the chairperson always sat, almost inconspicuously it seemed to Brenda, in one of the chairs at the side. Brenda wondered about the reason for this. Was it merely coincidence?

From time to time, the chairperson made a point of stressing committee responsibility. It was the *committee* that represented the organization; the chairperson was serving as chairperson simply because the by-laws specified he was the one to perform this function. When, on a seemingly inconsequential point, Brenda once suggested the matter be left to the chairperson's discretion, the chairperson said he thought it "would be good for the committee to act as a matter of record."

When members were to be appointed to special committees, the chairperson avoided personal selection by insisting the executive committee should use its collective judgment. In fact, to the best of Brenda's recollection, the chairperson had never once brought a slate of names or made suggestions. The democratic committee philosophy of the chairperson apparently made such direction unthinkable.

Apparently this is what is meant by a democratic committee, Brenda thought. At any rate, no one can accuse this chairperson of "railroading" business through the committee or riding roughshod over the members.

Brenda glanced at her watch again. Only one hour and 30 minutes more to go.

Questions

1. What is your evaluation of the chairperson and his role in this committee?

2. What, if anything, would you do differently if you were the chairperson?

3. Evaluate the use of an agenda for committee meetings.

4

Understanding Behavioral Aspects of Organizations

Objectives

1. Explain business organizations as *social systems* and the significance of interpersonal relationships in organizational life.
2. Identify the various forms of *informal organization* and show their relationship to the formal organization.
3. Point out *political* aspects of organizational behavior and explain the ways in which *political power* is built and exercised.

Chapter

Informal Groups and Relationships

The Social Structure of Industry
Work Groups and Informal Organization
Power and Politics

Case: The Blast Furnace Confrontation

Any organization is a social system, and its human relationships affect its performance. In this chapter, we consider the interpersonal relationships of organizations, especially informal ones that supplement the formal organization structure.

The Social Structure of Industry

The Human Side of Organization

A business firm requires people—a human organization—to provide the mental and physical services necessary in accomplishing its objectives. The official responsibilities and relationships of these people may be indicated in a general way by an organization chart. The lines on such a chart represent *interpersonal* relationships, and these relationships provide the skeleton for the social structure. When we say that a laboratory supervisor reports to a department manager, this involves more than one box on a chart reporting to another box. It means that Jones, the laboratory supervisor, reports to Wolfe, the department manager. It further means that Wolfe directs and evaluates the performance of Jones. Jones must satisfy Wolfe in order to progress in the organization.

The social structure of an organization encompasses more than the formal superior-subordinate relationships. Any member of the organization normally has contact with other members of the same organization. Two employees work side by side in a shop or share adjoining desks in an office. Employees also eat lunch together in the cafeteria or ride in the same car pool. All of these relationships, if they are continuing, are a part of the social structure of the organization.

An organization, therefore, is more than a collection of individuals. To understand its nature, we must recognize the social relationships that exist and understand their significance. An organization member is more than an isolated individual. Instead, he or she is located at some point in a web of relationships. The following studies were noteworthy in drawing the attention of managers and students of management to the nature and importance of these relationships.

Western Electric Illumination Experiments [1]

In 1924, the Western Electric Company, manufacturer of telephone equipment, initiated a series of experiments that were later to become famous. In one phase of these experiments, workers were divided into two groups—a test group and a control group. Lighting affecting the test group was increased from 24 to 46 to 70 foot-candles, while control group lighting was held constant. It was assumed that output of the test group would show some increase in contrast to that of the control group. Results were surprising, however, because production of both groups increased in roughly the same proportion!

In another experiment, lighting of a test group was reduced from 10 to 3 foot-candles, while lighting of the control group was held constant. Rather than declining, however, test group output increased—as did that of the control group! It is evident that some uncontrolled variables were at work. These

---

[1] Descriptions of the Western Electric experiments, including both the illumination and other phases, may be found in F. J. Roethlisberger and William J. Dickson, *Management and the Worker* (Cambridge: Harvard University Press, 1946); F. J. Roethlisberger, *Management and Morale* (Cambridge: Harvard University Press, 1941), Chapter 2; and Stuart Chase, *Men at Work* (New York: Harcourt, Brace, & World, Inc., 1945), Chapter 2.

factors were canceling any effects resulting from physical changes. We should note that the employees involved in the experiment were aware of the study and were apparently reacting to it in some way. The experiment disclosed that the human element in production was more significant than had been previously realized.

Following the illumination experiments, the researchers attempted to measure the effect of fatigue or rest upon output. In conducting the study, a group of six women assembling telephone relays was brought into a special test room.

The general plan was to measure output in different periods of several weeks each. In the early periods, the rate of output was established under "normal" conditions. In subsequent periods, rest pauses of various lengths were introduced. In Period IV, for example, two rest periods of five minutes each were introduced—one in the morning and one in the afternoon.

During the experimentation, which continued for more than a year, output increased as working conditions were improved. Professor Roethlisberger has summarized the results of these experiments as follows:

> During the first year and a half of the experiment, everybody was happy, both the investigators and the operators. The investigators were happy because as conditions of work improved the output rate rose steadily. Here, it appeared, was strong evidence in favor of their preconceived hypothesis that fatigue was the major factor limiting output. The operators were happy because their conditions of work were being improved, they were earning more money, and they were objects of considerable attention from top management. But then one investigator—one of those tough-minded fellows—suggested that they restore the original conditions of work, that is, go back to a full forty-eight-hour week without rests, lunches and what not. This was Period XII. Then the happy state of affairs, when everything was going along as it theoretically should, went sour. Output, instead of taking the expected nose dive, maintained its high level.[2]

Attitudes of the women toward their work, management, and work group were apparently affecting their work efficiency. According to William Foote Whyte, Period XII provided the birthplace for industrial sociology.[3] Realization of the <u>importance of human relationships</u> in industry increased rapidly from the date of this experiment.

Another phase of the Western Electric experimentation involved observation of a group of fourteen workers engaged in wiring certain types of telephone equipment. The group included wirers, solderers, and inspectors. It was discovered that this group operated as a team rather than as a group of individuals. The group recognized its own informal leaders and also shared various sentiments. For example, a member was expected to avoid turning out too much, thus becoming a "rate buster."

---

[2] F. J. Roethlisberger, *Management and Morale* (Cambridge: Harvard University Press, 1941), p. 13.

[3] William Foote Whyte, *Men at Work* (Homewood, Ill.: Richard D. Irwin, Inc., and The Dorsey Press, 1961), p. 8.

**The Business
Organization as a
Social System**

The effect of the Western Electric experiments was to turn a spotlight on the social structure of industry and its significance in business operation. In developing theory to incorporate these findings, researchers adopted the concept of the business organization as a *social system*. According to this view, the social system of a factory, store, or office has as its component parts the employees of those organizations. The social system involves more than a group of individuals, however. The component parts—that is, the people—function or work together through patterns of interaction that develop among the members. One part of a company—say the drafting room or typing pool—is a social system, and the entire company is also a social system. In other words, there are systems within systems.

A formal organization structure, if it were sufficiently detailed to include all employees, would show all component parts of the social system—that is, all personnel. It would also indicate the approximate formal relationships of these parts to each other. A manual or job description might detail all activities expected from a particular position and describe the intended relationships and methods of working with others.

Functioning of the system is only partially prescribed by the statement of formal organization, however. Employees devise arrangements and procedures that supplement or conflict with the formally prescribed structure. In the bank wiring observation room, the informal set of relationships did not appear on the organization chart or receive formal recognition. (The nature of informal organization will be discussed in more detail in the following section.)

**Work Groups
and Informal
Organization**

Management creates work groups by specifying interrelated job assignments and by locating employees in proximity to each other. The life and activities of such groups typically extend far beyond the minimum relationships stipulated by the formal organization. Formal work associations are supplemented by friendships that develop among members of work groups. Through luncheon groups, shared coffee breaks, general conversation about nonbusiness subjects, and in numerous other ways the life of formal groups is elaborated. In many cases, strong personal relationships develop along organization lines—that is, within immediate work groups. In other cases, individuals from different work groups are drawn together by some common interest.[4]

**Understanding
Organizational
Behavior**

One approach to an analysis and understanding of work group behavior draws attention to three factors—*activities, interactions,* and *sentiments.*[5] A study of *activities* shows us what an individual does. Job requirements specify some of the required activities. The job incumbent drives a truck, operates a machine, types invoices, or programs a computer. A job description does not list all details of job performance, however. The individual supplements, eliminates, or modifies the officially specified duties to produce the actual work activities

---

[4] The small face-to-face work groups and social groups discussed in this section are customarily referred to by sociologists as *primary groups.*

[5] William Foote Whyte, *Organizational Behavior: Theory and Application* (Homewood, Ill.: Richard D. Irwin, Inc., and The Dorsey Press, 1969), Chapters 4 and 5.

that can be observed. Examples of unrequired activities are drinking coffee, talking with a colleague, and engaging in horseplay.

Activities typically require some *interaction*, but jobs differ greatly in their interaction requirements. Interactions occur when individuals respond to each other, and they typically involve some communication. A supervisor talks with an employee, a machine operator obtains a tool from a tool room attendant, or an engineer dictates a letter to a secretary. Each of these activities involves an interaction.

Sentiments refer to feelings or attitudes. Some sentiments are acquired prior to, or apart from, employment. An employee may feel, for example, that people should have short hair or that idleness is wrong. Other sentiments are developed within the group, some of which are group norms that prescribe standards of conduct for the group.

As an example of these factors in a practical situation, consider a change in production technology that takes employees out of small work teams and distributes them along an assembly line. In all probability, the scope of the job (required activities) would be narrowed. Furthermore, a reduction in interactions would occur. As a result of changes in activities and interactions, sentiments would likewise be affected. If the individual enjoys interaction and the opportunity for performing a varied job, as would be true of most employees, the change to assembly-line work would create dissatisfaction and possibly bitterness. This feeling, in turn, might affect activities (the way work is performed or the quality of work) and interactions (with the foreman, for example).

Informal organization refers to those relationships, associations, and patterns of working together that develop spontaneously and that supplement the formal organization. The nature and practices of the informal organization are not stipulated by management. Indeed, this is the contrast between formal and informal organization. Both managerial and nonmanagerial employees are members of such informal groups.

Nature of Groups and Informal Organization

Every organization has some type of informal organization. The only way to avoid informal organization completely would be to eliminate all personal association among members of an organization. Because it is impossible to stipulate all relationships and procedures in detail and because employees are social beings, they naturally supplement formal relationships and adapt procedures that are formulated by management.

Employees in a primary work group, for example, often help one another informally. Also, one may discover that the way to get results is to "see Joe." "Joe" does not always appear on the organization chart. Other informal organizations are primarily social in their interests and activities. In one industrial plant, for example, a group of eight factory employees developed an active social life together outside the plant. On weekends, they often went fishing or boating together. One of the members owned a cabin on a lake, which was a frequent rendezvous for the group. The socializing after hours had no direct connection with work activities, although most of the group also worked together in the plant. These activities affected in-plant relationships, of course, but the principal bond was the social associations outside the plant.

Factors Contributing to Formation and Cohesion

Location stands out as a primary factor in regulating the formation and cohesion of informal groups. Although there are exceptions, individuals must be located sufficiently close to each other to permit the personal interaction necessary for development of group relationships. Groups of engineers, draftsmen, or other types of employees may have common interests but work in different parts of the plant.

Professional or occupational differences are likewise significant in determining the nature of informal groupings. There is a tendency for those in the same occupation or "job family" to find a common bond in this fact, particularly if there are status differences among the occupations. It is uncommon for engineers or accountants to develop strong informal ties with cooks or electricians.

The homogeneity of work groups likewise affects the degree of cohesion. If a group is composed primarily of Irish, old-timers, young women, or some other homogeneous group, it is easy for a strong informal group relationship to develop. Within any general work group, it is also natural for smaller informal groupings to form on the basis of such common features as age, race, or outside interests that provide a focal point for organization.

Pressure or threat of danger can likewise encourage the formation of informal groups. Supervisory behavior that is regarded as threatening by a group of employees has a tendency to bind employees together.

Informal Leaders

Informal leaders differ markedly from those appointed by management. In contrast to formally designated leaders, informal leaders are merely recognized or accepted by members of the group in which they exert leadership. They have no formal authority, so their leadership must be based upon other characteristics.

It is difficult to specify the qualities that enable an individual to assume leadership in the informal group. Degree of skill, age, and personality characteristics, for example, may all have a bearing on acceptance. Following is a suggestion of two general characteristics that informal leaders are thought to possess:

> a) *Ability to communicate*—the informal leader is both a transmitter and receiver of information. He is a sort of clearing house of information for the informal organization. He is "in on the know." And, probably more important, he is willing to transmit all information to his followers in the informal organization.

> b) *Ability to embody the values of the primary group*—this characteristic is somewhat more elusive than the first. The informal leader is a kind of living representation of the things the group stands for. He is able to perceive the values of the group, crystallize them into a coherent ideology, and verbalize them to others outside the group. Perhaps this is what is meant when the informal leader is referred to as the spokesman of the group.[6]

---

[6] William G. Scott, *Human Relations in Management: A Behavioral Science Approach* (Homewood, Ill.: Richard D. Irwin, Inc., 1962), p. 133.

The informal leader assists in working out problems among members of the group and in resolving their difficulties with outsiders. The following functions have been suggested for the informal leader:

1. He initiates action.
2. He facilitates a consensus.
3. He provides a link or liaison with the outside world: managers, other work groups, the union.[7]

Informal organization differs from one situation to another in its orientation toward the formal organization. In some cases, it accepts the formal organization's objectives and supports management in achieving them. On the other hand, some informal organizations owe their existence to conflict—real or imaginary—with company management or company policy. At any given time, each informal organization might be located at some point on a scale, such as that in Figure 9–1, on the basis of its relationship to the formal organization.

Orientation Toward the Formal Organization

Range of Possible Orientations Toward Formal Organization   **Figure 9–1**

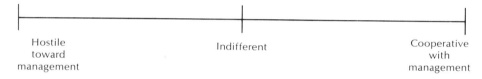

Hostile toward management   Indifferent   Cooperative with management

Formal and informal groups provide satisfaction for the social needs of members of the organization. Opportunity for social interaction can make a job or an organization bearable, even though it may also have undesirable features. Membership in cohesive groups also contributes to the emotional well-being of employees. Individual employees are aided in maintaining their emotional equilibrium, particularly in times of crisis or difficulty, by the support they receive from fellow workers.

Functions of Groups

A second function of work groups and the informal organization is that of communication. In this context, the informal organization is called the *grapevine*, and it supplies information to supplement that passed through formal channels.

Standards of conduct are also established and maintained by work groups. We are particularly interested in those standards directly connected with organizational objectives. These group standards may be either favorable or unfavorable from the standpoint of management thinking. As an example, the group may support a standard of punctuality in reporting for work and regularity in attendance.

Lupton has described the informal pressures applied in one English factory to enforce the group norm that "You should work hard when work is avail-

[7] George Strauss and Leonard R. Sayles, *Personnel: the Human Problems of Management*, 2nd ed. (Englewood Cliffs, N.J.: Prentice-Hall, Inc., © 1967), p. 83.

able." [8] About twenty minutes before finishing time, for example, an employee received a new batch of materials. He was reluctant to make a start on these materials so near quitting time, however. Consequently, he relaxed a bit until a remark from another member of the work group abruptly changed his intentions. With the eyes of the entire work team upon him, he felt uncomfortable and started reaching for materials to begin work.

On the other hand, a group may establish a limit on output and insist that no member of the group exceed that production quota. The primary method of control involves social disapproval of the offending member. The offender is ridiculed or ostracized in some manner. It takes a strong individualist to withstand such tactics. [9]

Still another function of the informal work group is its direct contribution to work accomplishment. Through the informal organization, individual members are able to share job knowledge and to give one another a hand in the accomplishment of work. One member of the organization may assist in training or supplying job tips to a newer member of the same informal group. If the group accepts management objectives, its control supports the supervisor's position and lightens his or her work.

We may summarize, then, the functions of formal and informal groups as follows: (1) provision of social satisfactions for organization members, (2) communication, (3) establishment and maintenance of standards of conduct, and (4) contribution to work accomplishment.

Working with the Informal Organization

The question now confronts us as to how management should relate itself to the informal organization. A constructive approach in dealing with these groups must begin with recognizing their potentially useful functions. The administrator must realize that activities of informal organizations are not necessarily opposed or hostile to management. Indeed, they may support the achievement of management objectives. At the same time, the manager must be aware of the sharp differences that exist among informal groups and strive to understand the real nature of existing groups.

While managers may recognize existence of the informal organization, they may choose to avoid any substantial contact or cooperation with it. Acceptance of the informal organization may be based upon a realization that it is necessary and is impossible to eradicate. Managers may, accordingly, attempt to avoid conduct that appears threatening to such informal groups, but still deal with employees on an individual basis.

Another, sometimes more fruitful, approach involves an attempt to work directly and constructively with the informal organization. This begins, of course, with a full appreciation of the positive values of informal organization. The administrator learns the identity of informal leaders and establishes close liaison with them. By maintaining the confidence and understanding of such

---

[8] T. Lupton, *On the Shop Floor: Two Studies of Workshop Organization and Output* (London: Pergamon Press, 1963), pp. 40-41.

[9] For the story of a crane operator whose fellow workmen refused to speak to him for 367 days as punishment for working during a one-day strike, see George A. Lundberg, Clarence C. Schrag, and Otto N. Larsen, *Sociology*, 3rd ed. (New York: Harper & Row, Publishers, 1963), p. 70.

individuals, a manager can expect a greater measure of support on the part of the entire organization. Managers may use informal leadership as one channel of communication. This is not to suggest, of course, that managers should use the informal organization in lieu of the formal structure or that they should attempt to manipulate employees, but rather that they should attempt to improve the general understanding among members of this group and the formal leadership.

The discussion of informal organization has revealed the existence of power outside the formal organization. Any empirical investigation of organizations in action substantiates the existence of such unofficial power. A review of the social structure is incomplete, therefore, without reference to informal politics and power.

Power and Politics

Decisions may be influenced by the judgment of individuals whose names do not even appear on the organization chart. There may be a power behind the throne. Staff advisors, by virtue of close association with the chief, may express opinions that are accepted with the force of commands (even though they technically may be called suggestions).

Political Techniques of Influencing Behavior

Observers of organizational behavior have come to recognize the fact of *political activity* in administrative situations. Unfortunately, the word "politics" has a connotation of unstatesmanlike conduct. As used here, however, political activity is concerned with the manner in which positions of power are established and influence is exerted in the administrative process. There is nothing to indicate the use of power for undesirable ends.

Through politics, an executive may first of all build and exert influence over subordinate personnel. Activities of this nature include any unofficial efforts to "take care" of subordinates with an expectation of their loyalty in return.

A new executive often acts to remove "old guard" officials and to replace them with those loyal to the new regime. The following statement explains the political tactics of a new department head, Moss, to establish his power by replacement of a subordinate, Queenie, whose primary loyalty was to Katz, Moss's superior:

> Queenie was in charge of the final quality control station. She had been at Zed for thirteen years but was not well-liked in the department. She refused to reduce the time she took to test a television set, thereby holding up production. Workers complained that she rejected sets for no reason and caused them to lose production bonuses.
>
> Moss would have liked to remove Queenie from the line; first, because she interfered with his aim to expand production and second, because of her loyalty to Katz, the production manager, who backed her solidly. Katz had an almost mystical faith in her unfailing ability to detect a faulty set, which he considered essential for establishing a market reputation for quality. Moss lacked the power to overrule Katz. Furthermore, no one knew how to operate the station well enough to win Katz's confidence, and Queenie consistently prevented her assistants from learning the complete job.
>
> When a new worker was hired and assigned by the production manager to

be assistant to Queenie, Moss resolved to break Queenie's monopoly on quality control with the new worker's help. The process took several months, and a variety of tactics were employed.

Moss was not able to damage Queenie's reputation for high quality. Instead he questioned the functional value of her high standards and insisted that it was at the expense of quantity which the company needed more. He argued that her pedantic standards were not in keeping with market requirements and that her slow pace was costing the company large sums in unearned profit.

Moss's tactic was to discredit Queenie by undermining the value of her contribution and even implying that she was an economic liability. Faced with increasing pressure from the Board to raise production levels, Katz relented. The new worker was promoted to the position of quality controller on the line. Queenie was taken off production. Moss thus succeeded in placing a subordinate of his own choice in a key position while ingratiating himself with the line workers.[10]

A manager's political activities, however, are not limited to influencing subordinates. The primary connotation of administrative politics, indeed, is concerned with the manager's relationships outside the manager's own department. Through political activities, an executive may exert some degree of control over colleagues and even superiors. Other managers at approximately the same level are potential competitors or allies, and the executive typically seeks to exert as much influence as possible in matters of mutual interest.

While some political activities are inevitable and even contribute to the accomplishment of organizational objectives, company politics may also be destructive. The company politician is often far more concerned with the advancement of personal interests than those of the organization. To prevent such situations from getting out of hand to the extent that political activities dominate rather than supplement normal management processes and personal ambition supplants organizational goals, top management must sense and prevent extreme or self-seeking forms of political action. A program and practice of objective evaluation of subordinates is one essential safeguard against the destructive company politician. Political intrigue that subordinates organizational goals to narrow personal objectives must be rejected. The climate must prevent an abuse of political power. This is difficult to accomplish, of course, because political action is often carefully camouflaged and rationalized.

The Power Structure   The combination of formal authority and political action creates centers of power or influence in an organization. The framework incorporating these centers of influence might be called the *power structure*.

The power structure differs from the formal organization structure only to the extent that the influence of particular individuals does not correspond perfectly to their positions in the formal structure. In view of the nature of political action, some such discrepancy between formal position and power is to be expected. It would be rare indeed if six vice-presidents each had precisely the same influence over company policy.

---

[10] Dafna Nundi Izraeli, "The Middle Manager and the Tactics of Power Expansion," *Sloan Management Review* 16, no. 2 (Winter, 1975): 65-66.

To maximize their effectiveness, therefore, managers must use political means to establish their positions of power. McMurry described this requirement of managers as follows:

> If he does not [own the business], and sometimes even when he does, his power must be acquired and held by means which are essentially political. Of crucial importance, since most of his power is derived or delegated, his power must be dependable. Nothing is more devastating to an executive than to lose support and backing in moments of crisis. It is for this reason that the development of continuing power is the most immediate and nagging concern of many professional managers.[11]

Political methods of acquiring power are varied and include such steps as developing alliances with peers, selecting and rewarding loyal subordinates, creating many clear channels of communication, and maintaining close contacts with superiors.

A Case Study of Power and Politics

One of the classic studies of organizational power was Melville Dalton's analysis of political activities and the power structure in the Milo Fractionating Center, a fictitiously named industrial organization having a work force of 8,000 employees.[12] Dalton's charts of the formal organization and unofficial influence in the management of this plant are shown in Figures 9–2 and 9–3.

In Figure 9–3, Dalton has ranked the individuals to show their relative influence in the organization. As an example, the assistant plant manager (Hardy) is shown at the same level as the plant manager (Stevens), thus indicating that their influence in the organization is roughly equivalent. Following is Dalton's explanation of the Hardy-Stevens relationship:

> In executive meetings, Stevens clearly was less forceful than Hardy. Appearing nervous and worried, Stevens usually opened meetings with a few remarks and then silently gave way to Hardy who dominated thereafter. During the meeting most questions were directed to Hardy. While courteous, Hardy's statements usually were made without request for confirmation from Stevens. Hardy and Stevens and other high officers daily lunched together. There, too, Hardy dominated the conversations and was usually the target of questions. This was not just an indication that he carried the greater burden of *minor* duties often assigned to assistants in some firms, for he had a hand in most issues, including major ones. Other items useful in appraising Hardy and Stevens were their relative (*a*) voice in promotions, (*b*) leadership in challenging staff projects, (*c*) force in emergencies, (*d*) escape as a butt of jokes and name-calling, (*e*) knowledge of subordinates, (*f*) position in the firm's social and community activities.[13]

Another position of unusual influence was occupied by Rees, who functioned officially as head of Industrial Relations and was presumably limited to

---

[11] Robert N. McMurry, "Power and the Ambitious Executive," *Harvard Business Review* 51, no. 6 (November–December, 1973): 140–41.

[12] See Melville Dalton, *Men Who Manage* (New York: John Wiley & Sons, Inc., 1959).

[13] *Ibid.*, p. 23.

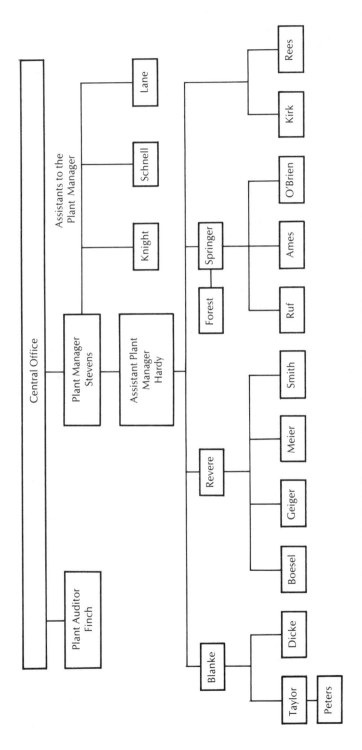

Source: Melville Dalton, *Men Who Manage* (New York: John Wiley & Sons, Inc., 1959), p. 21.

Figure 9-2 *Milo Formal Chart Simplified*

Milo Chart of Unofficial Influence   **Figure 9-3**

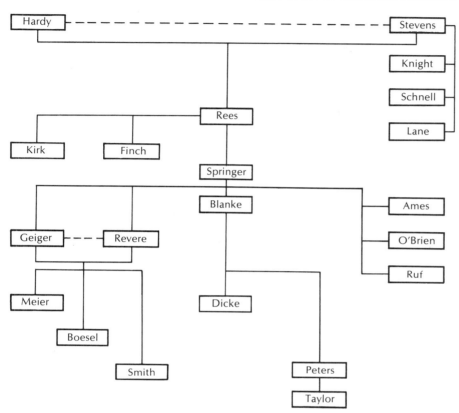

Source: Melville Dalton, *Men Who Manage* (New York: John Wiley & Sons, Inc., 1959), p. 22.

advising on these matters. In spite of this, Rees seemed to carry more weight and inspire more concern than the other managers subordinate to Hardy and Stevens. His influence was partly attributable to the fact that he had been sent from headquarters to strengthen the department. He had replaced a weak manager, Lane, who was made assistant to Stevens.

Dalton's depth study of the Milo plant reveals conditions of influencing organizational behavior that, to some extent, exist in every organization. The positions of power are not always evident on the surface and cannot be read with assurance from the organization chart. Only careful observation of the functioning of the organization reveals the true power centers and the extent to which they differ from the formal organization structure.

Summary

The Western Electric experiments revealed and increased understanding of the social nature of business organizations. These experiments demonstrated that business organizations are more than collections of individuals. Rather, they are *social systems* in which the relationships among people are of extreme significance in determining organizational behavior.

As a social system, the business organization includes not only the *formal* organization and groups but also *informal* groupings and relationships that supplement the formally prescribed structure.

Organizational behavior may be analyzed by examining the *activities, interactions,* and *sentiments* of organization members. *Informal organization* refers to relationships that develop spontaneously, supplementing or modifying the formal organization established by management. In a typical informal organization, certain informal leaders come to be recognized and to exert influence over other members. The informal organization performs various functions for the individual and also for the formal organization. Informal groups may operate constructively with respect to the formal organization, or they may adopt goals conflicting with those of the formal organization. Management sometimes attempts to work constructively with informal organizations and to use these relationships in achieving organization objectives.

In influencing behavior in organizations, the use of *political activity* supplements the manager's formal authority. The relationships and techniques employed in acquiring and exerting influence outside official channels are described as political. This does not indicate that they are necessarily underhanded or shady but simply that they involve alliances, relationships, and approaches that differ from those of the formal organization.

The *power structure* of an organization may be similar to the formal organization, but differences exist in the case of those who hold more or less power than the formal structure confers upon them. In the example of the Milo plant, it was discovered that subordinate managers sometimes held as much real power or influence as their superiors. Power of the manager is derived not only from a formal position of authority, but also from the manager's political relationships and activities.

Discussion Questions

1. The Western Electric experiments were designed to show the relationship between lighting and productivity. What were the results? Explain.

2. Why might the Western Electric Hawthorne plant be called the "birthplace of industrial sociology"?

3. Explain the concept of the business organization as a *social system.*

4. Identify a number of factors affecting the formation of *informal* groups and explain the significance of each.

5. What accounts for differences in the cooperation or hostility of different informal groups in their relationships to the formal organization?

6. Is the informal organization useful to management? What constructive role, if any, does it have?

7. What should a manager do about the informal organizations in which subordinates are involved?

8. Is it better for a supervisor to deal with subordinates as individuals or to encourage development of a cohesive work group? Explain.

9. What action should be taken by a manager whose subordinates have established an unreasonably low ceiling on work output?

10. Describe an "organization politician." What practices does such an individual typically follow?

11. What is the *power structure,* and why may it differ from an accurately drawn organization chart?

Supplementary Reading

Bell, Robert R. and Mascaro, Guillermo F. "Interpersonal Attraction as a Basis of Informal Organization." *Academy of Management Journal* 15, no. 2 (June, 1972): 233–36.

Katz, Fred E. "Explaining Informal Work Groups in Complex Organization: The Case for Autonomy in Structure." *Administrative Science Quarterly* 10, no. 2 (September, 1965): 204–23.

McMurry, Robert N. "Power and the Ambitious Executive." *Harvard Business Review* 51, no. 6 (November–December, 1973): 140–45.

Pettigrew, Andrew M. "Towards a Political Theory of Organizational Intervention." *Human Relations* 28, no. 3 (April, 1975): 191–208.

Zaleznik, Abraham. "Power and Politics in Organizational Life." *Harvard Business Review* 48, no. 3 (May–June, 1970): 47–60.

Case 9

The Blast Furnace Confrontation*

I worked one summer in the labor pool of a steel mill. During the summer, I worked all over the plant and consequently had many different experiences with the union laborers there.

The most remarkable experience occurred one hot July afternoon on the floor of the open-hearth furnace room. The temperature there hovered between 140 and 160 degrees, and two crews were used to do the clean-up work between the furnaces. During clean-up work, one furnace was normally in operation, but the adjacent furnace would shut down. Our crew was led by a soft-spoken lay preacher whom everyone in the crew seemed to like and respect.

The foreman ordered our crew to work between two furnaces which were both in operation. The temperature between the furnaces was extremely high and "Preacher," our leader, balked at the order. Preacher exclaimed loudly that he would have to talk to the Lord about the order. Standing in the middle of the furnace room floor, Preacher outstretched his arms, shut his eyes, and plaintively wailed to Heaven, "Oh Lord, this old foreman wants us to go in between those two furnaces where it is as hot as Hell." After a moment of si-

*Prepared with the assistance of David N. Moore.

lence, his head nodded and his arms fell back to his sides. Preacher opened his eyes and walked straight to the foreman. Preacher informed the foreman, "The Lord told me to take my crew in between those two furnaces, but to stop by the union hall on my way home and file a grievance against you!"

The whole labor force on the furnace room floor snickered, while the foreman turned on his heels and walked away. We later did what the foreman asked, and I don't think Preacher even intended to file a grievance. Nevertheless, he seemed to have gained the upper hand with the foreman. I waited to see what would happen on the next such occasion, but, for some reason, there was no recurrence of this situation.

Questions

1. What type of power conflict is evident in this situation? To what extent is it a management-union confrontation?

2. What sources of power, if any, do the work crew have in this case?

3. Who won in this incident?

4. What is the probable effect of this incident on future relationships within the work group and between the work group and the foreman?

Objectives

1. Explain the meaning of culture and its relevance to organizational life and managerial decision making.
2. Recognize status differences, the contributions of status systems, and the types of organizational problems created by status systems.

Chapter

10

Cultural Features of Organizations

Culture and the Business Organization
Implications of Culture in Management
The Nature and Functions of Status
Symbols of Status

Case: The Executive Lunchroom

As pointed out in the previous chapter, human interaction and human behavior are the core of organizational life. The business organization is a social organization, and its formal and informal groups vitally affect its operation, survival, and progress. An additional aspect of a firm's social structure—its cultural features—will be discussed in this chapter.

Culture and the Business Organization

What Is Culture?

Culture consists of the behavior patterns and values of a social group. These are patterns of belief and behavior that have been learned from other members of society. They are, as the cultural anthropologist would say, *socially transmitted.* They include the practices that we have learned and that we share.

Culture is often described as *custom,* and it includes not only actions but also ideas and manufactured objects called *artifacts.* Eating lunch at noon, or eating three meals a day for that matter, is an example of culturally determined behavior. Most of us do it as a matter of course. We consider it the normal method of receiving nourishment, and, in America, we use forks and knives (artifacts) instead of chopsticks. In America, such ideals as individual liberty are also widely accepted and are a part of our culture. The religious beliefs of any people likewise are a part of the total culture.

Components of Culture

Material Culture

The things that people produce—the artifacts mentioned earlier—are a part of their culture. These manufactured objects are created by technology and are often referred to as the *material culture.* Various types of artifacts are recognized—for example, food, clothing, housing, tools, and transportation devices. The material objects and material culture are not completely separate from the nonmaterial culture. As an example, food may be used for ceremonial purposes, and religious rules regulate its use.

In an industrial organization, we find artifacts similar to those of society generally. There are often minor variations, of course, as would be found in the variety of clothing evident in any organization. In a hospital, nurses and orderlies are dressed in white uniforms. On a police force, the officers wear an identifying uniform. A few years ago, one business firm even considered a distinctive blazer that would identify the "top brass" in the executive ranks!

Perhaps the most significant part of the material culture as far as business organizations are concerned is the tooling or equipment used. This aspect of our culture distinguishes it from other cultures preceding it and from many cultures existing elsewhere in the world today. The extensive use of tooling—machinery, power, and automated equipment—has resulted in an industrial culture.

The tooling and equipment and the technology associated with it also affect the nonmaterial culture of industrial organizations. The worker on the assembly line adopts practices and beliefs reflecting the technology and material culture. Some assembly lines, for example, are paced mechanically and are not subject to the control of the worker. This pacing of work may result in any number of behavior patterns and beliefs. As one example, a feeling of being driven by a "mechanical monster" can lead to resentment, resistance, and organization of unions.

There are many facets or aspects of nonmaterial culture. The very fact of social organization is one of these factors. As one feature of social organization, consider the status distinctions that exist among people in any social group. The status distinctions (discussed later in the chapter) are culturally determined and comprise a part of the total cultural pattern of the society.

Nonmaterial Culture

Another feature of culture is the use of *rituals.* Although they are often associated in our thinking with religious ceremonies, they are not limited to activities of this kind. Many practices in our society and in business institutions in particular have a ritualistic character. Graduation ceremonies of school systems, for example, involve elaborate ceremonies and an unusual (and uncomfortable) type of clothing specially designed for the occasion. In business organizations, there is a practice of awarding pins or gifts to employees who have faithfully served the organization for twenty or thirty years. Even business meetings may have a ritualistic, in addition to a practical, value. (In educational institutions, faculty members are often convinced that the *only* substantial value of many such meetings is the ritualistic value.)

Another feature of culture is known as a *taboo.* The nature of taboos, which are activities frowned upon or regarded as undesirable or immoral, depends upon the organization and its particular background and personnel who are in it. In some organizations, for example, no one calls the president by first name. Or it may be considered wrong to accept gifts from suppliers.

Another cultural feature is the language a particular social group develops. The special language associated with a particular group is called *jargon.* Teenagers, for example, develop a type of slang that is virtually incomprehensible to many adults. Occupational and industrial groups likewise develop somewhat similar terminology so far as its understanding by outsiders is concerned. The jargon identifies the group, and it also identifies those qualified to be recognized as participants and members of the particular group.

We are often unaware of the cultural patterns and values that characterize our own society. We tend to take our own practices and beliefs for granted rather than looking at them objectively. We learn the accepted way and assume that almost everyone behaves or believes in the same way. Whether these practices involve educational ceremonies, religious rituals, living patterns, or employment practices, we seldom think of them as aspects of culture.

Variations in Culture

Different patterns of culture characterize different societies. Over a period of time, for example, the culture of any society changes. Also, the background cultures of other nations differ significantly from those of our country. According to one story, a European businessman in New York, with his customary courtesy, held the door open for a New Yorker hurrying behind him. The New Yorker, with some bewilderment, exclaimed, "What are you—a wise guy?" Even within our own country, there are marked differences in culture. The internal variations within a general cultural system are referred to as *subcultures.*

The extent to which a given cultural pattern is accepted and followed is, of course, a matter of degree. Some cultural patterns are followed quite rigidly by everyone, while others have only a general degree of acceptance. Naturally, there must be some consistency in a practice or some uniformity of belief for it to be classified as culture.

Business Firms Within the Larger Cultural System

A business firm, branch plant, or any other institution for that matter functions within the cultural system of the society in which it is located.[1] A firm in Dallas must function within the American culture, including modifications or "wrinkles" peculiar to the state of Texas and the city of Dallas. Similarly, a company located in London must operate within the general British culture and that of London in particular.

Because a firm must function within the larger cultural system, some agreement between the practices of the firm and the culture is necessary. The expectations of the surrounding community with regard to the establishments located within it are based upon the community's cultural traditions. Employees also bring into the firm the cultural values they have assimilated from the community. Both the community and the employees are inclined to expect, therefore, some conformity to prevailing cultural values. As a general example, the American worker has been exposed to a political philosophy that emphasizes the importance of the individual. If the work place provides conditions degrading to personality and self-respect, as occasionally happens, a serious conflict with the broader cultural background is evident. The disparity may contribute to high personnel turnover, poor public relations, or unionization.

American communities differ, however, in their attitudes toward minority groups and their rights in society. These community attitudes constitute cultural values of obvious importance for company management. The Civil Rights Act prohibits discrimination in employment practices, but conflicting traditions still exist in some communities.

One national company, for example, with a national union, promoted a black employee to a higher, nonsupervisory position in its shop organization. This promotion was consistent with the law, company policy, and the constitution of the national union. The job had never previously been filled by a black, however, and other workers were conscious of the nature of the precedent. Because of the conflict between this act and the cultural values of most employees, they engaged in a wildcat strike that lasted for several days. It took considerable effort on the part of both the company and the union to persuade the employees to return to their jobs and to tolerate the conflict with the prevailing cultural pattern.

Other cultural variations between locations are more subtle and difficult to explain. One study of employee attitudes discovered differences between employees in "town" and "city" settings.[2] Town workers expressed high satisfaction with more complex or demanding tasks, but city workers were more satisfied with less complex tasks. There were obvious differences between the two groups in their expectations concerning work. Religious variations between the two settings may have accounted in part for the contrasting attitudes. Unfortunately, the causative factors could not be pinpointed easily.

---

[1] For a delightful description of certain aspects of American culture, see Horace Miner, "Body Ritual Among the Nacirema," *American Anthropologist* 58, no. 3 (June, 1956): pp. 503–7.

[2] See Arthur N. Turner and Paul R. Lawrence, *Industrial Jobs and the Worker: An Investigation of Response to Task Attributes* (Boston: Harvard University Graduate School of Business Administration, 1965), Chapters 4 and 5. This study was concerned primarily with technological determinants of attitudes and unexpectedly uncovered the variation reported here.

Subcultures of the Organization

Within any community, certain groups have cultural patterns that are distinct from those of the general community. For the most part, these are supplementary to the general culture. They are occasioned by the unique activities, interests, or beliefs of the particular group. Any business firm, as a social institution, develops such unique subcultures within its own organization.

It is possible to classify these subcultures as either *institutional subcultures* or *professional subcultures*. An institutional subculture involves the behavior patterns and beliefs of the company as a whole, a department within the company, or a particular work group. Some companies, for example, emphasize safety and accident prevention with an almost religious fervor. Personnel in such organizations would not think of operating equipment without appropriate safety glasses or driving a company car without a safety belt. The value attached to safety and the activities designed to implement this value become a part of the firm's subculture.

A given department within a company may likewise develop its own unique culture. The sales department and engineering department do not necessarily hold to all of the company traditions in precisely the same manner.

The professional subculture comprises those customs associated with a particular professional or occupational group within the company. Indeed, it is possible for certain values of a professional subculture to cross company lines and to characterize all members of the profession. These cultural differences are focused or centered on the work and the nature of the work. Some professional groups have developed codes of ethics applicable to their professions. Accountants, as an example, recognize principles that are supposed to be observed by accountants without deviation, irrespective of the consequences to the particular firm.

Occasionally the professional culture presents perplexing administrative problems for business managers. Direction of research scientists is an example. The orientation of researchers toward freedom of inquiry may conflict with budgetary controls and other administrative constraints. In supervising professionally trained personnel of this type, it is often necessary to adapt customary procedures.

Other practices that constitute a type of professional subculture are not professional in and of themselves. A group of laboratory workers, for example, develops a practice of wearing white coats and drinking coffee from laboratory beakers. These practices may have definite values attached to them. Other members of the organization are not granted indiscriminate access to the coffee beakers. The beakers and coats serve as a kind of badge to distinguish laboratory workers and to set them apart as a separate group.

Implications of Culture in Management

Importance of Cultural Values to Individuals

The significance of cultural patterns to management depends upon the extent to which they are of primary value to employees. If a practice is followed more from habit than from a strong attachment to it, management need have little apprehension about changing it. If, on the other hand, employees are vitally concerned with such matters, management's ignorance of them may be perilous.

Throughout their lives, members of a society are trained to follow the cultural patterns prevailing in society. One learns to sit on a chair in a house and to eat three meals a day. Within the business organization, a continuing process of training adapts the individual to the prevailing subculture. The result of this conditioning is that the culture (or subculture) becomes imbedded in the makeup of the individual and appears completely natural. In fact, effort is required to make changes in customary cultural patterns.

The extent to which a custom exerts control over the organization and its members depends upon several considerations. Some customs are carefully observed by the majority of employees. Other practices may be accepted by the majority, but rejected by a substantial minority. In addition, some cultural practices are habitual, with little pressure toward conformity. We may think someone a little odd who does not eat three meals a day, but no one worries greatly about it. In the case of other behavior patterns, however, there is a definite feeling that one should follow the customary pattern. In the extreme case, conflict with a code or pattern appears repugnant to most members of the organization and leads to the imposition of some type of sanction. Such views often find expression in formal rules or law.

Value of Cultural Awareness

Effective participation in a social system requires a knowledge of its culture, particularly for managerial personnel. The general customs and beliefs of the community and the special traditions of employee groups are all facets of the environment confronting a manager. To ignore them is dangerous in the same way that it is dangerous to fall asleep technologically. The facts of culture exist whether they are recognized or not, and they affect the business firm and its way of operation. Some negative attitudes toward American business abroad have been attributed to management's callous disregard for local customs.[3]

The manager also finds personal relationships with other managers conditioned by company traditions. Note the following description of beliefs about managerial associations in one factory:

> One of the strongest conventions in the Divisional Managers Meeting was that divisional managers should not criticize each other in front of the General Manager. When a difference occurred between divisional managers, the accepted convention was that the matter should first be taken up privately between the two. Failing a satisfactory solution, it would then be referred to the General Manager, the colleague having first been informed.[4]

It is evident that violation of such a tradition would incur the displeasure and probably the hostility of colleagues.

Introducing Changes Having Cultural Overtones

From time to time, management finds it desirable or necessary to introduce changes that affect established cultural patterns. If the cultural pattern is deeply established, it is important first to question the wisdom of a direct chal-

---

[3] John W. Houser, "The Delicate Job of American Management Abroad," *Advanced Management-Office Executive* 1, no. 1 (January, 1962): 20.

[4] Elliott Jaques, *The Changing Culture of a Factory* (London: Tavistock Publications, Ltd., 1951), p. 281.

lenge to it. If the custom is one that has been established over a long period of time and seems thoroughly practical and important to those in the organization, difficulty may be expected in the administrative change. In view of the probable opposition, the manager may well hesitate and consider from every angle the importance and necessity for the change. Opposition or conflict that may be engendered by administrative action may take a number of forms. Members of the organization may occasionally engage in open conflict. On the other hand, the opposition or sabotage may be subtle, or members of the organization may simply leave because of their dissatisfaction.

Of course, not all traditions can be regarded as inherently bad or unproductive. Some may contribute to progress or be used to encourage economic development. As Hoselitz has pointed out, even the Hindu's concept of the sacredness of cattle may be used by the government of India to induce peasants to take better care of cattle, to improve cattle strains, and, in this way, to contribute to economic development.[5] Also, the "extended family" kinship system of India facilitates the financing of small artisans' shops.

It is often necessary to make changes, however, and the fact that certain patterns have been established is no guarantee that they are good. In fact, progress is possible only at the expense of some changes. Existing culture represents a status quo that may be less than perfect. The desirable course is to proceed with good judgment in making the really important changes. As one noted industrialist has expressed it,

> Certainly, by innovating, we do stand to lose some traditions that have had value in the past. But right here is one of the tests of leadership: to know the differences between a tradition that is still good, one that needs to be modified, and one that should be abandoned altogether. Those who are to lead adequately in these times not only need to know the differences, but they need the fortitude to act on what they know, painful as this sometimes is.[6]

If the need to change is urgent, the manager must recognize the problem but get ahead with the process of accomplishing the necessary change. The manager's hope is in getting members of the organization to see the management position with regard to the need for such change. "We've always done it this way" is a good argument until one sees there is some reason we can't just go on doing it this way.

One feature of culture consists of judgments relative to the importance of various roles and groups.

Status is concerned with a person's prestige or standing within a group (or the standing of a group within a larger society). Different individuals are evaluated

The Nature and Functions of Status
What Is Status?

---

[5] Bert F. Hoselitz, "Tradition and Economic Growth," in *Tradition, Values, and Socio-Economic Development*, eds. Ralph Braibanti and Joseph J. Spengler (Durham, N.C.: Duke University Press, 1961), pp. 110–12.

[6] Frederick R. Kappel, *Vitality in a Business Enterprise* (New York: McGraw-Hill Book Company, 1960), pp. 13–14.

in terms of some common yardstick and are assigned positions of relative importance. These judgments about the relative prestige of individuals and groups are based upon consideration of the rights, duties, obligations, restrictions, and limitations applying to them.

Every organization has some type of *status system.* In a status system, all positions are assigned a standing relative to one another. This results in the classification of individuals as equals, superiors, and subordinates. There is no such thing as status apart from other individuals. Status suggests that one is better or more important than another. It is a relative matter. One who has higher status in an organization "carries more weight" than those with lesser status. Deference is generally shown to the individual with higher status.

Different individuals naturally use different weights or values in their individual judgments regarding status. Technically, therefore, there are as many different status systems as there are individuals making judgments of this variety. We often simplify this process, however, by making generalizations about status. These generalizations express a general consensus regarding the status of particular individuals, positions, occupations, or groups.

Status Differences in Organizations

Two kinds of status systems have been suggested by Chester I. Barnard.[7] The first of these, *functional* status, is based upon the type of work or activity performed. The professional, whether an engineer, attorney, or otherwise, enjoys greater prestige than nonprofessional members of the organization. The craftsman has a higher status than the unskilled employee. An accountant is a notch above a mechanic. In fact, a white-collar worker generally is viewed as superior to a blue-collar worker unless there are marked differences in income.

Scalar status, on the other hand, is concerned with the level in the organization's hierarchy or chain of command. In a position that is high in the organizational pyramid, the incumbent is considered an important executive or a "wheel." The top of the company is populated with very important people, while the bottom echelons contain the less important people.

In any functioning organization, these two status systems operate simultaneously and complement each other. Figure 10–1 presents a diagram in which the prestige or status of the position is indicated by its vertical level. In this diagram, we can see the influence of both functional and scalar status. It appears that the public relations function, for example, has less prestige than the other functions appearing near the top of this chart, even though the function is headed by a vice-president who reports directly to the chief executive.

The two types of status suggested by Barnard—functional status and scalar status—are both descriptive of the position, regardless of the incumbent. These types of status are supplemented by a third variety that might be designated as *personal* status. Although formal position, by virtue of its scalar and functional qualities, goes a long way in determining an individual's status, this status may be augmented or reduced by the individual's personal characteristics. When a brilliant or distinguished individual replaces a lackluster incumbent, the replacement enjoys higher status even though the position may be un-

---

[7] Chester I. Barnard, *Organization and Management* (Cambridge, Mass.: Harvard University Press, 1948), pp. 209–10.

changed. In a business organization this would be true whether the position is that of executive, supervisor, craftsman, scientist, or engineer. In a university, the same would be true of a new president, dean, department chairman, professor, or coach.

Business executives need an appreciation of the ubiquity and significance of status systems in order to understand the attitudes of those who work in the organization. This applies both to managerial and operative personnel. In addition, executives are constantly making decisions that affect status in various ways. They need, therefore, an awareness of the status dimensions of management action.

Status Levels of Key Individuals in a Business Organization **Figure 10-1**

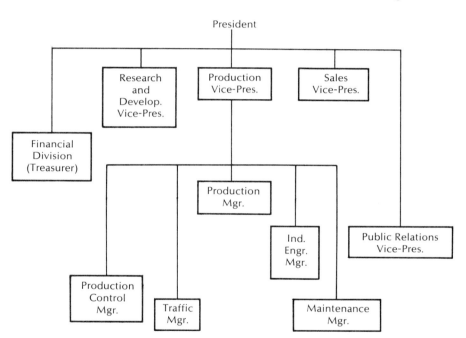

One of the most penetrating studies of status in industry was that conducted by William Foote Whyte in his investigation of human relations in the restaurant industry.[8] In Whyte's analysis of the social structure in restaurants, he discovered very marked distinctions in the status levels of the positions. In the kitchen, for example, he found that the work stations were socially ranked. At the top status level was the range station, where the cooking took place. At that station, the positions were most highly paid and involved the highest degree of skill. It served as a focal point, with other work in the kitchen revolving around it. Below the status level of the range station was the salad station, which involved products of high prestige value. Women vegetable cooks were

An Example of Status in a Business Organization

---

[8] William Foote Whyte, *Human Relations in the Restaurant Industry* (New York: McGraw-Hill Book Company, 1948).

respectful in their references to work at the salad station and indicated a willingness to work there if they were not already holding positions at the range. Below these two stations, in order, were the chicken preparation and meat preparation stations, the chicken cooking and vegetable preparation stations, and the fish station. The fish station was considered to have the lowest status of all kitchen stations.

Relationship of Industrial Status Systems to Those of Society

There is a reasonably close relationship between general social status as established in the community and status inside a specific formal organization. An occupation with low social standing in the eyes of society is unlikely to have much prestige in the work place, and vice versa.

Examples of high-status occupations in the United States are the following:

Physician	Architect
Scientist	Minister
College professor	Civil engineer
Lawyer	Airline pilot

There are differences in prestige among these occupations, of course, even though they are all near the upper end of the status scale. At the other end of the scale, the following occupations are widely regarded as having low status:

Taxi driver	Soda fountain clerk
Farm hand	Garbage collector
Janitor	Street sweeper
Bartender	Shoe shiner

Functions of the Status System

Status systems often appear undemocratic and undesirable. What is sometimes overlooked is the constructive role of status in our society and in business organizations in particular.

Maintaining Effective and Authoritative Communication

The existence of a status system makes possible effective and authoritative communication. This is essential if any group is to function as an organization rather than as a rabble. Someone must be in a position to provide direction and coordination to the members associated in the undertaking. The status system permits understanding who is to lead and who is to follow.

This need for a status system to provide authority in communications is particularly acute in emergency situations demanding quick, unquestioned decisions. The battlefield is no place for uncertainty in leadership. Military forces, as a result, employ a well-defined and widely recognized status system.

Providing Incentives for Advancement

The status systems and symbols of status that pervade our society provide strong motivation. Few individuals are content with the status quo, and their aspirations are often linked with conceptions of status as much as they are with hopes of purely material advancement. It appears important to most people that they should live in the "right" section of the city and drive a type of car befitting their positions.

No matter how much we may disparage status differences, it is important to recognize their powerful influence as a motivational force. Achievement in our society results from such motivation. In criticisms of status factors, therefore, we should consider the alternatives in terms of motivational power.

As a motivational device, status also operates negatively to enforce a sense of responsibility. An individual usually wishes to maintain an existing position and to avoid conduct or performance that would result in a reversion to lower status. The phrase *lose face* has been applied to this reduction in status, and most individuals find such a thought repugnant.

Developing Sense of Responsibility

Although status performs constructive functions as noted, it also has its disadvantages. Indeed, some are so conscious of its weaknesses that they refer to the *pathology* of status. One important negative feature concerns the *social distance* between organization levels. It is true, as discussed earlier in the chapter, that authoritative communication is desirable. However, organization levels must also work together in achieving the objectives of the organization. It is possible, consequently, that status distinctions may become so great or be emphasized to the point that active cooperation is reduced. The subordinate may follow orders but find it difficult to work closely with higher levels.

Problems of Status

An individual may also become so preoccupied with status symbols that the entire system is run into the ground. Getting a private office or a staff assistant or an electronic computer becomes important in and of itself, and little regard may be paid to the intrinsic need for these symbolic trappings. Instead, they are conceived as being important merely for the purpose of proving one's value to one's associates.

Status distinctions, furthermore, do not always correspond perfectly to the competence of the individuals involved. A doctor may be a quack, and an engineer may be only a poor mechanic. The vice-president may be the owner's son-in-law but lack administrative knowledge. The general may have more seniority than skill in military strategy. The fault is not so much with the basic idea of the status system as it is with errors in assignment of status.

Members of an organization may experience anxiety as a result of status considerations. For example, an inability to improve one's status may produce a sense of frustration within the individual. This feeling may be described as *status anxiety. Status inconsistency* may also lead to anxiety. The title of the position may be right, for example, but the incumbent may lack a private office that seems appropriate for the particular level.

Status levels are indicated by various external trappings or indicators closely connected with the individual. These *symbols* permit an observer to understand the prestige level of the individual in question.

Symbols of Status

Nature and Function of Status Symbols

As an example, the military services indicate rank by insignia worn by military officers. An officer wearing an eagle is outranked by an officer wearing a star. By the same token, the one-star general is outranked by those wearing two or three stars.

In most organizations, the symbols are more subtle than those of the military service. But the symbols are nonetheless real and widely recognized as indicating different levels of importance.

One of the widely recognized symbols in our society is the type of automobile that is driven. "Imporant" people drive Cadillacs or Lincolns, while those of lower status drive Oldsmobiles or Buicks. Those at the lower end of the social ladder drive old-model Fords, Plymouths, or Chevrolets.

Types of Status Symbols in Industry

Status symbols in industrial organizations vary considerably. They exist at all levels, however, from the vice-president to the operative employee.

One of the most obvious symbols is the title applying to the position. The title of president indicates that the individual is extremely important. The vice-president is obviously less important. A project engineer is above a junior engineer, and a junior engineer probably outranks a drafsman.

Vice-presidents usually have larger offices than those occupied by lower officials. Numerous other features of the office itself also reveal its status level. The very fact that an office is private indicates greater prestige than that of a desk in a larger office. The furnishings in the office similarly reveal status distinctions. At some level, the offices are carpeted, and metal desks give way to wooden desks. Even wooden desks have their rank, with walnut and mahogany outranking oak. Draperies at the window and paintings on the wall are also symbolic of prestige. Potted plants, lounge chairs, private washrooms, intercom boxes, and adjoining private conference rooms all suggest the prestige of the person occupying the office.

In addition to material trappings, there are privileges that indicate the status level of the incumbent. Some employees are required to punch a time clock, while higher-level employees are not required to do so. Higher management officials often report at a later hour than other employees, and no one checks closely regarding the precise time of their arrival.

Functional Value of Status Symbols

Status symbols communicate the facts regarding status to members of the organization. Without knowledge of status differences, the status system is unable to perform its customary function. By communicating the facts regarding status, therefore, status symbols contribute to the values inherent in the status system itself. They confirm and help maintain this status system.

For example, certain minimum status symbols are useful in providing a type of credentials to members of the organization. Members know that they can listen to a certain individual who speaks regarding certain situations because of that person's status. The manager may, therefore, need some status symbols in order to get a prompt hearing and reasonable acceptance of his or her position.

This requirement for status symbols does not demand their proliferation. A small number may well serve with sufficient forcefulness to establish and maintain the status system of the organization.

Summary

Culture refers to patterns of belief and behavior that have been learned from other members of society. Within an organization, two types of subcultures may be recognized—*institutional subcultures* and *professional subcultures.*

Cultural practices have significance for both members and managers of organizations. In introducing changes having cultural overtones, therefore, it is important to recognize possible conflicts with established cultural patterns.

Status refers to gradations in standing or rank that exist in any group. Status is *scalar, functional,* and/or *personal* and is determined by a combination of organizational and personal factors.

The status system performs useful functions in administration and in society generally. Among its values are its contribution to authoritative communication, the incentive that it provides for advancement, and the sense of responsibility that it develops. Problems connected with status include an increase in social distance, preoccupation with status symbols, assignment of status to incompetent individuals, status anxiety, and status inconsistency. Status is communicated by means of *symbols,* which include not only official titles but also such privileges and physical trappings as private offices, lunch room privileges, and office furnishings that surround the job and identify its status.

Discussion Questions

1. Explain carefully the concept of *culture.*

2. In the context of the business organization, what is the nature of *material culture?*

3. From your own experience, preferably in a business organization, give an example of a *ritual.*

4. Should management accept the larger cultural system as providing the basic rules for managing a particular plant, or should management risk conflict with the general culture if it seems necessary for efficient operation?

5. Explain the meaning of *subculture* and distinguish between *institutional subculture* and *professional subculture.*

6. Suppose a particular element of the subculture of one department is objectionable to management. What should management do about it?

7. "A lot of trouble has come from technical people trying to operate a company by scientific methods rather than by management methods." Discuss the cultural implications of this statement.

8. The Defense Department recently issued an edict barring employees from accepting any favor or entertainment from contractors. Defense employees were not even to dine at a contractor's plant as guests except on an infrequent basis and then only when the conduct of official business would be facilitated and payment for meals could not conveniently be made. How is this ruling related to culture?

9. When the president, in a well-known novel, told a younger executive to call him "Tony," the young man went home in great excitement. Both he and his wife considered it a cause for celebration. How would you interpret this incident in the light of this chapter?

10. Probably few of us would agree on the prestige ranking of the various individuals in an organization of any size. What, then, is the *status system?*

11. What is the basic distinction between *functional* status and *scalar* status?

12. Consider a recent change of personnel in a public or private position with which

you are acquainted. Was any change of status involved? If so, what caused this change?

13. How is the status system of a business organization related to that of society?

14. Explain the effects of a status system upon vertical communication.

15. Do you believe that the average American works more for money (and the goods and services that money will buy) or for status and the symbols that signify status?

Supplementary Reading

Alexander, C. Norman, Jr. "Status Perceptions." *American Sociological Review* 37, no. 6 (December, 1972): 767–73.

Berger, Joseph; Cohen, Bernard P.; and Zelditch, Morris, Jr. "Status Characteristics and Social Interaction." *American Sociological Review* 37, no. 3 (June, 1972): 241–55.

Evan, William M. "Culture and Organizational Systems." *Organization and Administrative Sciences* 5, no. 4 (Winter, 1974/1975): 1–16.

Margulies, Newton. "Organizational Culture and Psychological Growth." *The Journal of Applied Behavioral Science* 5, no. 4 (October/November/December, 1969): 491–508.

Rosenzweig, James E. "Managers and Management Scientists *(Two Cultures)*." *Business Horizons* 10, no. 3 (Fall, 1967): 79–86.

Case 10

The Executive Lunch Room

A company cafeteria provided the only practical food service because of the rural location of the plant. The subsequent creation of an executive lunch room was intended to provide managers and professionals with a better lunch-time atmosphere and, perhaps more importantly, to enable them to entertain visiting guests properly.

Because of the limited size of the new dining room, management was forced to restrict its use. This space problem was solved by printing a limited number of executive lunch room tickets (that is, cards to be carried by the executives) and apportioning them to the major divisions on the basis of their overall personnel strength. Divisional managers were asked to distribute them to their professional and managerial personnel in any way they considered best for their divisions.

Division managers soon found they must make some unpleasant decisions because of the active interest of managerial, professional, and even subprofessional personnel in gaining access to the lunch room. Some relatively low-level professionals argued that they were frequently visited by outside professionals in connection with their official duties. Middle-level managers who carried their lunches felt they needed executive lunch room tickets for those occasions when they might wish to eat out or on rare occasions when they might have outside visitors.

One divisional manager solved the problem by limiting the issuance of tickets to the top portion of the management structure and the top ranking professionals, without trying to measure individual need for access to the executive lunch room.

Questions

1. Should scarce tickets be given to executives who usually carry their lunches?

2. Should a ticket be issued to a low-ranking professional whose project requires entertaining a relatively important outside visitor from two to four days per month? If the professional's boss is not eligible for a lunch room ticket, would this affect your decision?

3. What are the consequences, if any, of the creation of the lunch room on rank-and-file employees who have no expectations of being admitted to it?

4. On balance, does it seem desirable to establish an executive lunch room? How many levels of lunch rooms would be appropriate for a plant having thousands of employees?

Objectives

1. Review the management personnel requirements of contemporary business organizations.
2. Recognize strengths and weaknesses of various sources of management personnel.
3. Identify methods of *management development* and their respective contributions and limitations.
4. Explain the purpose of *organization development* and point out the forms it may take.

Chapter

11

Staffing the Organization

The Managerial Job
Recruitment of Managerial Talent
Development of Managerial Personnel
Organization Development

Case: The Banker and the Beard

Staffing activities build and develop the human organization. The specific emphasis of this chapter is upon *recruitment, management development* in its traditional sense, and various types of group training known as *organization development.*

The Managerial Job

Quest for Qualified Managerial Personnel

In recent years, we have witnessed a surge of interest in human resources development, including executive recruitment and development. College recruitment programs have multiplied, with campus visits by industrial organizations becoming commonplace. A few corporations have even established their own management institutes. Others have sent management personnel back to school to participate in executive development programs.

Such activities are based upon a growing awareness of the need for capable management personnel. The success of a firm is seen to depend upon its leadership. And, when an organization pauses to examine its managerial potential, glaring deficiencies are often apparent. The need for developing managerial personnel becomes particularly pressing in the case of rapidly changing and expanding organizations. Leaders are needed who can assume the broader responsibilities of the current decade.

Managerial Specialization

A modern business organization needs both specialists and generalists in its management structure. Specialists are managers whose responsibilities are concerned with one functional area of the business—sales, finance, research, personnel, and so on. Managers in these functional areas develop expert knowledge and abilities in their respective fields of specialization. The typical business organization needs far more functional specialists than its does generalists. In recruiting, therefore, the search is ordinarily for those who can contribute directly in some functional area.

This creates two staffing problems. First, the specialist tends to view business problems from a functional viewpoint. The production executive sees a problem as a production problem, while a marketing manager most appreciates its marketing aspects. To minimize this weakness, each functional manager must acquire some conception of the values inherent in the other functional areas and an ability to take an overall point of view in management decisions.

The second problem concerns the need for general managers. At some level, managers must rise above specialized compartments and provide direction for a number of functional areas. The president or executive vice-president or manager of a product division must resolve production, sales, and financial differences for the overall benefit of the business.

Qualities of Successful Managers

There have been many attempts to identify characteristics of effective managers. Efforts to rate such traits as dependability, initiative, fairness, cooperation, and ambition, however, have been largely futile. The primary difficulty in appraisals of this type is that they often distinguish better between good people and bad people than between good managers and bad managers. An effective manager usually has these qualities in some measure, but this has not told us much about his or her management ability.

Even though we lack proof of those attributes that make good managers, we intuitively sense that some elusive human characteristic or mixture of characteristics significantly affects management performance. In speaking of the "mysterious, indefinable x-factor that is the personality and style of the manager," Levitt commented as follows:

> Exactly what that is is seldom clear, but it is never consciously learnable or transferable from one manager to another, from teacher to student, or from textbook to reader.[1]

Even though indefinable, the style and temperament of the manager can apparently be recognized. They must, according to Levitt, be congruent with the character and needs of the organization at a particular time. Even though prescriptions vary, therefore, it seems likely that highly personal qualities interact with professional skills in some way to produce successful management. Technical skills and specialized knowledge may be necessary but insufficient to guarantee success.

The approach to analysis of executive capacity suggested by Robert L. Katz concentrates upon skills rather than personal characteristics.[2] The three basic skills serving as the basis for successful management are thought to be *technical, human,* and *conceptual.*

Types of Managerial Skills

Although managerial positions differ in the technical skill required, most necessitate some ability of this nature. A laboratory supervisor, for example, needs to understand the nature of laboratory tests conducted under his or her supervision. A controller requires a knowledge of accounting. A production manager should have some conception of production technology.

Technical Skills

No doubt, the hierarchical level has some bearing on the need for technical knowledge and competence. Near the work level, the appropriate technical skills and knowledge are almost imperative. At higher levels, decision making is concerned with broader issues. Even here, some technical knowledge may be extremely useful.

Competence in interpersonal relations is an important asset to the administrator, since a manager accomplishes work through the efforts of other individuals. Managers who are able to develop the confidence and support of others have an advantage over those who rub people the wrong way.

Human Relations Skills

A manager must blend the efforts of subordinate managers who frequently differ in backgrounds, areas of specialization, and viewpoints, particularly top-level managers whose subordinates represent different functional areas or dif-

---

[1] Theodore Levitt, "The Managerial Merry-go-round," *Harvard Business Review* 52, no. 4 (July-August, 1974): 127.

[2] Robert L. Katz, "Skills of an Effective Administrator," *Harvard Business Review* 33, no. 1 (January-February, 1955): 33–42.

ferent product lines. The ability to integrate diverse interests and simultaneously to preserve the loyalty and enthusiasm of team members contributes directly to organizational effectiveness.[3]

Conceptual Skills   It has often been suggested that an education which teaches one to think is a good education. In business management, the problems challenge the thinking and mental abilities of managers. They must be able to discern problems, devise solutions, analyze data, and exercise judgment. These tasks are often difficult and intellectually demanding.

Many business problems, unfortunately, do not lend themselves to easy solutions. Like difficult mathematical problems, it takes both skill and effort to think them through. In production management, in questions of location, in financial administration, and in other areas, the issues may call for the very best thinking of which the manager is capable.

Recruitment of Managerial Talent

Planning Managerial Requirements

The staffing process must begin with a determination of executive requirements and the steps necessary to fulfill them. Questions to be answered are both quantitative and qualitative. One question is simply, "How many managers will be required?" A supplementary question concerns the types of duties involved and the qualifications necessary for staffing these positions. While the staffing plan is concerned with managerial requirements for the following year, it may also be a type of long-range planning in which estimates are formulated for the next five or ten years.

Inside Sources of Management Talent

The story is told of a young advertising executive who, feeling stymied in his job, submitted a detailed application in response to a blind ad calling for a marketing director at a salary of $50,000. He later discovered that the ad had been placed by his own company!

> Summoned by the president, he said: "I expect you want me to leave immediately."
>
> "On the contrary," the president beamed, "we're making you marketing director. We never dreamed you had done so much here until we got your letter."[4]

The moral of this story is that there is a need for evaluation of available sources of management talent and a determination of the extent to which each may be profitably used.

The organization itself is one source of executive personnel. In filling vacancies, many corporations emphasize promotion from within. This method has the advantage of rewarding outstanding performance on the part of the existing staff. It also secures executive personnel who have experience with the

---

[3] See Henry Mintzberg, *The Nature of Managerial Work* (New York: Harper & Row, Publishers, 1973), Chapter 4, for a discussion of the manager's roles as leader and disturbance handler.

[4] "Where are the $50,000 Jobs?" *Dun's Review and Modern Industry* 80, no. 2 (August, 1962): 33.

organization and its methods of operation. A danger in internal recruitment, or at least in extensive reliance upon this source, is the inbreeding that may occur. This problem is particularly serious in positions requiring originality and new ideas.

Some firms have developed so-called *assessment centers* for use in locating potential managerial talent within the organization. According to the typical format, one or more six-person groups are brought together to participate in group exercises over a period of two or three days. During this time, they are also given interviews, psychological tests, and in-basket tests. They are observed by a staff that includes line managers, personnel specialists, and staff psychologists. Leading users of this method have been AT&T, IBM, General Electric, and Sears. Results of assessment evaluations in selecting the prospects with management potential have been encouraging.[5]

Outside Sources of Management Talent

Other business organizations—often competitors—may also be used to train or supply managerial talent. This leads to the practice of executive recruitment or *piracy*. The practice has both rewarding and perilous aspects. College-trained personnel who have been seasoned by experience are superior to college graduates of the same caliber without work experience. A possible weakness is that second-rate ability is most abundant in such markets. The employing corporations differ in their ability to stand as raid-proof against the enticements of competitors. By using the incentives of attractive salary and challenging opportunity, however, it may be possible to hire executive personnel away from some competitive organizations. Of course, the assumption here is that such recruitment is not based upon the unethical objective of stealing secrets or customers from one's competitors.

There are mixed feelings on the part of management concerning the ethics or desirability of recruitment from other companies. It is an increasingly common practice, however, and is not limited to the lower levels of the organization.

College Recruitment

To provide a supply of management potential, many firms bring a new crop of college graduates into the business each year. This practice permits hiring at a salary that is initially lower than that required for direct recruitment from other employers. In addition, the employer has access to capable applicants before they have made commitments to other concerns.

The type of graduate to be selected is a continuing question. One key controversy concerns the extent to which the graduate should have a liberal education versus specialized training. Another problem in college recruitment concerns the type of young person who may be attracted to a managerial career. Can business organizations obtain a reasonable share of the ambitious, able, educated young people? Or must business content itself with those less-qualified students who fail to respond to the opportunities in college teaching, scientific research, public service, and other nonbusiness positions?

---

[5] William C. Byham, "Assessment Centers for Spotting Future Managers," *Harvard Business Review* 48, no. 4 (July-August, 1970): 150-68.

**Development
of Managerial
Personnel**
Methods
*The Principle of
Self-Development*

Although an organization can provide opportunities for managerial development, it cannot actually develop managers. In the final analysis, the managers themselves must accomplish their own development. This viewpoint assumes that the process of education or development is not passive. If any real development is to occur, managers must assume some responsibility for their own progress.

*Job-Centered
Training*

Perhaps the most basic or fundamental approach to management development is that of managerial experience. The manager learns to manage by managing. Every manager owes some debt to his or her own opportunities for experience as a manager.

Such experience may be more or less productive depending upon the type of direction and guidance provided by higher management. Extensive delegation of authority, for example, seeks to maximize development through managerial experience. A manager who has no opportunity to make significant decisions has little opportunity to develop decision-making ability.

*Management
Responsibility for
Executive
Development*

The philosophy of some companies holds that no planned executive development is necessary. Even some who believe in recruiting people with potential feel that the cream will come to the top by itself. Another point of view holds that management must assume a responsibility for actively planning the executive development program. Haphazard methods are thought to produce unpredictable and unsatisfactory results.

As an example of managerial responsibility for development, Exxon provides for close monitoring of the program by top-level managers. The chairman, president, and seven other inside directors constitute a compensation and executive development committee which meets each Monday to review the development programs in each of Exxon's operating units.[6]

Job Rotation

One method of expanding direct job experience is to broaden that experience through a system of rotation. Such a job rotation plan seeks to maximize experience by shifting managers periodically from one job to another. Individuals selected for such programs are moved at the end of a stipulated period—say one year—and the positions they hold at any given time are viewed as training positions.

*Supervisory
Coaching*

The supervisory manager is expected to provide guidance to subordinates. In some cases, this guidance is formalized to the point of prescribing periodic interviews for the purpose of analyzing the work of subordinates and their training needs. If coaching can be conducted in the right atmosphere, it provides an excellent type of developmental experience. Its major limitation is its dependence upon the skills of the coach. It has the practical advantage of being centered in the "real world"—the manager's work activities—and provides guid-

---

[6] "How Companies Raise a New Crop of Managers," *Business Week*, no. 2371 (March 10, 1975): 48.

ance from the one best able to evaluate performance and to supply help—the employee's superior.

Managerial personnel are often brought together for company or departmental training conferences. The purpose of such conferences is to impart knowledge or to improve skills of participants. Conferences of this type are particularly appropriate in cases in which a number of managers have similar training needs. It may be discovered, for example, that certain basic policies can profitably be discussed with an entire group. Or a chief executive may wish to review with subordinate management overall personnel problems or the outlook for the business as a whole.

Training Conferences

Some companies use outside activities or schools in supplementing inside development or in providing a type of training not available within the firm. Of particular interest are the management development programs conducted by university schools of business. These programs typically range from one to six or eight weeks in length and deal with general aspects of administration. Many of them make extensive use of the case method of instruction. One of the best-known of these programs, the Sloan program for executive development at the Massachusetts Institute of Technology (with a thirty-year history), brings its executive trainees into contact with top government officials in Washington and with prominent corporate leaders in New York, London, Paris, Rome, and other West European capitals.

Outside Developmental Activities

Modification of conventional development programs to introduce a greater degree of individual initiative and choice can be accomplished by a system known as *career management.* Rather than visualizing management development merely as a way to solve *organizational* staffing problems, career management emphasizes the mutual objectives of *both* parties. Individual managers formulate career plans, which are integrated into an organizational staffing plan. According to this type of thinking, individuals should have some freedom in planning their own lives in a way that reflects their personal aspirations, and the employing organization must at the same time make necessary staffing plans to guarantee its own future.

Career Management

The following statement of an experienced personnel manager conveys an idea of the basic approach involved in career management:

> How does career management work? To put it simply, the individual programs his own career, drawing on selected expertise and information. When he chooses to affiliate with a particular institution as the best way to meet his personal objectives, he cooperates fully with organization systems; yet he still is free to change his affiliation should his personal targets make this desirable. In turn, the institution completely opens its career systems to employee initiatives while retaining the right to select people for its open positions. Development programs designed for career advancement purposes are treated as joint man-management ventures.[7]

---

[7] Marion S. Kellogg, *Career Management* (New York: American Management Association, Inc., 1972), p. 21. © 1972 by American Management Association, Inc. Reprinted by permission of the publisher.

**Management
Development and
Pressure for
Conformity**

An important issue in the direction and development of managers and even nonmanagers is the extent to which corporations should mold managers in their own image. In deciding what type of behavior may reasonably be expected, the employer must consider the degree of conformity that is proper and the degree of independence that must be allowed. A requirement of strong loyalty to the organization and an insistence upon minutely specified types of behavior may conflict with the member's expectations of freedom.

In his bestselling work, *The Organization Man*,[8] William H. Whyte, Jr., drew attention to the nation's drift toward the social ethic. He voiced provocative questions about the nature and extent of this trend and in general expressed a critical point of view concerning it. Although Whyte's study was not limited to the business organization, the business manager was one of the prime examples of the organization man he described.

A thorough application of the social ethic in a business organization is thought to produce the type of executive known as the *organization man*. This individual inoffensively shares the values of the group. As a conformist, the organization man is a "yes-man," gets along well with others, and has a special knack for finding a path of compromise and harmony. This person is not a troublemaker or a rabble-rouser but is one who accepts and internalizes the values of the organization.

One primary danger to recognize is that of stifling the creative spirit. Many brilliantly creative people, those with great achievements, have been nonconformists. Another objection to the trend toward the social ethic is the extent to which the organization should be allowed to invade the privacy of the individual. Must people sell themselves body and soul to the corporation, or should they be permitted to retain their personal lives with their own choices and convictions?

**Organization
Development**

**Basic Elements of
Organization
Development**

In management development programs, the individual skills of managers receive attention. Some programs, however, have gone beyond individual development to group or team development. This latter type of training, which is designed to improve organizational relationships and encourage teamwork, has been labeled *organization development* and is popularly known as *OD*.

The field of organizational development is nebulous, and practitioners do not agree on a definition of its scope. The following statement by Beckhard provides a useful, working definition:

> Organization development is an effort (1) *planned*, (2) *organization-wide*, and (3) *managed* from the *top*, to (4) increase *organizational effectiveness* and *health* through (5) *planned interventions* in the organization's "processes," using *behavioral-science* knowledge.[9]

OD is *planned* in the sense of involving a systematic diagnosis of the way an organization functions and a prescription of certain organization development

---

[8] William H. Whyte, Jr., *The Organization Man* (New York: Simon and Schuster, Inc., 1956).

[9] Richard Beckhard, *Organization Development: Strategies and Models* (Reading, Mass.: Addison-Wesley Publishing Company, 1969), p. 9.

methods to improve its functioning. The analysis involves an *entire organization*, although this may be a corporation, an autonomous division, or even a local unit.

In saying the development is *managed from the top*, Beckhard is stressing the desired commitment of top leaders to it. Increasing *effectiveness* and *health* of an organization would entail improvements in intergroup and interdepartmental collaboration, development of undistorted communication, identification of shared values, and reduction of interpersonal friction.

By *planned intervention*, managers and other organizational members step back and analyze the way the organization is functioning and look at alternative ways of working together. The *behavioral science* knowledge deals with such features of organizations and management as "motivation, power, communications, perception, cultural norms, problem-solving, goal-setting, interpersonal relationships, intergroup relationships, and conflict management." [10]

A central figure in most types of organizational development is the *change agent*, who is also known as an *OD consultant* or *OD practitioner*. The change agent provides the technical or professional leadership necessary to improve the functioning of the organization. The change agent must inspire confidence, which, in turn, requires an ability to understand and diagnose organizational problems as well as a knowledge of behavioral science and OD methodology. The client organization, however, must accept responsibility for the program and for its implementation if the program is to be taken seriously.

Organization Development Methods

The various methods of changing organizations tend to overlap, and a given OD program may use more than one method. For the most part, the methods discussed here deal directly with teamwork in the various organizational systems.

Laboratory Training Groups

One approach is described as *laboratory training*, and its best-known variety is *sensitivity training*. Its purpose is the development of interpersonal skills of organizational members. Through participation in group projects and exercises, managers are taught to look at themselves and their behavior as it may affect others and to attempt to understand the behavior and attitudes of others. Laboratory training emphasizes the way that individuals "come across" in their face-to-face interactions with others.

Team-Building Conferences

Team-building conferences are intended to improve the functioning of managerial groups or work teams. Activities of this type begin with a review of team purposes and priorities and areas in which improvement may be helpful. In one of the first sessions, for example, participants may establish an agenda by identifying the problems needing attention.

Grid Organization Development

One of the most widely used team-building programs is Blake and Mouton's *grid organization development*.[11] The *managerial grid*, a key tool in this program,

---

[10] *Ibid.*, p. 13.

[11] Robert Blake and Jane Srygley Mouton, *Building a Dynamic Corporation Through Grid Organization Development* (Reading, Mass.: Addison-Wesley Publishing Company, 1969).

portrays managerial orientation in terms of two variables—concern for people and concern for production. See Figure 11-1.

Figure 11-1   *The Managerial Grid*

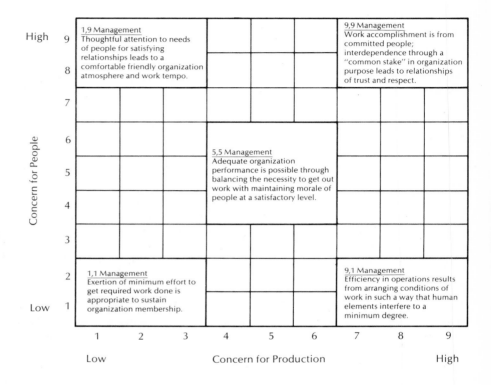

Source: Robert R. Blake and Jane S. Mouton, *The Managerial Grid* (Houston: Gulf Publishing Co., Book Div., 1964), p. 10.

A series of exercises is used to permit managers to analyze their own positions on the grid and to work toward the ideal 9,9 position. The complete grid OD program also involves additional steps designed to carry the grid approach to all parts of the organization.

Summary

The management of many firms has become concerned with the need for *recruitment* and *development* of a competent managerial staff. In part, this concern is based upon a realization of managerial limitations in the face of the growing complexity of management and the tendency toward managerial specialization. Staffing functions are designed to produce managers with the necessary *conceptual, technical,* and *human relations* skills.

Recruitment of managerial personnel may draw upon various sources of management talent. A company has available not only internal sources, through promotion from within, but also other business organizations and universities.

A great number of management development methods are available. Regardless of what training opportunities management may provide, the development must ultimately be *self-development.* Each individual must assume a personal responsibility for training. The most fundamental type of development occurs in the actual performance of managerial duties. Other methods of development include *job rotation, supervisory coaching,* and *training conferences. Career management* involves a cooperative effort of each employee and the company in formulating individual career plans. One danger in management development and direction involves the specter of the *organization man,* with an emphasis upon *conformity* to fit into an organizational mold.

Organization development, which is broader than management development, trains teams of managers or groups to work together effectively. Some of its better-known methods are *sensitivity training, team building,* and *grid organization development.*

Discussion Questions

1. Does it appear likely that the increased complexity of management will have a greater effect upon staff management or general line management? Can a general manager solve the problem by proper reliance upon staff assistants?

2. In view of the proportional numbers of specialists and generalists in management, what policy would you recommend in recruitment of management trainees?

3. What is the relative importance of *technical* skills, *human relations* skills, and *conceptual* skills at the top-management level versus the first-line supervisory level?

4. Is it possible to overemphasize human relations ability as an essential element of effective managerial importance?

5. Compare the advantages and difficulties in recruiting managerial personnel from competitive organizations.

6. What factors should be considered in choosing the specific colleges or universities to use in recruitment of management trainees?

7. Evaluate the placement service provided by your college or university. What benefits do employers receive from such service?

8. Explain the reasoning underlying the concept or principle of *self-development* in managerial growth.

9. Describe the ideal conditions for effective on-the-job management development.

10. To what extent are the *career management* interests of the employing organization and the individual congruent or conflicting?

11. What is the nature of the problem of *conformity* in modern organizations? What causes the problem to exist?

12. How does *organization development* differ from *management development?* Are not both intended to improve organization effectiveness?

Supplementary Reading

Argyris, Chris. "Personality and Organization Theory Revisited." *Administrative Science Quarterly* 18, no. 2 (June, 1973): 141–67.

Bray, Douglas W. "Management Development Without Frills." *The Conference Board Record* 12, no. 9 (September, 1975): 47–50.

Foulkes, Fred K. "The Expanding Role of the Personnel Function." *Harvard Business Review* 53, no. 2 (March–April, 1975): 71–84.

Mills, Ted. "Human Resources—Why the New Concern?" *Harvard Business Review* 53, no. 2 (March–April, 1975): 120–34.

Schein, Edgar H. "How 'Career Anchors' Hold Executives to their Career Paths." *Personnel* 52, no. 3 (May–June, 1975): 11–24.

Case 11

The Banker and the Beard

Phil Harris, B.B.A. graduate of a northeastern university, accepted a work-study assistantship offer from another university. These assistantships involved a combination of study and part-time work with a local business organization. The awarding of the assistantships was subject to employer acceptance of the students after they arrived to begin graduate study. When the director of graduate studies welcomed Phil, she noted that he was neatly dressed and wearing a luxuriant moustache and beard.

Phil was tentatively assigned to a local state bank. When he reported for the initial interview, with moustache and beard neatly trimmed, he talked briefly with a junior officer who ushered him into the office of the president. The president looked at him carefully and then proceeded directly to the main issue. "Young man," he asked abruptly, "how important is that beard to you?" Phil squirmed and gave a noncommital answer. The banker explained that the bank was determined to present a good image to its customers and that they could not tolerate employees who did not maintain a clean-shaven look.

After a brief discussion of other aspects of the work, Phil got into his car and drove back to campus. He recalled a comment by the director of graduate studies that this position was one of the few remaining openings for graduate students.

Questions

1. What rational basis, if any, does Phil have for objecting to the banker's requirements?

2. What is the apparent basis of the banker's policy? Can it be justified?

3. What are the potential dangers for the bank in its present personnel policy?

4. Does the banker believe in individualism and free enterprise?

5

Directing and Motivating Members

Objectives

1. Explain the leadership role and the types of leadership style that managers may use.
2. Identify types of participative management, the prerequisites for effective participation, and the values of using a participative approach.
3. Recognize situational constraints and their effect upon choice of leadership style.

Chapter

12

Managerial
Leadership

The Manager's Leadership Function
Participative Management
Situational Factors in Leadership

Case: Monitored Phone Calls

An effective manager needs leadership ability, that is, the ability to direct and inspire other members of the organization. This chapter examines leadership and its contribution to organizational performance.

The Manager's Leadership Function

Importance and Nature of Leadership

Organizational performance is closely related to quality of leadership. Although competent leadership is not the only important ingredient for successful operation, it is essential. A bungling leader can wreck morale and destroy efficiency. Strong leadership, on the other hand, can transform a lackluster group into a strong, aggressive, successful organization.

Through leadership, a manager secures the cooperation of members of an organization. The office manager, production foreman, laboratory supervisor, and company president each has a leadership role to perform. Through leadership, the manager accomplishes an objective by mobilization and utilization of people.

Not all that an executive does represents leadership. Leadership activities are directed to getting effective work from team members. The unique ability of the leader is a social talent—that of getting the best effort of the organization's members.

The term *leadership* is sometimes used with the connotation of *positive* leadership—*leading* versus *commanding*. As used here, however, the term includes all aspects of leadership. Any approach, positive or negative, that elicits the efforts of one's subordinates, and even one's colleagues, represents an exercise of leadership. An industrial leader may get results by inspiring followers to give their all for the company or by threatening to fire them. One appeal may be superior to the other, but the use of either constitutes leadership.

Patterns of Leadership

Leadership may be classified in various ways. One common distinction involves the element of authority in the relationship between superior and subordinate. According to this classification, leaders may be *autocratic, democratic,* or *laissez-faire.*

Autocratic leadership emphasizes commanding and order giving. Such leaders make most important decisions, entrusting relatively little authority to subordinates. Their supervision uses negative sanctions and develops a sense of fear in those at lower levels.

The industrialist of the past is an extreme example, even though the authoritarian leader is not extinct in the present generation. The colorful John H. Patterson, founder of NCR Corporation, was an autocratic leader who coupled a flair for the dramatic with his use of authority.[1] In a somewhat bizarre episode, he once abolished a cost accounting system he considered inefficient. The erring department produced reams of statistics, but the data were too late to be of value. After fretting over the matter for some time, Patterson reached the boiling point one day, jumped up from his desk, and headed for the cost accounting department. He gave the accountants little time for reflection, walking

---

[1] The incident from Patterson's career is taken from the following account prepared by Stanley C. Allyn, a subsequent NCR board chairman: Stanley C. Allyn, "Fiery Furnace Claims Erring Department," *NCR Factory News,* (November, 1961): 4–6.

from desk to desk and asking each employee to pick up his accounting books and to follow him. The procession, carrying armloads of accounting records, headed straight for the power house, where they met the engineer in charge.

> "Will these furnaces burn anything except coal?" he asked.
> "Well, sir," said the engineer, "we've never tried anything else."
> Mr. Patterson then threw one of the accounting books into the fire.
> "That burns," he said.
> And with that he ordered the others to do the same with their books. In a little while all of the books had gone up in smoke while the clerks stood speechless. Finally, Mr. Patterson pulled out his watch and said: "Gentlemen, it has taken us just ten minutes to get rid of the Cost Department."

Of course, Mr. Patterson did not mean to operate without some cost data. But, as is evident from this account, he devoted little time to sampling employee thinking about changing the existing cost accounting system.

In contrast to autocratic leaders, democratic leaders show greater deference for subordinates. They value the ideas and suggestions of subordinates and consult with them to secure their contributions. The *laissez-faire,* or *free-rein,* leader, on the other hand, goes a step farther and turns an entire problem or project over to subordinates. Subordinates may be asked to set their own objectives and to develop plans for achieving them. Although laissez-faire leadership may be effective in occasional situations in which the group is capable of a constructive response, chaos may also result from this type of leadership.

Degrees of Leadership Authority

The preceding leadership categories are presumably distinct and mutually exclusive. One contrasting analysis of leadership suggests a broad range of possible leadership behavior.[2] Rather than forcing all leadership into two or three sharply defined classes, this study contends that the variety in leadership approaches may be viewed as a continuum.

As shown in Figure 12–1, leadership behavior may involve any of various combinations of authority of the manager and freedom for subordinates. We should note that neither extreme constitutes an absolute. The leader always has a minimum of authority, and subordinates never surrender all discretion.

Other Classifications of Leadership

It is also possible to classify leadership in terms of the leader's orientation. In such schemes, a distinction is made between leaders oriented toward followers and leaders oriented toward work.

One such leadership classification, used extensively in research studies of the Institute for Social Research of the University of Michigan, distinguishes between *job-centered* supervision and *employee-centered* supervision.[3]

The managerial grid, cited in Chapter 11 distinguished between *concern for production* and *concern for people.* The two concerns are visualized as independent variables, the horizontal axis of the grid indicating concern for production and

---

[2] Robert Tannenbaum and Warren H. Schmidt, "How to Choose a Leadership Pattern," *Harvard Business Review* 36, no. 2 (March-April, 1958): 95–101.

[3] See Rensis Likert, *New Patterns of Management* (New York: McGraw-Hill Book Company, 1961), Chapter 2.

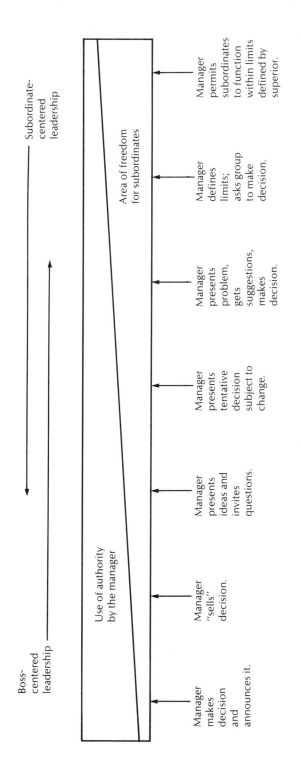

Figure 12-1 *Continuum of Leadership Behavior*

Source: Robert Tannenbaum and Warren H. Schmidt, "How to Choose a Leadership Pattern," *Harvard Business Review* 36, no. 2 (March-April, 1958): 96.

the vertical axis indicating concern for people. There is an obvious similarity between these two variables and the preceding job-centered and employee-centered categories.

Leadership studies at the Ohio State University have used two dimensions of leadership behavior—*consideration* and *initiating structure*.[4] Consideration is related to the leader's consideration of followers and warmth of personal leader-follower relationships. Initiating structure involves the leader's actions that define leader-follower relationships and establish definite standards of performance.

There appears to be much similarity among the leadership styles described above. There are technical variations, however, which lead to some differences in research results.[5]

Much research effort over the past twenty-five years has probed the relationship between leadership style and group performance because group performance provides the ultimate test of the leader's efforts. Although leadership is not the only factor affecting performance, it is probably the most important variable. As coaches and coaching styles are judged on the basis of win-loss records, other leaders and leadership styles are likewise evaluated in terms of group accomplishments.

Leadership Style and Group Effectiveness

Rather intuitively, we expect employee-centered, considerate leadership to be better than task-centered leadership. To date, however, research results have been disappointing. Some studies have reported significant correlations, but they are offset by other studies with conflicting findings. It may be that significant relationships are obscured by situational differences in the various studies. Under particular circumstances, one leadership approach may lead to higher productivity, while in other circumstances, a different type of leadership may be necessary for maximizing performance.

There does seem to be a positive correlation between employee-oriented, considerate leadership and employee morale. In other words, employee-oriented leadership tends to enhance employee satisfaction.[6]

Even in those cases showing positive correlations between person-centered leadership and productivity, we are unsure which is the chicken and which is the egg. An assumption that leadership causes superior performance is merely an assumption. The leader may be merely responding positively to effective performance of subordinates. Farris cites a delightful cartoon appearing in *Look* magazine several years ago, picturing two rats in a Skinner box. Said one rat to the other: "I've really got this psychologist conditioned. Every time I press the bar, he gives me a pellet of food."[7] Similarly, followers may condition leaders to respond in a particular way, rather than vice versa.

---

[4] For discussion of these dimensions, see Lyman W. Porter, Edward E. Lawler III, and J. Richard Hackman, *Behavior in Organizations* (New York: McGraw-Hill Book Company, 1975), pp. 424–25.

[5] Ralph M. Stogdill, *Handbook of Leadership: A Survey of Theory and Research* (New York: The Free Press, 1974), p. 403.

[6] See Porter, Lawler, and Hackman, *Behavior in Organizations*, p. 424 and Stogdill, *Handbook of Organizations*, p. 404.

[7] George F. Farris, "Chickens, Eggs and Productivity in Organizations," *Organizational Dynamics*, (Spring, 1975): 10.

Participative Management

Nature and Benefits of Participation

One type of democratic leadership that has received much attention in recent years is known as *employee participation.* In general, a program of participation attempts to involve subordinates—sometimes managerial subordinates and sometimes the rank and file—more directly in the management of the business. Subordinates are allowed and encouraged to participate in some aspects of their superior's decision making—an activity that would not be expected, or even tolerated, in many organizations. As one example of a participative approach, a unit supervisor may ask subordinates for suggestions or ideas in tackling some problem confronting the unit.[8]

Much work, even in some supervisory positions, seems monotonous and uninspiring. An opportunity for participation provides a contrast to such unchallenging assignments and is welcomed by many employees. From a psychological point of view, there is a vast difference between *activity* and *participation.* Participation may add meaning to work and permit employees to become *identified* with it. In contrast to a system in which all important thinking is limited to the superior, participative management places subordinates on an entirely different footing. Soliciting the assistance of subordinates assumes they have something valuable to offer and that their opinions have significance. This approach adds dignity to the jobs and to the incumbents.

Benefits of participation are not limited to the employees. In tapping the thinking of employees, management gets the benefit of their contributions as well as their enthusiastic work. Increased output and product quality improvement have been experienced in some uses of participative management. Also, in introducing changes, participation can help to minimize employee resistance. In fact, some changes occur in direct response to employee participation.

It is possible, of course, that a participative approach may be adopted insincerely. A manager may know what he or she intends to do but ask employees so they will "think it is their idea." Such an attempt is doomed to failure. An employee does not need a Ph.D. to detect insincerity.

Types and Degrees of Participation

Participative management takes many different forms. In some organizations, a gesture is made in this direction through use of a suggestion system. Employees are rewarded financially for submitting usable suggestions. Success of these systems has been spotty. Some systems have garnered valuable ideas from a large number of employees, whereas others have been disappointing in their results. Competent administration of the suggestion system is essential. At best, a suggestion system alone gets the participation of only a minority of the employees. Also, the participation is usually limited to an occasional, specific suggestion.

Perhaps the more usual form of participation is the type of supervision that might be labeled as *consultative management.* Managers simply use participation in the day-to-day administration of the organization. Rather than deciding matters unilaterally and passing the decisions on to subordinates, they bring

---

[8] In contrast to delegation of decision-making authority to a subordinate, the concept of participation is primarily concerned with a sharing of the decision-making process between a superior and a subordinate or subordinates.

subordinates into the supervisory process. They seek the thinking and comments of group members on matters confronting the group.

Managers differ greatly in the degree to which they use participation. The amount of participation is normally greater at upper levels of the organization. At any level, a relatively autocratic manager may check an occasional issue with subordinates. A distinction may also be made between issues directly affecting employees—such as scheduling vacation periods—and general problems of management. Managers who make the most extensive use of participation consult with employees frequently on all types of issues.

It seems likely that participation may function more successfully in some settings than in others. The type of subordinates, for example, is one significant variable. Participation assumes that subordinates *can* contribute something worthwhile. This contribution depends, however, upon their ability and background.

Prerequisites for Participation

Effective participation also requires a set of necessary psychological conditions.[9] Subordinates must be capable of becoming psychologically involved, possess a minimum amount of intelligence, and be in touch with reality. They must favor participation and not feel that the boss always knows best. They must also see the relevance of the problem to their own lives and be able to express themselves satisfactorily.

The atmosphere of the organization must also be conducive to participation. If a highly autocratic management prevails throughout an organization, a particular manager may have difficulty in adopting a participative approach. Subordinates in such an organization, accustomed to taking orders, may interpret consultation as a sign of weakness.

Whether the difficulty was organizational atmosphere, need for quick decisions, or otherwise, American Airlines failed in an attempt to increase participative management between 1968 and 1973.[10] Prior to 1968, American Airlines had been managed by Cyrus Rowlett Smith, described as a "tough old pioneering leader" who ran the airline the way a "George Patton-type general would run an army." Smith was followed by George Spater, described as an "easy-going" man and a "nice guy."

Spater believed in management by participation and in sharing decision making with others. In American Airlines, however, participative management failed to work. Delays caused by committee deliberation and indecision were disruptive. The president of American's pilot association was quoted as follows:

> "Pilots spend much of their lives making split-second decisions, and they don't understand an operation that has to wait for a committee to decide everything.[11]

---

[9] These conditions are discussed in Robert Tannenbaum, Irving R. Weschler, and Fred Massarik, *Leadership and Organization: A Behavioral Science Approach* (New York: McGraw-Hill Book Company, 1961), pp. 94–98.

[10] "Casey at the Bat," *Forbes* 114, no. 10 (November 15, 1974): 38–48.

[11] *Ibid.*, p. 39.

The condition of the airline deteriorated—both its reputation for service and its profitability declined— and Smith came out of retirement to take over again in 1973. This example points out clearly that participation is not always the answer to organizational problems.

Situational Factors in Leadership

Discussion of leadership to this point has revealed a lack of uniformity in leadership situations. These differences in leadership situations are extremely significant in understanding leadership behavior.

Leadership in a Systems Context

Managers function as parts of complex organizational systems. As such, they are related in decision making and other managerial activities to other levels of management, and they function in relationship to them.

This viewpoint suggests that leadership style may be affected by the treatment that supervisors receive from their own superiors in the organization. The fact of such systems' constraints upon leadership style has been established by a number of research studies. One investigation, reported by Fleishman, evaluated a leadership training course for foremen in the International Harvester Company.[12] Leadership attitudes of foremen were found to vary with the type of manager under whom the foremen served. Foremen who worked under considerate supervisors tended to express more considerate attitudes toward their own subordinates. The training course improved leadership attitudes during the training session but failed to produce permanent changes in either the attitudes or behavior of the foremen when they returned to their regular jobs. Apparently the training was inadequate to counteract the influences coming from higher organization levels.

The Leadership Situation

An analysis of managerial role in the context of the organizational system reveals the *situational* nature of leadership. Different kinds of organizational circumstances call for different kinds of leadership. Any of a variety of supervisory styles may be effective under appropriate conditions. Leadership is always exercised in a specific situation involving real people and a given physical environment. There is a specific leader who has individual followers. The most appropriate type of leadership and the traits of the successful leader depend, to some extent, upon the particular situation.

As one factor in the leadership situation, consider the type of subordinates. If the work is professional, the organization's members may be college trained and possibly hold graduate degrees. This could be true, for example, in a research laboratory. Another organization's personnel, in contrast, may lack even a high school education. In a building maintenance department, for example, such a situation would not be unusual. The extreme contrast between the two groups presents the respective leaders with quite different challenges.

Other factors also distinguish the leadership situation. The traditions of a given organization may discourage certain types of leadership. Autocratic management may be traditional and have general acceptance by the member-

---

[12] Edwin A. Fleishman, "Leadership Climate, Human Relations Training, and Supervisory Behavior," *Personnel Psychology* 6, no. 2 (Summer, 1953): 205–22.

ship. The stable or dynamic nature of an organization, the variable or routine nature of the work, the degree of turbulence in the environment, the possibility of emergency situations, the capability of the leader, and other factors could also be cited.

One research study which verified the situational nature of leadership examined leadership differences at various hierarchical levels of a hospital.[13] Variations in the supervisor's "skill mix"—that is, the combination of technical skill, human relations skill, and administrative skill—were analyzed. At lower levels, technical and human relations skills were most highly related to subordinates' satisfaction with the supervisor. At higher organizational levels, however, the supervisor's administrative skills were more closely related to satisfaction of subordinates, with human relations skills only a poor second.

Over the last half century, the typical leadership situation in American industry has changed. As one factor in the change, the average educational level of the labor force has risen from an elementary school level, or lower, to an average level involving some college work. In the past, autocratic management was characteristic. Changes in the situation may have prompted the movement toward democratic leadership.

Contingency Model of Leadership

In view of the situational differences noted, the most effective type of leadership may well depend on the situation. This possibility, in fact, helps explain the inconsistencies in research results reported earlier. The next logical step in analyzing leadership approaches, therefore, is to classify leadership situations in a meaningful way and find the best leadership style for each class of situations.

The most ambitious step in this direction is Fiedler's *contingency model of leadership*.[14] Fiedler and his associates have classified situations in terms of their "favorableness" for the leader. The favorableness is defined as follows in terms of three properties:

1. *Leader-group relationships.* A close leader-follower relationship, in contrast to a distant relationship, is favorable for the leader.
2. *Task structure.* Well-defined tasks with a minimum of ambiguity provide the most favorable conditions for the leader.
3. *Leader position power.* The leader who possesses formal authority and who has rewards and sanctions available has a favorable situation.

The most favorable situation, then, combines close leader-follower relationships, well-defined tasks, and strong formal position power. Leadership situations involving combinations of these properties may be found when we classify the situations as either favorable or unfavorable in terms of each property. In other words, we may visualize eight possible leadership situations, in terms of these properties, ranging from highly favorable to highly unfavorable.

---

[13] Robert Dubin *et al., Leadership and Productivity* (San Francisco: Chandler Publishing Company, 1965).

[14] This theory of Fred E. Fiedler is widely discussed in the literature. For one recent source, see Fred E. Fiedler and Martin M. Chemers, *Leadership and Effective Management* (Glenview, Ill.: Scott, Foresman and Company, 1974).

The leader's orientation, according to the Fiedler model, is classified by measuring the leader's perceived psychological distance from his or her *least preferred coworker.* A *high-LPC* leader tends to see even a poor coworker in a relatively favorable light. A *low-LPC* leader, on the other hand, tends to reject the weak coworker. The measurement apparently takes account of variations in a leader's human relations intensity or consideration of others. A high-LPC leader, therefore, is a strong human-relations-oriented leader.

A substantial body of research based upon this model has shown a positive correlation between high-LPC (positive human relations) leadership and group productivity in *moderately difficult* situations. However, the correlation was negative in situations that were either *very favorable* or *very unfavorable.* In other words, high-LPC (positive human relations) leadership apparently works well in average situations but not in very good (very favorable) or very bad (very unfavorable) situations.

The contingency theory is not yet firmly established, and various questions remain to be answered.[15] For example, the theory apparently fails to consider the possibility that leaders may change their behavior depending on the situation. Nevertheless, Fiedler's model represents a significant attempt to move beyond the vague statement that leadership depends on the situation. More practical guidelines should emerge as its propositions become better substantiated or modified to reflect a growing understanding of organizational life. In any event, it seems clear that situational differences interact with leadership. It is the nature of significant situational variables that needs further study.

Summary

Through the function of leadership, a manager secures the effort and teamwork of members of an organization. Different types of leadership are noted—particularly the extent to which leadership is *autocratic* or *democratic.*

Studies analyzing the general relationship of leadership style to group productivity have failed to establish any consistent correlations. However, there does seem to be a positive relationship between employee-centered leadership and employee satisfaction.

Democratic leadership is often expressed through *participative management.* In this approach, management attempts to secure the thinking and suggestions of subordinates in the decision-making process. Although participation may occur in many different forms, one of the most common varieties is the informal consultation by a supervisor with subordinates. The prerequisites for effective participation include the necessary minimum ability and psychological conditions on the part of the participants, a permissive atmosphere, adequate available time, reasonable cost requirements, and satisfactory union relationships.

Differences in leadership situations appear to be extremely significant in determining the effectiveness of leadership. Fiedler's *contingency model of leadership*

---

[15] Victor H. Vroom, "The Search for a Theory of Leadership," in Joseph W. McGuire, ed. *Contemporary Management: Issues and Viewpoints* (Englewood Cliffs, N.J.: Prentice-Hall, Inc., 1974), pp. 396–99.

is a situational model that classifies leadership situations according to their favorableness or unfavorableness for the leader. High-LPC (human-relations-oriented) leaders are more effective in moderately favorable situations, whereas low-LPC leaders are more effective in either highly favorable or highly unfavorable situations.

Discussion Questions

1. With what type of subordinates would each of the three patterns of leadership—*autocratic, democratic,* and *laissez-faire*—be most effective?

2. Evaluate the leadership approach of John H. Patterson as described in this chapter. Do you think it may have been effective then? Would it be effective now?

3. Distinguish between a *job-centered* supervisor and an *employee-centered* supervisor. On the basis of your own experience, describe the leadership approach of one manager (or teacher) in each category.

4. Explain the distinction between the following two dimensions of leadership behavior: *consideration* and *initiating structure.*

5. Disregarding situational factors, what general relationship exists between leadership style and group effectiveness? What is the most obvious explanation for this relationship?

6. What is the relationship between leadership style and employee satisfaction?

7. In those cases which do show a positive correlation between employee-centered leadership and productivity, how can one know which is the cause and which is the effect?

8. Is there evidence that shows *employee participation* contributes to productivity?

9. How can a manager allow *participation* by subordinates and still retain a position of leadership?

10. What is the significance of the *leadership situation* in choosing a pattern of leadership?

11. What is meant by a leadership measurement in terms of *LPC* (least preferred co-worker)?

12. Explain Fiedler's *contingency model of leadership.*

Supplementary Reading

Fiedler, Fred E. and Chemers, Martin M. *Leadership and Effective Management.* Glenview, Ill.: Scott, Foresman and Company, 1974.

Greiner, Larry E. "What Managers Think of Participative Leadership," *Harvard Business Review 51,* no. 2 (March–April, 1973): 111–17.

Hill, Walter A. "Leadership Style: Rigid or Flexible?" *Organizational Behavior and Human Performance 9,* no. 1 (February, 1973): 35–47.

Stogdill, Ralph M. "Historical Trends in Leadership Theory and Research." *Journal of Contemporary Business 3,* no. 4 (Autumn, 1974): 1–17.

Case 12

Monitored Phone Calls*

On a Friday afternoon Gil Harris, National Insurance Regional Manager, called his accounts division manager, Earl Bennett, into his office and explained to him that he had, for some time, been considering a program which he felt could reveal any possible problems with customer service. Now he was prepared to implement it. Over the weekend the telephone company was to install new equipment allowing incoming and outgoing phone calls to be monitored. The program involved three managerial and nine clerical employees, all of whom had either agent or policy holder contacts. Mr. Harris was to maintain the tapping device in his office. Not only did he wish to supervise the program personally, but he felt that employees would be enthusiastic about an opportunity to prove themselves before higher management. As Bennett attempted to express his reservations, Harris ended the talk by saying that his decision was good and that Bennett should notify his people of it. Monday morning Bennett called the twelve employees together and told them of Mr. Harris's wishes.

The announcement was followed by a great deal of grumbling. One woman was overheard telling her coworkers, "I've always prided myself in doing a good job. We should go in there and complain, but he would probably fire the lot of us."

During the first month of monitoring, absenteeism nearly doubled, and two employees notified Bennett they wished to transfer to another section. When asked why, they replied they couldn't stand being "watched" all the time. Bennett knew he would be held responsible for this activity and didn't know what to tell Harris. His problem compounded when he received the following memo from Harris:

"Earl, it appears as though I have been successful in uncovering problem areas. Your people don't seem to spend enough time with agents or policy holders. They act as though they are in a hurry and on occasion are downright 'rude.' Be in my office at 10 a.m. tomorrow morning with your recommendations on how you are going to straighten this out."

Questions

1. What type of leadership style did Harris use? How effective was it?

2. Evaluate Bennett's performance as a leader.

3. How should Bennett respond to the memo from Harris in their morning conference?

*John V. Murray and Thomas J. Von der Embse, *Organizational Behavior: Critical Incidents and Analysis* (Columbus, Ohio: Charles E. Merrill Publishing Company, 1973), p. 190.

Objectives

1. Explain the nature and methods of effective communication in organizations.
2. Analyze the significance of organizational roles and relationships in communication, particularly the superior-subordinate relationship.
3. Explain informal communication channels (the "grapevine") and identify possible management strategies for dealing with informal communication.

The Communication Process

Nature of Communication

The process of communication is an integral part of the functioning of any organization. Leadership is exerted and coordination is achieved through communication. As managers improve their understanding of communication problems and increase their skill in communication, therefore, organizational performance will become more effective.

Management Through Communication

The manager's world is a *world of words.* Much, perhaps most, of the time is spent in communicating with those about him or her. On the basis of studies of managers in action, we know that most managers show a strong preference for verbal over written communication. Mintzberg's observation of chief executive behavior revealed that 78 percent of their time was devoted to verbal interaction.[1] Figure 13–1 shows the relative importance of various types of interaction.

Figure 13–1 *Distribution of Hours*

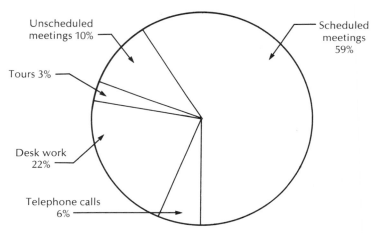

Abridged and adapted from Fig. 4 (p. 39) in *The Nature of Managerial Work* by Henry Mintzberg. Copyright © 1973 by Henry Mintzberg. By permission of Harper & Row, Publishers, Inc.

Any type of organized activity, in fact, demands communication. There is no other way to direct the work of the individual members and work groups of the firm. In laying out work assignments, changing the direction of work or projects that are under way, instructing subordinates, and coordinating the different activities of the organization, the manager must communicate in some way.

It should be evident, on the basis of these comments, that communication in the business organization may be upward, downward, or horizontal. The need for downward communication—giving orders, instructions, and so on—is easily recognized. Downward communication is often incomplete, however. Al-

---

[1] Henry Mintzberg, *The Nature of Managerial Work* (New York: Harper & Row, Publishers, 1973), p. 38.

though instructions and directions are given, there is often failure to communicate the rationale or "why." Upward communication is even more troublesome and is often neglected. Horizontal communication is particularly important among positions or components involving extensive coordination or teamwork. In some administrative situations, the volume of necessary horizontal communication is as great as the volume of vertical communication.

The general nature of communication requires little explanation. It is obvious that the manager's contacts with subordinates involve communication. To understand better the strengths and weaknesses of communication in the administrative process, however, it may be helpful to note certain underlying concepts.

Definition of Communication

First of all, communication implies both *transmission* and *reception* of a message. The communication process is not complete unless reception occurs. All of this seems clear enough. In the administrative situation, however, there is danger in assuming that reception occurs whenever there are listeners. In reality, this does not always happen. The message may not be received, even though it may be physically read or heard. In such a case, no communication has occurred.

It is also important to note *what* is transmitted through communication. Factual information, of course, is exchanged. The manager explains the nature of an assignment to the subordinate, and the subordinate reports work progress to the superior. But communication involves more than the intellect; feelings and attitudes are also expressed. An employee may come to know a supervisor's attitude quite well. Opinions, predictions, suggestions, ideas—all of these are involved in communication. To understand communication, therefore, we must see that it includes a great deal more than mere facts.

Methods of Communication

We all know that language—written and spoken—provides tools for communication. What we sometimes overlook is that language may be supplemented by other less obvious forms of communication. Consider the physical expression of a speaker, for example. What can the listener detect from this? If a supervisor scowls, the subordinate discovers the supervisor's unhappiness or displeasure. This may lead to various conclusions about the real meaning of the scowl, such as "He's hot under the collar and will forget all about this when he cools off." Or, "He's unhappy about my performance, and my future is clouded." Or, "He really means business, and I'd better get to work immediately." If the supervisor wears a smile, the same message may carry quite a different meaning. Almost instinctively, a subordinate picks up and interprets such signals. By looking at the boss, a subordinate knows whether the time is ripe to ask for a raise or to request a day off.

Not only physical expressions and gestures but also voice inflections may tell the listener more than the words themselves reveal. The tone of voice can transform words of praise into sarcasm. No wonder mistakes occur in oral communication.

Even silence, the absence of language, can communicate! Occasionally, someone communicates contempt for another by refusing to speak to that person. In management, the same effect may be achieved by silence. If an employee performs exceptionally well or completes a project outstandingly, he or she might logically expect some word of commendation. Silence, however, communicates indifference or disrespect, whether intended or not.

Perhaps the most forceful method of communication is not language at all. There is an old saying that "Actions speak louder than words." We observe an individual's behavior and infer something about the person. One who is constantly late in meeting appointments, for example, apparently has little regard for punctuality or little respect for the other party. One who is not well-groomed apparently does not value personal appearance.

In the administrative situation, subordinates watch the behavior of higher management. If management promotes on the basis of favoritism or family connection, for example, what do subordinates assume? If supervisors reflect indifference about their own responsibilities, what is the effect on subordinates? From the standpoint of employees, such actions provide the most eloquent expression of management policy and values.

If there is a discrepancy between management's words and actions, a conflict in communication results. The listener is asked to believe a written or oral communication in the face of behavior that suggests it is not so. Almost without exception, the observer takes the actual behavior as representing the truth and assumes that contrary talk is so much "hogwash." Managers need to be unusually careful, therefore, in insuring that their actions communicate the same message as their words.

Distortion in Communication

Perfect communication would accurately transmit an idea from one mind to another. Unfortunately, transmission is often imperfect. Something goes wrong in the process of verbalizing an idea and then extracting the idea again from the words. A semblance of the message may be transmitted, but distortion may also be present.

Some distortion occurs almost automatically as communications are passed through channels. Errors creep into the original message as it is passed on. At each point in the communication chain, certain details may be unintentionally omitted or changed. The net effect may be substantial change in communications that are repeated a number of times.

Another reason for distortion in communication is based upon semantics. The same words do not always carry the same meaning for both parties. A supervisor, for example, may intend to commend subordinates by commenting upon "satisfactory" performance. Subordinates may take offense at such commendation, however, because they know they are "superior" and not *merely* "satisfactory"!

Another factor interfering with clear communication is the inclination of listeners to hear what they expect to hear. They may have preconceived ideas of what others are trying to say. If so, it is difficult for them to hear anything that differs from their preconceptions. Regardless of the accuracy of an employee's perceptual world, it does affect the interpretation placed upon communications. Suppose the boss commends a subordinate who is convinced a supervisor is prejudiced and unfair. The subordinate may think, "The boss must be trying to pull a fast one."

Emotions also color one's understanding and interpretation of a communication. Anger or fear, for example, tends to distort communications. In recognition of this fact, an effective supervisor may emphasize an employee's strong points before attempting to correct a weakness.

Some causes of distortion may be described as *noise,* a type of interference similar to radio static. Irrelevant talk, emotions that block communication, and preconceived ideas that affect the receiver's understanding are all types of noise.

Two-Way Communication

Management literature often emphasizes the importance of two-way communication. A communication interchange that permits discussion back and forth between two parties, superior and subordinate, for example, presumably communicates more effectively than a one-way flow. Managers who engage in two-way communication do more than *tell* their subordinates. They *tell* and *listen* or, in other words, engage in conversation with subordinates.

Two-way communication offers several advantages, possibly the most significant being greater accuracy. The receiver can check on any unclear matter by asking questions. The give-and-take of discussion may also clarify issues in a general way. In the case of superior-subordinate communication, furthermore, the subordinate gains a sense of greater involvement and self-respect through two-way communication.

The following comments by Leavitt point out strengths and imply weaknesses of a one-way communication flow:

> If speed alone is what is important, then one-way communication has the edge. If appearance is of prime importance, if one wishes to look orderly and businesslike, then the one-way method again is preferable. If one doesn't want one's mistakes to be recognized, then again one-way communication is preferable. Then the sender will not have to hear people implying or saying that he is stupid or that there is an easier way to say what he is trying to say.[2]

Although two-way communication is usually preferable, it does not occur automatically. The manager must work at it to make sure it happens.

Much of the study of communication has stressed the transmitter and has tended to ignore the receiver. As we have discovered, however, the listener is not completely passive. A good listener hears more than a poor listener. We say that a person is "all ears" to emphasize attentive listening.

By aggressive listening, then, management may act to improve communication. Such listening requires effort to understand precisely what the other person is saying and removes certain barriers that block or distort communication. The sensitive listener, for example, carefully weighs a speaker's words to make sure of their meaning. "What does this employee mean by that statement about the rate of pay? Is that really the problem?" The unusually sensitive listener is quick to detect statements or indications that a less alert listener would completely miss.

---

[2] Harold J. Leavitt, *Managerial Psychology,* 3rd ed. (Chicago: The University of Chicago Press, 1972), p. 118. Reprinted by permission, © 1972 by The University of Chicago.

Feedback in Communication

Feedback is necessary to determine the extent to which a message has been understood, believed, and accepted. In face-to-face conversation, this process often occurs through facial expression. A puzzled look on the face of the receiver indicates that the message has not been transmitted as intended. The listener's remarks may also reveal understanding or misunderstanding. Compliance with communicated instructions also shows that communication has occurred.

Feedback does not always occur automatically, however. Silence guarantees neither consent nor comprehension. In the absence of feedback, an executive may become isolated from the lower levels of the organization, not knowing whether messages are getting through or whether they are properly understood. The sender must therefore arrange for, or be alert to, feedback to determine the effectiveness of either written or oral communication.

In face-to-face verbal communication, one can attempt to check the accuracy of communication by asking questions. The listener may ask the other party, "Would you tell me a little more about that?" or "Do you mean that—?" or "Is it your feeling that—?" Responses to probing questions of this type may reveal the listener's initial impression to be completely inaccurate. In seeking feedback, however, a manager must be alert to the danger of phony feedback—of asking questions that produce pleasant but incorrect answers.

Organizational Role and Communication

The Significance of Role in Communication

The roles of organization members affect and even distort communication within the organizational system because each individual tends to interpret information in the context of his or her own position. The role furnishes the frame of reference, therefore, in classifying and understanding messages received from outside. A production manager and laboratory researcher see things differently, hear things differently, and generally live in two different worlds.

Functional areas such as production, sales, and finance are organizational subsystems with their particular perceptions or viewpoints of organizational reality. This presents a difficulty in communicating across subsystem boundaries. Rather than functioning as cooperative allies, such functional groups tend to act as competitors. As a result, communication among them is poor. Moreover, their communications to higher levels carry the "slant" that reflects the special interest or viewpoints of the functional specialty.

In a middle-management training seminar, twenty-three managers were asked to identify the major problem of the unnamed company described in a long case history.[3] The managers' backgrounds evidently influenced their judgment. Eighty-three percent of sales managers considered the *sales* problem to be most important. However, eighty percent of production managers specified the *organization* problem as the most important. (The parts of the case pertaining to manufacturing featured an organization problem.) It is evident that these managers responded to the same communication on the basis of their past experience, task orientation, and organizational frame of reference.

Of all the conflicting roles that interfere with the process of communication,

---

[3] DeWitt C. Dearborn and Herbert A. Simon, "Selective Perception: A Note on the Departmental Identifications of Executives," *Sociometry* 21, no. 2 (June, 1958): 140–44.

few are more troublesome than those of superior and subordinate. Let us now turn our attention to some of the specific features of this relationship and its effect upon communication.

The difference in organizational levels makes communication between Supervisor *A* and Subordinate *X* distinctly different from communication between Supervisor *A* and Supervisor *B* or between Subordinate *X* and Subordinate *Y*. The subordinate occupies a position of dependency with respect to the superior, making the relationship much more than casual. To a great extent, the subordinate's future depends upon the superior's judgment. If the subordinate is to advance, earn pay increases, or receive choice work assignments, the decision must be the superior's.

The Sensitive Superior-Subordinate Relationship

In view of the critical importance of the superior's opinion, it is small wonder that *upward communication* is affected. It is only natural for the subordinate to wish to control all factors serving to influence supervisory judgment. In communication, therefore, the subordinate desires to transmit a message and *also* to influence the superior favorably. If possible, every message will convey not only the appropriate information but also a favorable impression.

It takes little imagination to see that the subordinate's personal desires may introduce distortion into the communication. Achieving the goal of favorably influencing the supervisor may require some alteration of the communication itself. In its extreme form, this could involve misrepresentation of facts that would be damaging to the subordinate. But, perhaps more likely, this simply involves a subtle, perhaps almost unconscious, adaptation of the subordinate's communication. If the communication goes upward through several levels, it may become increasingly rosy and at the same time farther and farther from reality.

Downward communication may also be distorted as a result of this same sensitive, supervisory relationship. In this case, it is the concern and eagerness of the subordinate that causes trouble. As an eager student of the boss, the subordinate tries to read between the lines and tends to react too strongly to communications from the superior. The subordinate may attach unusual importance to purely casual comments of the superior.

Not all difficulties in superior-subordinate communication can be attributed to the hierarchical relationship. The rush of work, so characteristic of many management positions, also makes communication difficult. In some organizations, it takes much effort even to see the boss. Other activities and other individuals are constantly competing for management time. Contacts that are not urgent must frequently be postponed. In discussions that do occur, the relaxed, leisurely atmosphere necessary for certain types of communication is missing. It is impossible for a subordinate to convey any personal feelings or even job ideas very adequately to a busy supervisor who has a telephone in one hand and a stack of red-bordered "rush" orders in the other.

Other Difficulties in Superior-Subordinate Communication

The subordinate may also lack an ability in self-expression. The position of the supervisor normally requires a great deal more talking than that of the subordinate. Consequently, the superior acquires experience in speaking and may be able to speak quite readily. Unless the subordinate's work involves much communication, however, an ability for self-expression may never develop.

Furthermore, as human beings, many superiors simply enjoy speaking more than listening. By having control of the conversation, it is easy to do that which is most fun—the talking. Listening, as noted earlier, calls for greater effort and self-discipline.

Overcoming Barriers to Superior-Subordinate Communication

To some extent, of course, weaknesses in superior-subordinate communication are little different from those in any other type of communication. Semantics, for example, may be a problem here as elsewhere. Accordingly, elimination of communication problems includes all steps designed to foster improvement in general communication. Our concern at this point, however, is with those steps that are particularly significant in the context of the superior-subordinate relationship.

An emphasis upon status distinctions widens the gulf between hierarchical levels. In contrast, a de-emphasis of status should facilitate the flow of communication. Creating a private office and establishing a battery of secretaries through which visitors must proceed, for example, makes communication difficult, to say the least. Part of the difficulty is based upon the physical separation. In addition, such features emphasize the distinction between levels and thus decrease ease of communication by increasing social distance. Achievement of a freer flow of communication depends upon minimizing both physical and status barriers.

Regardless of existing physical barriers, much can be done by creating a tolerant atmosphere. A superior who wants to improve the upward flow of communication must be conscious of the restraints placed upon subordinates. While a superior cannot tolerate *extreme* disrespect, it is natural to react with antagonism or hurt feelings if *any* criticism is implied by subordinates. Any superior who can tolerate a moderate amount of criticism, however, can develop the necessary condition for encouraging subordinates to speak up. If the superior's behavior appears threatening, the subordinate can hardly be blamed for silence. Only by assuring subordinates, by action as well as by words, of willingness and ability to accept their critical expressions without retaliation can the superior foster a strong upward flow of information. Asking for their comments and opinions, where pertinent, is one of the simplest and most effective approaches in stimulating upward communication of this type.

Informal Channels of Communication

Nature of the Grapevine

The *grapevine* refers to the network of informal relationships used in transmitting information through unofficial channels. Although formal channels presumably carry all official communications, much of what any organization member knows is gathered through other channels. In daily work associations, lunch contacts, coffee breaks, and social activities, an employee is constantly trading ideas and information about the organization.

Reflection upon the grapevine shows that it involves a normal, rather than an abnormal, set of relationships. Informal communication occurs naturally wherever individuals are thrown together in work or social contacts. If employees had no interest in discussing work matters with fellow employees, they would appear peculiar.

Occasionally, one gets the impression that only false rumors are circulated by the grapevine. It is true that rumors occur and that wild ones may be rapidly transmitted through informal channels. But other, more substantial information is also conveyed in this fashion. As a matter of fact, the grapevine usually carries some mixture of truth and error. A few details are often distorted in an otherwise correct account. In one study of thirty rumors occurring in six different companies, sixteen of the rumors proved to be groundless.[4] Nine turned out to be accurate, however, and five were partly accurate. Emphasis upon the errors circulated through the grapevine may have obscured the extensive amount of substantially accurate information transmitted in this way. Some organizations could hardly function without the grapevine because of the paucity of their formal communications.

The grapevine is often visualized as a long chain, with *A* telling *B* who in turn passes it on so that it eventually reaches *Z*. Such a pattern of transmission would clearly maximize the chances for error. Studies of the grapevine, however, have provided evidence that conflicts somewhat with this concept. The general pattern, as discovered by one researcher, is that of a *cluster chain*.[5] One link in the communication network informs a number of people instead of just one. One or two of each cluster of receivers, in turn, pass the communication on to another group.

The speed of the grapevine is too well-known to require extensive comment. Formal communication has difficulty maintaining a similar pace. The problem of keeping secrets from the grapevine is likewise known by experienced managers. Despite precautions, stories have a tendency to leak out at some point and to become general grapevine information.

Truth is the best antidote for error. If facts are not available, the imagination is capable of devising "facts." Some plausible explanation or interpretation occurs to one individual who passes it on to another. As the idea is passed on, it becomes regarded as fact rather than a tentative interpretation. Providing complete information, when possible, is thus a first step in minimizing grapevine errors.

Once a rumor or error has started, some corrective action is called for. Once again, the error is best removed by a statement of the facts. If a manager discovers an unfounded rumor among subordinates, for example, he or she may simply call them together and discuss the matter with them. Whether the facts will be accepted as such depends upon management's reputation for accuracy and candor in previous communication.

Some organizations have established special programs to detect rumors, asking employees to bring them to the attention of management. The rumor is

Dealing with Errors in the Grapevine

---

[4] Robert Hershey, "The Grapevine—Here to Stay But Not Beyond Control," *Personnel* 43, no. 1 (January-February, 1966): 62–66.

[5] Keith Davis, *Human Relations at Work*, 3rd ed. (New York: McGraw-Hill Book Company, 1967), p. 225.

then presented along with the facts. The employee newspaper and bulletin boards, among other media, have been used for this purpose.

Constructive Value of the Grapevine

Any attempt to develop a constructive attitude toward the grapevine requires recognition that the grapevine is not entirely bad. Although its errors and distortions may be lamented, its inevitable existence makes complete condemnation irrational. The grapevine exists whether we like it or not—an emotional blast against it accomplishes little, if anything.

We should note the constructive values inherent in informal communication. Unless managers wish to multiply their own communication efforts many times, they cannot channel all information through the official chain of command. Informal communications supplement and amplify those emanating from official sources. Much information about work assignments and company policy, for example, is picked up from fellow employees. Official announcements are likewise heard by some employees and passed on to others.

The grapevine transmits useful information and messages that cannot be easily transmitted through formal channels. Orders and proclamations of management may be explained by employees to each other in language that they can understand. Also, the grapevine supplies the manager with information about subordinates and their work experiences, thereby increasing the manager's understanding and effectiveness.

A constructive approach to dealing with the grapevine begins with the effort to furnish complete and accurate information. In addition, a manager may recognize the informal communication leaders. By keeping them well informed, the manager can come closer to assuring the accuracy of information entering the grapevine. Also, listening to the grapevine as much as possible will keep the manager in closer touch with subordinates' thinking.

Summary

Communication is an integral and necessary aspect of management. Through the process of communication, information, facts, feelings, and ideas are transmitted from one person to another. Communication is accomplished not only through language, but also through physical expression and gestures, silence, and behavior. *Distortion* often occurs in communication as a result of emotions, differing points of view of the communicators, and semantics. The *listening* side of communication is an important part of two-way communication. Through *feedback*, a communicator can determine the extent to which a message has been understood, believed, and accepted.

The role or position occupied by an individual affects the process of communication, because each person speaks and understands in the context of a unique personal world. The roles of superior and subordinate are a special case of this phenomenon. A subordinate's dependency upon a superior makes the relationship between them unusually sensitive—a fact that tends to interfere with the process of communication. The subordinate is constantly concerned with the impression that he or she creates and tends to color information transmitted to the superior. Furthermore, the rush that characterizes the activities of many managers is not conducive to *upward communication*. In overcoming barriers to communication, the superior can de-emphasize status distinctions and strive to create an atmosphere which tolerates freedom of expression by subordinates.

The informal network of communication in an organization is known as its *grapevine.* The grapevine is a natural outgrowth of interpersonal contacts and circulates some combination of truth and error. In dealing with errors or unfounded rumors, management may be able to make corrections by supplying factual information. Although the grapevine may contain errors, it performs a useful function in transmitting information that cannot be conveyed easily in other ways.

1. In view of the close relationship between communication and the management process, what communication skills seem necessary for managers? Is extensive training in writing and in public speaking desirable?

2. Communication includes more than the transmission of facts. What are the other aspects of communication? Of these, which is most difficult to transmit in writing?

3. Suppose a state governor or the President of the United States personally inspects a flood-stricken area. Explain the significance of such a visit from the standpoint of communication.

4. Explain the factors leading to *distortion* in communication.

5. How does one become a more effective listener?

6. Why is *upward communication* often less effective than *downward communication?* How can a manager improve upward communication from subordinates?

7. What should a manager do about erroneous stories circulated on the *grapevine?*

Discussion Questions

Bromage, Mary C. "The Management of Communications." *Advanced Management Journal* 38, no. 2 (April, 1973): 42–46.

Hall, Jay. "Communication Revisited." *California Management Review* 15, no. 3 (Spring, 1973): 56–67.

Harriman, Bruce. "Up and Down the Communications Ladder." *Harvard Business Review* 52, no. 5 (September-October, 1974): 143–51.

Lillico, T. M. *Managerial Communication.* New York: Pergamon Press, 1972.

Okun, Sherman K. "How To Be a Better Listener." *Nation's Business* 63, no. 8 (August, 1975): 59–62.

Supplementary Reading

Case 13

Has the Worm Turned?*

The foremen watched as Alan Boswell, assistant to the factory manager, posted a memorandum on the bulletin board of the management lounge. It seemed as if there had been an endless stream of memoranda relating to policies, procedures, rules, and regulations since George Parker became

* Prepared by Professor John E. Schoen and Jerry L. Crowder of Baylor University.

factory manager five months ago. In addition, too many of the old department heads and management staff had been replaced by M.B.A.'s in vested suits, with Boswell being the worst.

For five months, Parker and his boys had harped on efficiency and had managed to drop the plant from second to fifth place in the division by stumbling over one another. However, Parker was a hard man to talk to—and not a man to cross because of his temper and autocratic style. Poor old Jimmy Collins found out about that after he spoke up in the annual budget meetings last month.

When Boswell had gone, the foremen approached the bulletin board, shaking their heads wearily, to read the message.

C O N F I D E N T I A L

TO: ALL DEPARTMENT MANAGERS   May 10, 1977
      ALL GENERAL FOREMEN

FRIDAY STAFF MEETING

"15 Minutes From The Jaw"

As mentioned in the last staff meeting, we will devote the last 15 minutes of each weekly staff meeting to a review and answer period (a chance to get acquainted). Subjects may be presented verbally or in writing; the latter may be in a sealed envelope, unsigned, and directed confidentially to the writer.

The purpose of this discussion is to strengthen our managerial team by communication, affording all managers an opportunity to have their questions concerning plant administration thoroughly analyzed, clarified, and answered.

A well-informed management team is one of our key objectives. This team's knowledge and skill, ability to plan and organize effectively, direct and control, evaluate and critique thoughtfully are requisites for effective, outstanding management.

We deal mostly with people, and we must be adequately prepared to:

1. Set goals and meet quotas
2. Work efficiently and effectively
3. Build sound, effective, and loyal teams
4. Stimulate and motivate
5. Develop others for promotion

Topics for discussion should not be limited, but must be meaningful and objective. They may relate to (1) improving individual performance, (2) clarifying procedures and policies, (3) improving leadership styles, or (4) any appropriate subject of your choice. Let's communicate and direct our efforts toward making the management team outstanding in each of its responsibilities.

signed

Factory Manager

1. Evaluate the probable effectiveness of the message in stimulating two-way communication in the staff meeting and/or generally.

2. Evaluate the content of the message with respect to management principles and/or a participative approach to management.

3. Who has responsibility for establishing communication after managerial succession?

4. Evaluate the method the factory manager has used to communicate instructions regarding the Friday staff meeting.

Objectives

1. Identify the unique contributions of first-line supervisors as connecting links between higher management and employees.
2. Explain the supervisor's special difficulties and contributions in such areas of production/operations as time and motion studies, quality control, cost control, and management of time.
3. Point out the strengths and weaknesses of the motivational approaches available to supervisors.

Chapter

14

Practical Supervision

Concentration upon the important issues of top management sometimes causes neglect of the practical problems of supervision. This oversight is unfortunate, because supervisors are the "first-line troops" of management. In this chapter, we consider some of the practical management problems in the lower echelons—a level where much of the action is, even in today's business world.

The Supervisory Job

The First-Line Supervisor

Managers who direct the work of operative employees—machine operators, typists, draftsmen, sales clerks, truck drivers, electricians, writers, and so on— are referred to as *first-line supervisors*. In manufacturing, they are often called foremen. In other settings, they are known by such titles as office manager, department head, head teller, unit chief, key punch supervisor, sales manager, or laboratory supervisor.

A significant feature of supervisory jobs is that they direct the work for which the organization exists. Business organizations are created to produce goods or services, and nonmanagerial, operative employees produce those goods and services. First-line supervisors who interact with and direct those operative employees thus occupy a strategic position in determining organizational success. Without belittling the role of higher management in any way, we can readily see that the immediate supervisor directly regulates the total productive effort of the corporation.

The Supervisor's Management Functions

Although management functions are part of every management position, their importance varies from position to position. Figure 14–1 shows estimated variations in emphasis based on management level. According to this figure, first-line supervisors are particularly concerned with the directing and controlling functions.

Figure 14–1 *Time Spent on Management Functions*

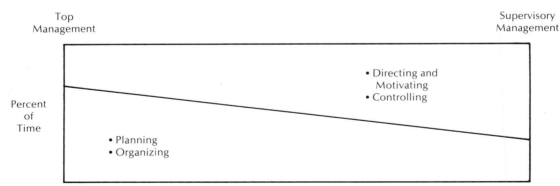

This does not mean that supervisors perform no planning or organizing. Their work is action oriented, however, and involves directing, instructing, and keeping in touch with the progress of operative employees. Their planning tends to be short-run, and their organizing decisions tend to be infrequent.

The first-line supervisor has been described as "the man in the middle," meaning that the supervisor stands between two different groups and, indeed, brings these two groups into working harmony with each other.

The Supervisory Link   **Figure 14–2**

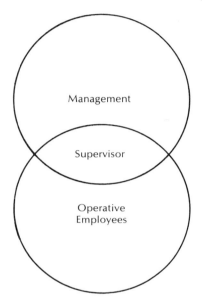

First-line supervisors are closely identified with the employees they supervise. In fact, supervisors have in many cases been promoted from the ranks. Moreover, they constitute "management" in the eyes of employees who interact primarily, if not exclusively, with this one management level. As a result, employees expect supervisors to understand their problems and to reflect their viewpoints in dealing with what is to them a relatively unknown world of top management. They also expect the supervisor to "go to bat" for them on occasion and to represent them well.

Higher-level managers, on the other hand, see the supervisor as their representative in keeping employees in line, getting out production, and enforcing company policy. The supervisor is expected to think and act like a manager.

In many companies, these expectations are sufficiently different that they create a condition known as *role conflict*. This condition means that the *role* of *supervisor* is seen differently by subordinates and superiors. Both groups may not approve a given decision because of their conflicting expectations. Supervisors in such positions are subjected to the stress and tension inevitable in conflict situations. This factor, among others, makes the position requirements difficult.

At one time, the first-line supervisor was the top craftsman in a group. The supervisory role was tacked onto the craftsman role. In recent decades, however, managerial requirements of these positions have been more clearly recognized. No longer do properly managed companies allow supervisory activities

Qualifications for Supervisory Positions

to flow automatically to the most skilled operator or craftsman. First-line supervisors are expected to function as managers.

Even so, the requirement for technical knowledge is probably greater at this level than at higher levels of management. Some familiarity with the work of subordinates who perform technical work is necessary for intelligent supervision. Supervisors need not be the most proficient or most skilled, but they typically need some expertise.

This is one reason that supervisors are often appointed by promotion from the ranks. In taking this step from employee to manager, the new supervisor must make a substantial change—from doing to supervising. This change is difficult for two reasons. First, operative work and managerial work are fundamentally different and require different abilities. Second, social ties are broken as an employee leaves the association of peers and moves to a higher level. At best, this upward movement calls for significant adjustments on the part of the new supervisor. Fortunately, many make the adjustment satisfactorily and go on to productive careers in management.

Supervision of Production

Supervision of production operations is required not only in manufacturing but also in service, financial, and other institutions. Many of the management processes are best explained, however, in the context of manufacturing.

Production Planning and Control

Production operations must be carefully planned if production is to be efficient. Unless specialized production planning units are used, the detailed work planning becomes the responsibility of first-line supervisors. In job order production, in which each production run consists of only one or a very limited number of products, each production project must be planned individually. The goal of supervisory production planning is efficient use of facilities and personnel and also prompt completion of production operations to meet customer needs.

Unless a specialized production planning unit is used, the supervisor's production supervision must include the determination of the path or sequence of the work, scheduling the time for different operations to begin, and giving orders to begin work on various parts of the production process. The supervisor must also follow each job to see that it is proceeding according to plan and to correct any conditions interfering with progress.

Time and Motion Study

The field of time and motion study is concerned with two basic goals—efficient work methods and standards for employee performance. Production foremen, in particular, are often involved, directly or indirectly, in the process of time and motion study. Time study is used to develop performance standards for repetitive production operations. Many wage incentive systems are based on standards developed in this way.

An industrial engineer typically sets the standards by using a stopwatch to time the various segments of the job. Some of the supervisor's problems in administering a wage incentive system derive from the difficulty in making completely objective measurements. Although use of a stopwatch provides some precision, it is impossible to eliminate all human variability, such as the relative speed of an employee's movements.

Motion study, which should precede time study or which may be used without time study, seeks to maximize efficiency by finding the best or most efficient methods. Unnecessary motions are eliminated, and the presumably best methods are specified for use by production employees.

First-line supervisors must understand time and motion study in order to relate properly to the questions and problems of employees whose work is studied. Understanding the concept of productivity necessitates a knowledge of the principles involved in motion study. By increasing productivity, it becomes possible to increase wages and profits. A knowledge of time study practice, furthermore, permits supervisors to answer employee questions and to provide practical information and advice to time study specialists.

Control of Quality

First-line supervisors play a crucial role in maintenance of high quality standards. Quality, to the extent that it is achieved, results from the work of production personnel. Quality cannot be inspected into the product. Through training, emphasis upon quality, insistence upon quality performance, provision of proper equipment, and correction of errors in production, supervisors regulate the quality level of a plant.

Even in nonfactory situations, first-line supervisors carry the major responsibility for quality of output. In an accounting office, for example, errors in bookkeeping may be minimized through proper selection, training, and supervision of office personnel. If supervisors fail to train employees or to supervise adequately, a reduction in quality is inevitable.

Cost Control

Some costs, such as property taxes and depreciation, are not controllable. Of those that are controllable, most are under the control of first-line supervisors. In most business organizations, for example, labor cost is a significant controllable cost. The productive efficiency of labor depends upon training, scheduling, and motivating personnel. The major role of direct supervision in each of these areas makes supervision the key to control of labor cost.

Because of their strategic position, supervisors must bear the brunt of management efforts to control costs or even to cut costs. If the company's profit margin disappears or even begins to slip, the pressure becomes intense. At any time, therefore, supervisors must be analyzing costs and finding ways to minimize them. Cost savings are available through saving time, increasing output with a given labor cost, introducing labor-saving equipment, reducing waste, improving methods, and increasing effectiveness of space utilization.

Management of Time

Any individual, and particularly supervisors, can make their work more effective by managing the use of their own time. Time is a scarce resource, even though each person has exactly the same amount. Haphazard use of the time resource is fully as wasteful as careless use of money or machinery. Supervisory schedules are highly susceptible to interruption. In fact, managerial activities are characterized by fragmentation, with numerous brief interactions during the day.

In view of such demands, supervisors typically profit from some planning of their own activities. Even though they can expect interruptions, establishing a daily schedule can lead to some saving of time. In fact, planning can allow slack in the schedule with full knowledge that unexpected demands will occur.

One approach to time planning begins with listing required activities in their order of priority. The supervisor can then work on the most important project first and complete it before proceeding to the next one. Another practice found helpful by some supervisors is the designation of a specified time each day for a given task, such as answering correspondence.

Various types of time-saving practices are available. To the extent that decisions can be passed on to others, for example, the supervisor gains time for other purposes. An extremely busy schedule of a supervisor may, though not necessarily, indicate excessively close supervision. The pattern of time usage by a supervisor must be carefully analyzed to find causes for waste and possibilities for improvement.

Supervision of Employees

An important part of successful supervision is the motivation of followers. Highly motivated employees can make the difference between a marginal firm and one that sets sales and profit records. In this section, we will look at the nature of motivation and the approaches used by supervisors to elicit the cooperative, enthusiastic efforts of their subordinates.

Motivational plans and approaches reflect an underlying set of assumptions on the part of supervisors about the nature of people and their probable response to various types of motivation. The best-known classification of assumptions was provided by McGregor under the labels of *Theory X* and *Theory Y*.[1] Although these concepts are often regarded as leadership approaches, they are more appropriately described as assumptions.

Theory X represents a pessimistic view of human nature and holds that most people, employees in particular, tend to be lazy, lacking in ambition and requiring supervision to "keep them moving." The opposite assumptions of Theory Y may be explained as follows:

> Theory Y states, in essence, that man is capable of integrating his own needs and goals with those of the organization; that he is not inherently lazy and indolent; that he is by nature capable of exercising self-control and self-direction, and that he is capable of directing his efforts toward organizational goals.[2]

The assumptions produce differences in motivational efforts. Theory X managers tend to rely more on disciplinary methods and penalties, while Theory Y managers tend to emphasize positive motivation and self-management.

No doubt, both types of individuals—the lazy and the ambitious—exist in organizational life. The basic question, therefore, concerns the extent to which

[1] Douglas McGregor, *The Human Side of Enterprise* (New York: McGraw-Hill Book Company, 1960).

[2] Edgar H. Schein, "In Defense of Theory Y," *Organizational Dynamics* 4, no. 1 (Summer, 1975): 20.

Theory Y assumptions can be intelligently followed. Use of Theory Y assumptions permits a manager to consider a broader range of motivational methods, including some that might be described as positive approaches. Only the total facts of the work situation, however, including the education and experience of employees, can determine whether a particular approach such as participative management is workable or logical.

One theoretical scheme for integrating the various elements of the motivational system is known as *expectancy theory*.[3] This theory rests in a general way on a number of key points. The concept of *expectancy* concerns an individual's perceived probability of attaining a particular work goal—"I can do it" or "That goal is impossible"—and the perceived probability that the achievement will be rewarded in a particular way—"I can get the raise if I sell enough" or "They won't even notice." The degree to which an individual desires a particular outcome is termed the *valence* of that outcome. The valence may be based upon the direct satisfaction received from an outcome (for example, enjoyment in performing work) or upon the fact that the immediate outcome makes possible other outcomes (performance, for example, resulting in money and money resulting in purchase of food, which satisfies a physiological need). Valence is basically related to the dominant needs of the individual at a particular time.

Expectancy Theory

According to expectancy theory, therefore, motivation depends upon both expectancy and valence. The motivational force in a particular situation is a function of expectancies about outcomes (attaining work goals and obtaining rewards) and valences of those outcomes (intensity of desire for them).

The discussion of expectancy theory has dealt with the concept of motivation in a general way. We now turn to the practical application of motivation theory by considering a number of specific motivational tools or approaches available to supervisors.

Some degree of authority exists in almost any administrative situation. An emphasis on the use of authority, however, carries with it the threat of penalty—"Do your work or you'll be fired."

Authority

Authority provides strong motivation in certain cases. A person who has great respect for higher authority may respond almost automatically to the orders of a superior. Furthermore, the threat of being fired may stimulate one to supreme effort if the job seems extremely important. If one's family depends upon the job and no other jobs are available, the danger of job loss is serious. On the other hand, the effectiveness of authority as a motivating factor is diminished by the existence of a strong union or conditions of labor scarcity and numerous job opportunities.

In addition, there is a question as to the degree of effort that can be obtained by use of an authoritative approach. A minimum performance may be secured in this way. At the same time, outstanding performance may be lacking. In

---

[3] Two of the better-known formulations are found in Victor H. Vroom, *Work and Motivation* (New York: John Wiley & Sons, 1964) and Lyman W. Porter and Edward E. Lawler III, *Managerial Attitudes and Performance* (Homewood, Ill.: Richard D. Irwin, Inc., 1968).

other words, the individual may perform sufficiently well to avoid dismissal but lack the incentive to do an outstanding job.

Financial Incentives

In one sense, the use of authority entails an application of financial incentives. Loss of a job means loss of income associated with that job. But money may also be used as a positive motivator. Financial rewards may be stressed, and employees may be offered higher pay for increased output or superior performance.

No doubt, most employees find some motivation in financial rewards. The important question concerns the effectiveness or extent of such appeals. In devising their incentive plans, the scientific managers assumed a worker who acted rationally to maximize economic gains. Such an extreme concept of the *economic man* has, of course, been discredited. Even though the theory has been generally rejected, however, management often acts as if it were still true.

Studies of the effectiveness of financial incentives have revealed many shortcomings. Although occasional examples of outstanding results have been discovered, they are by no means universal. In fact, the more customary experience seems to involve unsatisfactory, or only partially satisfactory, results. Unofficial work quotas are often recognized by employees, with no production above a "normal day's work."

Establishment of piece rates frequently becomes a matter of matching wits between employees and the management's industrial engineers. Conflict and hostility often seem characteristic of such systems.

Such experience with incentive plans and the improved understanding of the social structure of industry have served to reveal the limitations of financial motivation. Money is one, but only one, of the factors of importance to the worker. The major error in using such an approach is the attachment of undue importance to it. It is wrong to see financial incentives as the only goal of the employee. In many cases, it may not even be the primary motivating factor.

Competition

Closely related to the use of financial incentives is motivation by competition. Advancement to higher positions and higher pay scales is based upon individual performance. By using a *merit* principle, the employee is stimulated to excel in order to earn a promotion.

Various difficulties are involved in motivation through competition. In some areas, particularly in unionized plants, seniority has largely replaced merit as the basis for advancement. The most effective use of competition also requires accurate measurement of performance—a process that is notoriously difficult. Furthermore, excessive competition can be disruptive to the group, particularly in situations in which teamwork is required.

Paternalism

Another approach to motivation is paternalism. The paternalistic attitude is expressed by being "good" to employees and providing benefits for them. In return for such gifts, the employee is expected to respond with loyalty and enthusiastic performance. In the early 1900s, many concerns followed this philosophy of paternalism in employee relations. Paternalism may characterize an entire company, but it may also be used by individual supervisors.

The paternalist expects a favorable response from employees and experiences bitter disappointment if they appear ungrateful. Unfortunately, the paternalistic approach does not consistently produce the expected results. Indeed, some paternalism seems to operate in reverse, creating resentment rather than loyalty. Violent strikes have occurred in the plants of employers who prided themselves in their good treatment of employees.

There are a number of weaknesses in the paternalistic approach. First of all, the philosophy assumes that the employer and supervisors are superior and know what is best for the employee. This attitude of superiority is offensive to most employees and runs counter to their desire for independence.

Implicit Bargaining

One form of motivation that may be practiced by a supervisor has been described as *implicit bargaining*.[4] It differs from explicit bargaining in which management formally bargains with a union. In implicit bargaining, an informal understanding develops between the manager and subordinates. It is not explicitly stated but simply arises on the basis of behavioral patterns worked out or tolerated by the superior.

Implicit bargaining involves a live-and-let-live attitude. The supervisor permits conduct or performance that employees consider reasonable. In return, the employees perform in a manner reasonably acceptable to the supervisor. For example, the superior may be rather liberal in interpreting plant rules—accepting employee excuses for tardiness or absences or looking the other way when minor offenses occur. Employees, in turn, support the supervisor with at least average production, rather than complaining or constantly raising grievances.

The nature of the bargain from the worker's point of view is indicated by the following comments of an employee:

> Our policy is to live and let live. We give the foreman reasonable production. He protects us from the time-study man who tries to jack up the output rate and looks the other way if we take a smoke. We look out for each other.[5]

One of the weaknesses of such a motivational approach is its failure to stimulate more than a minimum or average performance.

Need Satisfaction Through Work

The preceding motivational approaches have in common a view of work as unpleasant and unrewarding in itself. The employee must be paid in some way for the unpleasantness involved. A different view of work is involved in an approach that attempts to satisfy the worker's need through the job.[6] Rather than considering work as drudgery, it views work as potentially satisfying and rewarding.

In this approach to motivation, consideration is given to all the employee's

---

[4] For an excellent discussion of implicit bargaining, see George Strauss and Leonard R. Sayles, *Personnel: The Human Problems of Management*, 3rd ed. (Englewood Cliffs, N.J.: Prentice-Hall, Inc., 1972), pp. 128–30.

[5] *Ibid.*, p. 129.

[6] This motivational approach is carefully analyzed in Robert N. Ford, *Motivation Through the Work Itself* (New York: American Management Association, 1969).

needs, including not only a need for money but also social and egoistic needs. An attempt is made to create an atmosphere in which satisfaction of all such needs is achieved. The nature of industrial technology admittedly makes this difficult or even impossible in some types of work.

In providing satisfaction of egoistic needs, an emphasis is placed upon the significance of the job. Even if a job requires little skill, it may be an important part of an overall operation. In addition, some jobs may be improved through job enlargement or other changes that make them more interesting. The style of leadership is also important in this connection. Social satisfactions are realized more easily in situations involving democratic supervision. Friendships and teamwork may occur more readily in such an atmosphere.

Undoubtedly, this motivational approach calls for understanding and skill on the part of the manager using it. It cannot be applied so easily as some of the other approaches. It has the potential advantage, however, of stimulating better-than-average performance. It also has the potential advantage of contributing to the happiness and satisfaction of employees apart from any contribution to organizational efficiency.

Management by Objectives

An approach to motivation, particularly applicable to management personnel, that has received much attention in recent years is known as *management by objectives* (MBO). Organizational objectives are subdivided to form a hierarchy of objectives. As a final step in factoring these objectives into more specific goals, each supervisor and employee eventually formulates his or her own objectives. Individual objectives are stated, as much as possible, in specific and measurable terms and are established with the collaboration of the individual's superior. Individual action plans are then formulated, implemented, and monitored as shown in Figure 14–3.

Figure 14–3 *The MBO Process*

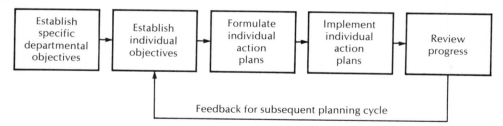

Both active individual participation in setting one's own goals and action plans and self-control in implementing individual plans are distinctive features of MBO programs—features that enhance their motivational impact. Objectives set in this way should also reflect a realism lacking in unilaterally imposed goals. Performance can likewise be evaluated more objectively by comparing it with stated objectives.

Summary

First-line supervisors act as the "first-line troops" of management, directing the work of operative employees. They are a link between employees and higher levels of management and often experience role conflict as a result of the conflicting expectations of these groups.

First-line supervisors have unique responsibilities in such areas of production/operations as production planning and control, time and motion study, quality control, cost control, and management of time. These supervisory responsibilities are particularly evident in the supervision of manufacturing processes but are also applicable to other types of business activities.

Two broad categories of managerial assumptions, proposed by McGregor, are known as *Theory X* and *Theory Y*, the latter being more optimistic. *Expectancy theory* provides an overall conceptual scheme which relates the various elements of motivation. According to this theory, motivation depends upon individual *expectancies* concerning particular outcomes and the *valences*, or attractiveness, of those outcomes.

Managers have a variety of motivational approaches available. Those discussed include *authority, financial incentives, competition, paternalism, implicit bargaining, need satisfaction through work,* and *management by objectives.*

Discussion Questions

1. How do the first-line supervisor's management functions differ from the president's management functions? Explain.

2. What causes the general role conflict problem of the first-line supervisor?

3. Explain the first-line supervisor's unique contribution to quality control.

4. Explain the relationship between delegation of authority and effective use of time.

5. Explain the distinction between *Theory X* and *Theory Y* and indicate the type of leadership or motivation that might be associated with each.

6. Explain the basic ideas involved in *expectancy theory.*

7. What are some of the difficulties involved in using a wage incentive plan as a tool for *motivation?*

8. Explain the concept of *paternalism.*

9. *Implicit bargaining* was suggested as one form of motivation. Can you give an example of implicit bargaining from your own experience or observation?

10. What are the distinctive features of *management by objectives?*

Supplementary Reading

Eckles, Robert W.; Carmichael, Ronald L.; and Sarchet, Bernard R. *Essentials of Management for First-Line Supervision.* New York: John Wiley & Sons, Inc., 1974.

Ficker, Victor B. *Effective Supervision.* Columbus, Ohio: Charles E. Merrill Publishing Company, 1975.

Meyer, Herbert H. "The Pay-for-Performance Dilemma." *Organizational Dynamics* 3, no. 3 (Winter, 1975): 39–50.

Raia, Anthony P. *Managing by Objectives.* Glenview, Ill.: Scott, Foresman and Company, 1974.

Steers, Richard M. and Porter, Lyman W. *Motivation and Work Behavior.* New York: McGraw-Hill Book Company, 1975.

Case 14

The Supervisor*

John Benson was recently promoted to the position of shop foreman in a large electronics firm. His department's major task was shipping parts; and, although the shop was usually on a schedule, emergency orders were not infrequent. Since becoming shop foreman, John found several major problems beginning to crop up. First, he had worked at the plant for eight years prior to becoming foreman. He had developed a number of personal friendships which now seemed to be presenting problems. Being a member of the gang was something John had really enjoyed. When he had to remind his friends recently about safety procedures, they had laughed. When he repeated the warning more sternly, many had sulked about him now being some kind of big shot.

A second problem was trying to get the men to follow orders. Recently an emergency order needed to be shipped the same day. Because of some mishandling, the order was finished late, and John found himself doing the final processing alone in order that it be sent out. When he asked the others to stay, they simply said it was his problem now that he was the boss.

At meetings, held frequently, John had stressed that he needed the support of all the men. He continued to do the work he had always done and trusted everyone else to get his job done. When this failed to work and the men began to take advantage of the friendships, John cracked down. He told them to do as they were told and that they had better shape up, since management had noticed how the work had been slipping.

Although John continued to do his work, the firm hired another person to take John's old place. He had been assigned to help out wherever necessary. John was determined to prove he was just as effective a worker as ever and turned out even more work than before in an effort to impress both his crew and management. The new worker was left to assist wherever he could, and he soon joined in with the man who had been John's closest friend.

After four months, John requested that the new man be moved to another department on the basis that he wasn't needed. At this time, John was called in by the director of personnel. John related the situation in the manner in which he felt it had happened. He discovered then that the workers had been griping among themselves and had openly complained over the request that this new man be transferred. The personnel manager had a series of questions ready for John on supervisor performance.

---

*Victor B. Ficker, *Effective Supervision* (Columbus, Ohio: Charles E. Merrill Publishing Company, 1975), pp. 38–39.

1. Why was John not effective in developing a team feeling? What should he have done differently?

2. Why did the crew become resentful of John's position? What strategy could John have used to avoid this?

3. What do you see as John's basic supervisory weakness, and what should he do to correct it?

4. John encountered some of the problems of a supervisor promoted from the ranks. What are others that might arise?

5. What strong points does John have, and how should he use them?

6

Controlling Individual and Organizational Performance

Objectives

1. Identify the basic elements of the control process and explain their role in regulating performance.

2. Recognize the nature and causes of dysfunctional consequences of control.

3. Point out management practices that improve the effectiveness of control.

Chapter

15

Fundamentals of Control

Organizations seldom function perfectly in the execution of plans. As a result, a manager must monitor operations to discover deviations from plans and to be sure the organization is functioning as intended. These management activities that check on performance and correct it when necessary are a part of the managerial control function.

Basic Factors in Control

Nature of the Control Function

Control activities are often visualized in negative terms—reproof, correction, and surveillance. As a matter of fact, control is less sinister than this viewpoint suggests and is a necessary part of the managerial process. Newman has captured the nature and essence of control in the following comments:

1. *Control is a normal, pervasive, and positive force.* Evaluation of results accomplished and feedback of this information to those who can influence future results is a natural phenomenon. The cook watches the pie in the oven; the orchestra conductor listens to his orchestra—and its recordings; the doctor checks his patient; the oil refiner tests the quality of his end-product; the farmer counts his chickens; the football coach keeps an eye on the scoreboard. . . .

2. *Managerial control is effective only when it guides someone's behavior.* Behavior, not measurements and reports, is the essence of control. We often become so involved with the mechanics of control that we lose sight of its purpose. Unless one or more persons act differently than they otherwise would, the control reports have no impact. Consequently, when we think about designing and implementing control, we must always ask ourselves, "Who is going to behave differently, and what will be the nature of his response?". . . .

3. *Successful control is future-oriented and dynamic.* Long before the Apollo spacecraft reached the moon, control adjustments had been made. Similarly, we don't wait until next year's sales are recorded to make adjustments in packaging or pricing which are necessary to achieve the goal; instead, we use early measurements to predict where our present course is leading, and modify inputs to keep us on target. . . .

4. *Control relates to all sorts of human endeavors.* The need for evaluation and feedback is just as pressing in charitable organizations as in profit-seeking corporations. Each is concerned with attaining its goals and each has limited resources. Moreover, control should not be confined to easy-to-measure results. The quality of service in a hospital or bank, the training and promotion of minority workers, and the resourcefulness of a purchasing agent in developing alternative sources for important supplies—all need to be controlled.[1]

Types of Control

The control function encompasses a much broader range of subject matter than is commonly assumed. Budgetary control or expense control often comes to mind when managerial control is discussed. In reality, the manager's control responsibilities are much more diverse. He or she must use many different types of controls.

---

[1] William H. Newman, *Constructive Control: Design and Use of Control Systems* (Englewood Cliffs, N.J.: Prentice-Hall, Inc., 1975), pp. 3–5. Reprinted by permission of Prentice-Hall, Inc., Englewood Cliffs, New Jersey.

Some controls, for example, check directly on work performance. Examinations, for example, are designed to measure the quality of student performance. Inspection of completed products in a manufacturing plant and comparison of output records with production schedules likewise are control activities.

Other controls are intended to protect company assets—for example, requiring an invoice before writing a check or requiring a requisition before issuing tools or supplies. Organizational objectives and policies likewise regulate performance by providing guidance for the different segments of a firm.

The primary emphasis of managerial control is the regulation of performance from month to month and day to day. Consequently, sales forecasts, financial budgets, cost standards, and income statements are key features of most corporate control systems.

Controls obviously affect most, if not all, facets of the business. Without systematic control, therefore, a manager has no assurance that all elements of the organization will contribute to organizational achievement.

The Control Process

As noted, the concept of control includes the regulation of many different aspects of business activity. At the top corporate level, for example, it involves the appraisal of a firm's operating results and the institution of any necessary corrective action. At a much lower level, it entails the supervisory activities of shop foremen in checking the work progress of employees subject to their control. In every unit of the organization, management must regulate in some way the contributions of the organization members.

Formal, detailed reports are often associated with the control process. The accounting department prepares periodic analyses of operating results. These reports typically break down overall operating results by the use of department-by-department and product-by-product analyses. In themselves, however, these reports are of only historical value. They do not constitute control, although they provide a basis for control.

Control is concerned with the present—a regulation of what is happening. In controlling, the manager regulates the way in which members of the organization apply their efforts. Controlling is particularly concerned with locating operational weaknesses and taking corrective action. The project that is getting behind schedule or the quality that is slipping below standard is detected and corrected.

Predetermined Standards or Objectives

The function of controlling assumes the existence of some type of target or objective. A firm has certain overall objectives as well as more specific goals applying to its individual departments and members. Individual and organizational performance is directed toward the accomplishment of these goals, and performance may be evaluated in terms of such objectives. These goals, which are determined through planning, are the standards employed in the controlling process.

Some examples may clarify the nature of such standards. For the enterprise as a whole, the projected profit provides a checkpoint for measuring overall performance. Such broad control standards are essential tools of the administrator. These general control standards are supplemented, however, by a vast number of more specific controls. In manufacturing, for example, product specifications provide predetermined standards that regulate the manufacturing process. A given dimension may be specified as fifteen inches with a tolerance of plus or minus one-fourth inch. A monthly sales quota establishes an output standard for a salesperson. A budgeted expense item sets a standard for expenditures. A standard operating procedure specifies a standard to regulate the order or method of performance. A work schedule provides a standard controlling time and order of work.

From the standpoint of the company as a whole, there is a wide variety of standards that may be used. Many factors may be selected to supplement the overall profit figure. The rationale for selection of performance criteria is discussed later in this chapter.

Quantification of the objective or standard is obviously difficult in the case of certain factors. Consider the goal of product leadership, for example. In evaluating its product leadership, a company compares its products with those of competitors and determines the extent to which it pioneers in the introduction of basic products and later product improvements. Such standards may exist even though they are not formally and explicitly stated. Similarly, at the operative level, a supervisor may find it difficult to express in quantitative terms the exact amount of output required of a particular employee. Inability to quantify the output standard, however, does not indicate the absence of some conception as to what constitutes reasonable or standard output or performance. This conception, in effect, is a standard for controlling.

Comparing Performance with Standards

In controlling, managers attempt to make sure that the organization is functioning properly in the accomplishment of its goals. They must periodically check on the organization's position to answer the question, "How well are we doing?" This requires a measurement of performance so that it may be compared with the predetermined standard. A company's return on investment, for example, is calculated and compared with prior results or with other figures that are accepted as standards. In the manufacturing process, an inspector measures the product to make sure it falls within tolerance limits established by the specification.

A critical stage is reached in the comparison of actual or measured performance with projected or standard performance. If the standard is explicitly expressed and performance accurately measured, the direct comparison is simple enough. Considerable interpretation may be required, however, to make sense of the figures. Some deviations from standard are justified because of inaccuracies in the standard, changes in environmental conditions, or other reasons. The data must be examined in the light of existing circumstances.

Corrective Action

Control is not confined to measurement of performance, detection of errors, and preparation of reports. Managerial action is required to correct existing weaknesses or mistakes. This means that control is never completed by the analysis and reports of a staff officer even though he or she may be designated as the "controller." The responsible manager must act to bring performance back into line or to hold it in line. If labor cost is becoming excessive, supervisors must take steps to secure more efficient personnel utilization.

What action is appropriate to correct out-of-line performance depends upon the unique nature of each situation. Delays and excessive cost in production, for example, may result from defective equipment or from inefficiency of labor. The former would require repair or replacement of equipment. The latter might be corrected by any of a number of actions, depending upon the cause of the inefficiency. It might result from such factors as poor personnel selection, inadequate training, poor motivation, lack of discipline, or confusion in work assignments. To be effective, corrective action must locate and deal with the real cause.

In the design of control systems and the application of controls to the organization, unanticipated and undesirable effects are often realized. Instead of, or in addition to, controlling organizational activity as intended, the controls produce side effects, a sort of by-product of the control system. Such dysfunctional side effects result from the human reactions of members of the organization.

Dysfunctional Consequences of Control

One such undesirable effect is the tendency of some control systems to narrow one's viewpoint unduly. The controls act as a set of blinders to limit the individual's vision or concern to his or her own sphere, with possible disregard for broader organizational values. A pay incentive system in manufacturing, for example, may base the reward upon output to the extent that quality suffers. Such a system may give the individual little or no encouragement to think beyond the daily production record to the broader objectives of the organization and the contributions one might make to these. There may be absolutely no incentive for improvement in the operations and methods. The incentive system has conditioned the employee to believe that only daily output is important.

The Narrow Viewpoint

At a managerial level, an example may be found in the restricted viewpoints of divisional managers in a decentralized corporation. In the eyes of a division manager, a good investment decision may depend upon the rate of return on investment expected by corporate management on the part of the particular division. And all divisions would not necessarily be expected to produce the same rate of profit. One division might be permitted to operate with little or no profit, whereas others might be expected to produce as high as 30 percent after taxes.

The divisional manager would normally approve any investment that would tend to raise the rate of return of the one division. This could lead to approval of investments promising a 5 percent return in some divisions and rejection of proposals promising a 25 percent return in other divisions. From the standpoint of the company as a whole, such decisions are clearly unwise.

> In a highly profitable division of a multidivisional company, the purchasing agent requested permission to increase the inventory in order to take quantity discounts; the return on investment would have been 25% on the inventory increase. His request was refused because the division was already earning 35% on its book investment. Therefore, a 25% investment would

have averaged down the 35%. Incidentally, the company as a whole was earning less than 10%! [2]

The Short Run Versus the Long Run

Another unfortunate consequence of some control systems is the premium
they may unwittingly place upon the short run. The control system encourages
a short-run course of action that may run counter to the long-run interests of
the organization. Consider, for example, the profit control applied to the different divisions of a decentralized company. The profit goal of the division
serves as a powerful incentive for the divisional manager who is under tremendous pressure to achieve that objective. Under certain conditions, this presents a strong motivation to win in the short run, even though the long-run effects may be disastrous.

The following decisions by division managers illustrate this type of undesirable short-run reaction to a control system.

> In order to increase his rate of return, a division manager reduced his re-
> search costs by eliminating all projects that did not have an expected payout
> within two years. He believed that if he did not improve his rate of return, he
> would be replaced.

> A division manager scrapped some machinery that he was not currently
> using in order to reduce his investment. Later, when the machinery was
> needed, he purchased new equipment.[3]

As another example, the behavior of production supervisors is illuminating.
One study of efficiency controls in large corporations has reported the reactions of department supervisors to efficiency ratings of their departments.[4] In
this company, monthly efficiency ratings of each department were compiled to
show the accomplishment of the department for the monthly period. The
plant manager took these ratings seriously and was quick to investigate any
deficiency revealed by the monthly reports. As a result, department supervisors were under pressure to show up well each month.

This led to a number of undesirable short-run expediencies. As the end of
the month approached, attention was shifted to *completing* units in order to get
them beyond the checkpoint into finished stores. In this way, they would show
up as completed work in the department's efficiency ratings. This practice is
known as *bleeding the line,* and one foreman described it as follows:

> What actually happens is that in the beginning of the month I have to put
> all of my men at the beginning of the line to get pieces going for the month's
> production. This is because we cleaned out the department in the previous
> month. Then, during the last two weeks I have to put all of the men at the
> end of the line to finish up the pieces.[5]

---

[2] Bruce D. Henderson and John Dearden, "New System for Divisional Control," *Harvard Business Review* 44, no. 5 (September-October, 1966): 149.

[3] *Ibid.,* p. 150.

[4] Frank J. Jasinski, "Use and Misuse of Efficiency Controls," *Harvard Business Review* 34, no. 4
(July-August, 1956): 105–12.

[5] *Ibid.,* p. 107.

It is apparent that a great deal of inefficiency would result in this and other departments from such practices.

Department supervisors were similarly inclined to neglect necessary maintenance in their rush to achieve the month's production goal. They would run a machine to the breaking point in order to make the right efficiency rating. One foreman's explanation ran as follows:

> We really can't stop to have our machines repaired. In fact, one of our machines is off right now, but we'll have to gimmick something immediately and keep the machine going because at the end of the month, as it is now, we simply can't have a machine down. We've got to get those pieces out. Many times we run a machine right to the ground at the end of the month trying to get pieces out, and we have to spend extra time at the beginning of the month trying to repair the machine.[6]

Interestingly enough, a strong control system has produced strikingly similar results in a completely different culture. In Soviet Russia, factory managers also work under a monthly output plan.[7] Plant managers have tremendous pressure to achieve their output quotas. They may double their income, for example, by producing the proper amount. This has led to the practice of *storming*—that is, concentrating great effort upon production in the last part of each month. The problem has been sufficiently widespread to merit attention at the highest levels of government.

> This practice of "storming" leads to a number of uneconomic consequences. States of emergency constantly arise; men and equipment are subject to periods of unnecessary idleness; during the days of storming the rate of spoilage increases, overtime pay mounts up, the machines suffer from speed-up, and customers' production schedules are interrupted.[8]

Individuals who are subject to a control system may also be tempted to beat the system by making themselves look good on paper. They may use various stratagems for this purpose. In the Jasinski study cited earlier, top supervisors were sometimes guilty of fudging figures.[9] In a desire to equalize efficiency ratings of departments under their direction, supervisors would go so far as to transfer personnel "on paper" from low efficiency departments to high efficiency departments. The effect, of course, was to produce a more consistent ratio of output to manpower in the various departments.

Soviet managers also practiced the *sharp pencil* technique at times to make their records appear satisfactory.[10] In effect, this amounts to tinkering with the

Evasion of Controls Through Falsification of Reporting

---

[6] *Ibid.*

[7] The practice described here is reported in Joseph S. Berliner, "A Problem in Soviet Business Administration," *Administrative Science Quarterly* 1, no. 1 (June, 1956): 86–101.

[8] *Ibid.*, p. 89.

[9] Jasinski, "Efficiency Controls," pp. 107–8.

[10] For a discussion of this practice, see Joseph S. Berliner, *Factory and Manager in the USSR* (Cambridge: Harvard University Press, 1957), Chapter 10.

figures so that they will show what the manager wishes them to show. One of the most common methods involves borrowing output from the next period. For example, work in process may be valued at an unreasonably high percentage of completion.

An opposite type of falsification occurs in the manager's tendency to avoid exceeding quota too much in any period. Because of the *ratchet* principle, an attained quota in one period may be established as a minimum for a later period. For this reason, it is dangerous for managers to look too good. In fact, this may lead them to fall below quota occasionally. A Soviet informant is quoted as follows with respect to this practice:

> Sometimes the plan is deliberately underfulfilled. This may happen once or twice a year. They underfulfill it because they want to remove any suspicion that might arise if the plan is fulfilled every single month. The purpose of this is to give the assistant commissar the impression that he is really putting pressure upon the enterprise. Because if month after month the plan is fulfilled, then the commissar might crack down upon them. But if in some months the plan is not fulfilled, then it will seem like a very hard program. They are willing to give a few months' premiums for this.[11]

Adverse Morale Effects In view of the malfunctioning of control previously described, it is hardly surprising that morale may be impaired at times. The combination of pressure and seemingly necessary but illogical behavior would hardly make one wildly enthusiastic about the organization. In fact, management personnel may easily experience a strong reaction against such a control system.

Consider the attitude expressed by one department store salesperson concerning sales quotas:

> Every day we are assigned a quota based on what was sold a year before. No account is taken of economic conditions, whether a holiday (such as Easter) comes early or late this year, or other such factors. In other words, only one criterion is used. When the quota is either too high or too low, my performance suffers. If it is too low, there is no challenge. If the quota is too high, which is worse, the quota is just out of reach. Management is plain being unrealistic. Why should I try to reach such an arbitrary quota? My attitude is negative.

If management appears unreasonable in the application of controls, the subordinate naturally becomes disturbed. A superior, for example, may refuse to accept reasonable explanations for delays. As a consequence, the subordinate must be content with an unfavorable evaluation by the superior or resort to one or more of the devious means available in combating the situation. A straightforward, honest effort may not secure the approbation of the superior. Those subject to such types of control are understandably critical.

---

[11] "Joseph S. Berliner, *Factory Manager in the USSR* (Cambridge, Mass.: Harvard University Press, 1957), p. 165.

It is clear that managers, in installing and using controls, do not desire the unfortunate effects described above. Nor are these effects an inescapable consequence of all control systems. Establishing controls, however, does create pressures often leading to these undesirable effects. Managers should, therefore, be aware of this tendency and attempt to minimize the harmful effects.

The control system may be poorly designed. The adequacy of controls must be evaluated by examining their results. Do they produce the operational results desired? Or do they encourage undesirable short-run expediencies, narrowness of viewpoint, and distortion of reports? All controls need to be examined from this point of view in evaluating their overall effects on company operation.

To gain general acceptance, standards must be established in such a way that they are perceived as fair by those whose performance is controlled. The use of participative management, for example, tends to induce acceptance of standards as reasonable. Standards which recognize some range of acceptable performance and which appear to be established objectively, as is the case with statistical quality controls, also encourage acceptance by those whose performance is controlled.

In addition, controls must be recognized as means and not as ends in themselves. Higher-level management can assure this, however, only by a reasonable interpretation of results being controlled. The threat of being sent to Siberia, either literally or figuratively, in spite of an outstanding effort, would make one wary of the control system. If all explanations, regardless of validity, are unacceptable, the control system will almost inevitably become an end in itself.

The management-by-objectives (MBO) approach discussed in Chapter 14 tends to minimize undesirable behavioral effects. The principal feature of this type of management is the establishment of specific performance goals for each position, particularly for each managerial position. By stressing these objectives, overall control is achieved through self-control by individual participants. Rather than applying control from above, the emphasis is placed upon control from within.

A system of management by objectives may not sound appreciably different from any other method of management. Its distinction is found in its careful delineation of formal objectives for a specific time period. There is danger, of course, if this type of management is not supplemented by the use of other controls. Ignoring other aspects of performance could lead to an undesirable Machiavellian attitude among managers. There is no need for this management approach to be pushed to such extremes, however.

The effectiveness of control partially depends upon the selection of the points at which control is applied. Consider a process or activity, for example, starting at point X and proceeding through stages a, b, and c to reach completion at point Y.

Improving Effectiveness of Control

Minimizing Adverse Behavioral Effects

Management by Objectives

Use of Strategic Control Points

To control the process, checking may be employed at various points. The work may be checked at the end of the process, at the end of each stage, or at various points during each stage. The best combination of control points would keep the process in line with a minimum of cost and control effort.

Management by Exception

Economy of control effort uses the principle of *management by exception.* In using this approach, the manager devotes effort to unexpected or out-of-line performance. Some standard is established, and significant deviations from that standard are the exceptions. If performance conforms to anticipations, time spent in reviewing this fact is largely wasted. Managing by exception permits the manager to isolate nonstandard performance and to concentrate upon it.

Suppose that six sales territories are each expected to produce $50,000 in sales. If one produces $40,000, another $60,000, and four others between $49,000 and $51,000, the manager can focus upon two territories.

The management-by-exception principle was recognized by the pioneers in professional management and has been followed by professional managers for many years. Frederick W. Taylor's strong support for this type of management is indicated by the following comments:

> It is not an uncommon sight, though a sad one, to see the manager of a large business fairly swamped at his desk with an ocean of letters and reports, on each of which he thinks that he should put his initial or stamp. He feels that by having this mass of detail pass over his desk he is keeping in close touch with the entire business. The exception principle is directly the reverse of this. Under it the manager should receive only condensed, summarized, and *invariably* comparative reports, covering, however, all of the elements entering into the management, and even these summaries should all be carefully gone over by an assistant before they reach the manager, and have all of the exceptions to the past averages or to the standards pointed out, both the especially good and especially bad exceptions. . . .[12]

In the customary operations and activities of business firms, some variation occurs. There are dozens of reasons for such variation, and much of it must be regarded as normal. In managing by exception, then, managers must first distinguish that performance which varies sufficiently to constitute an exception. They often rely upon experience in making this type of judgment. If their experience is extensive and if they are sufficiently alert, they may readily locate unusual situations that deserve attention.

Statistical quality control provides an example of a more systematic and objective search for exceptional performance. By using the laws of probability, management is able to distinguish between typical variation in a process and a process that is definitely "out of control."

Simplification of Control Procedures

It is a mistake to assume that elaborate controls are always best and that simplicity inevitably spells weakness in a control system. Some forms and procedures are desirable and indeed necessary for proper control. The forms and procedures in control systems have a way of proliferating and becoming elab-

---

[12] Frederick Winslow Taylor, *Scientific Management* (New York: Harper & Row, Publishers, 1947), p. 126.

orate, however. New forms are added and others made more complex. A vast amount of time may be spent in making reports, and mountains of data may be handed over to executives. The excessive complexity of these data prevents their serving as a sharp tool of management.

The only correction of undue complexity is through eliminating unnecessary reports and procedures and streamlining those that are retained. Such pruning is often painful. Control systems become clothed with tradition as time goes on. Periodic review of control procedures and systems is essential, however, in making the control system completely functional.

Use of Feedback in Control

In controlling an operation, management requires a system like the thermostat for measuring performance and reporting the results back to the manager. Performance information of this type that is channeled back to management is known as *feedback.* It is designed to show just what kind of job is being done. It tips off management as to deficiencies or variations from expected results.

Not all feedback is highly formalized. Personal observation and informal discussions are used extensively in many organizations in keeping managers in touch with organizations under their direction. In fact, informal feedback systems are most appropriate for certain types of control situations. Most first-line supervisors, for example, must rely heavily upon such methods for keeping in touch with their subordinates.

Informal feedback is typically inadequate for the organization as a whole, however, and must be supplemented with more formal methods, particularly as organizations grow in size. In the large corporation, extensive reliance must be placed upon formal techniques. Top management comes to live in a world of financial statements, statistical analyses, and other formal reports. But even though the emphasis shifts to formal feedback, no organization dispenses completely with informal methods.

Summary

In the exercise of the controlling function, a manager regulates the operation of an organization, holding performance in line or taking corrective action where necessary. On the basis of either implicitly or explicitly stated *standards* or objectives, the manager *evaluates* performance and *takes corrective action* to rectify errors or remedy deficient performance.

The control process has a tendency to produce certain unwanted *behavioral consequences* in the organization that is being controlled. To some extent, they reflect weaknesses in the control system, but it is difficult to perfect the control techniques sufficiently to avoid them completely. Some of these undesirable reactions are narrowness of viewpoint, short-run expediencies with long-run disadvantages, evasion of controls through falsification of reporting, and reduced morale.

A number of possible variations or changes in control systems are available to managers who wish to improve their effectiveness. Harmful behavioral consequences may be minimized, for example, by careful development of the elements of the control system and its equitable administration. *Management by objectives,* use of *strategic control points, management by exception, simplification of control procedures,* and *use of feedback in control* also contribute to a workable control system.

Discussion Questions

1. The function of controlling assumes the existence of some type of *standard.* What kinds of standards are used for the following: (1) quality of product, (2) work pace of a crew of employees, (3) travel expense for company executives, and (4) inventory level?

2. Suppose that a comparison of labor expense with the budgeted figure reveals the expenditure of 10 percent more than had been budgeted. What corrective action is called for?

3. How is closeness or looseness of control related to decentralization?

4. How can controls cause undesirably narrow viewpoints in individual members or departments of an organization?

5. Evaluate the practice of *storming* in Russian factories. Is this a consequence of Communism?

6. Explain the principle of *management by exception.*

7. How is *feedback* of information related to the control function?

8. An office manager commented as follows: "It is my responsibility to keep up with all aspects of every activity and project that are assigned to this office." Evaluate this statement in the light of managerial control theory.

Supplementary Reading

Fleming, John E. "The Spectrum of Management Control." *Advanced Management Journal* 37, no. 2 (April, 1972): 54-61.

Mockler, Robert J. *The Management Control Process.* New York: Appleton-Century-Crofts, 1972.

Newman, William H. *Constructive Control: Design and Use of Control Systems.* Englewood Cliffs, N.J.: Prentice-Hall, Inc., 1975.

Vancil, Richard F. "What Kind of Management Control Do You Need?" *Harvard Business Review* 51, no. 2 (March-April, 1973): 75-86.

Case 15

A Crisis of Control*

"I am probably the best anthropologist in Arkansas and the worst businessman in the state. I have totally lost control of this business. Tell me what you want to know, and I'll see if I can get it." After this opening statement, Brett Kerlo proceeded with the tale of an inherited printing firm, rapid expansion through the purchase of new high-capacity equipment, large losses, and a current state of impending bankruptcy.

It all started when the thirty-year-old printing firm with annual sales of $150,000 decided to purchase new high-speed presses for $100,000 and ex-

*Case prepared by Professor Richard C. Scott of Baylor University.

pand the building for another $125,000. All this was financed with a $250,000 SBA 90 percent guaranteed loan through the First State Bank of Arkadelphia. The extra $25,000 was allowed for working capital during the transition.

A review of sales and cost of goods sold (in thousands of dollars) was as follows:

	Nov.	Dec.	Jan.	Feb.	Mar.	Apr.
Sales	18	20	19	23	22	27
C of GS	10	19	14	25	15	28
Gross Profit	8	1	5	(2)	7	(1)

Job cost sheets (itemized lists of all costs associated with a job) were not processed or totalled until the end of the month when the bookkeeper closed the books. It was found that most jobs were priced when they were picked up by the customer. Losses were incurred on 50 percent of the jobs. A discussion with the vice-president revealed that fixed costs were roughly $15,000 per month, that a "normal" cost of goods sold was 68 percent of sales, and that the 50 percent of jobs on which money was lost represented about 25 percent of sales.

Questions

1. What additional information would you like to have in order to bring this business situation under control?

2. What would be your sequence of steps to start gaining control of this organization?

3. When do you expect to reach the break-even point—that is, the point at which sales revenue covers all expenses?

4. How much cash do you need to survive until then?

Objectives

1. Explain the relevance and limitations of accounting concepts in controlling performance.
2. Summarize and explain the problems and special features of quality control, production control, and inventory control.

Chapter

16

Special Types of Control

Accounting Control
Quality Control
Production Control
Inventory Control

Case: The Case of Matt Hopper

General concepts of control are applied in special ways as the manager seeks to regulate particular aspects of the total operation. This chapter reviews a selected group of such specialized types of control.

Accounting Control

So much accounting is involved in managerial control that the accounting executive is often called the *controller* of the firm. The following review of accounting concepts, however, considers them more from the viewpoint of the general manager than from that of the controller.

Control Through Profit Analysis

The profit objective is critically important to any privately owned business organization. Profits are essential for survival and are regarded as a major objective by owners and managers. As a control device, the profit figure provides an overall measure of managerial success or failure. Profits, for example, may be too low as measured by some pertinent standard and thus be indicative of unsuccessful management.

To interpret the dollar profit figure, we must relate it to other figures. One customary comparison relates profits to sales. A profit of $100,000 provides a 5 percent return on sales of $2 million or a 10 percent return on sales of $1 million. The percentage return for a given year can be compared with the rate of return for earlier years or for other firms in the same industry. In this way, one can evaluate the operating efficiency of the company as it has secured its sales.

Another comparison relates the amount of profit to the size of investment. This is intended to reveal the efficiency and intensity of utilization of facilities and other resources. A profit of $500,000, for example, represents a 10 percent return on an investment of $5 million or a 20 percent return on an investment of $2,500,000.

The Use of Conventional Statements

One major function of an accounting system is the reporting of pertinent financial information to managers. It may be helpful to begin with a general review of conventional financial statements and their functions. The *balance sheet* reports the company's financial position at a specified time. This requires a presentation of *assets* (the things it owns), *liabilities* (what it owes), and the stockholders' *equity* (net ownership). The balance sheet balances because the owners' equity must be the difference between the total assets and the outstanding debts. The statement makes no attempt to describe what has happened over a period of time. By comparing balance sheets for different dates, of course, one might discover changes that have occurred.

In contrast to the balance sheet, an *income statement* summarizes financial results for some period of operation. It typically begins with a *gross sales* or *revenue* figure for the period and subtracts the *cost of goods sold* in arriving at a *gross profit*. From the gross profit are subtracted the *selling* and *administrative expenses* to discover the *operating profit*. Ordinarily, corporate income tax represents the principal deduction that must be made from the operating profit to determine the *net income* accruing to stockholders.

The income statement is typically supplemented with a statement of *retained earnings*. A primary purpose of the latter statement is to disclose errors made in previous accounting periods that would affect retained earnings and to report other extraordinary transactions not included in the income statement.

Another, less frequently used financial statement is known as the *statement of application of funds* or *statement of changes in working capital*. It is the function of this statement to analyze changes in a firm's working capital from one point of time to another. It is sometimes described as a "where-got, where-gone" statement, showing the sources of funds (such as profits or long-term borrowing) and the applications or uses of those funds (such as purchase of fixed assets). The change in funds is ordinarily different from the net profit for the same period. A company that earned $500,000, for example, might invest $250,000 of it in new facilities, thereby cutting the potential working capital increase in half.

To use financial statements with any degree of sophistication requires some appreciation of their limitations. Only the naive manager accepts such statements as the simple truth. As a matter of fact, there are many limitations, only a few of which can be noted here.

Limitations of Conventional Statements

As one example of these difficulties, the changing value of the dollar presents continuing problems. Assets are typically shown at cost or, in the case of inventory, at the lower of cost or market. But when general price levels change markedly, the worth of assets as shown on the books becomes unrealistic. Charging depreciation on the basis of cost, therefore, may be insufficient to make possible replacement of fully depreciated assets.

Another related difficulty is associated with the valuation of inventories. Some companies use a FIFO (first-in, first-out) method, while others use a LIFO (last-in, first-out) method. The FIFO method, for example, treats inventory costs as if items purchased first are sold or consumed first. When inventory is purchased at different prices over a period of time, asset values and profits differ according to the method of inventory valuation used. Someone's judgment regarding inventory valuation is involved, therefore, in "scientifically" determining profit results.

Many accounting figures must be approximations. Although a given obligation—a promissory note, for example—may be valued down to the exact penny, such precise calculations are not possible in all phases of the accounting process. As an example, the portion of equipment cost to be charged as an expense in a particular period must be estimated. The useful life cannot be predicted with complete accuracy. A particular machine may last well beyond its expected life or become obsolete earlier than anticipated. Either of these eventualities could cause depreciation estimates to prove inaccurate.

Accounting information, furthermore, supplies only part of the total relevant information for control purposes. Some aspects of business operations are difficult to reduce to a dollar basis for inclusion in financial statements. Suppose, for example, that two managers are being compared on the basis of the profit performance of their respective divisions. The fact that one division suffered the loss of several key executives during the year or that unexpectedly strong competition developed for one division may not be shown on the financial statements.

Internal Control Systems

Internal control refers to the organizational plan and the operating methods and procedures employed within a company to safeguard its assets, insure accuracy of accounting data, and encourage compliance with management policy. An arrangement whereby one employee checks the work of another is a simple example of such control. Most internal control measures involve some application of the *checks and balances* principle.

A major purpose of internal control is the prevention of errors—intentional or accidental—in the accounting records. Fraud, for example, is made difficult by designing a set of controls to regulate the use of company assets. Unintentional errors are likewise detected by systems that provide for cross checking of records and transactions.

Internal control is frequently defined in such a way as to limit it to control methods for protecting cash and other liquid assets. The control concept involved, however, can apply to all aspects of the accounting process. In fact, the principle of internal control may be applied to operations that are unrelated to accounting controls. A production manager, for example, might be required to secure the approval of the personnel manager before dismissing an employee. Such an arrangement, whether wise or unwise, is a type of internal control. Our concern at this point, however, is with those aspects of internal control closely related to the accounting process.

Nature and Importance of Budgeting

As planning becomes formalized in any business organization, budgeting typically becomes a major part of the planning process. But the budget is more than a plan; it is also a device for controlling operations. As originally formulated, the budget is a plan of operation, expressed in financial terms, and prepared to cover a month, quarter, year, or other period of time. During the period to which it applies, management may use it to regulate decision making and to check performance.

Most companies use their fiscal year as the time period for budgeting. It is common practice to prepare the budget during the quarter preceding the start of the fiscal year, with final adoption just prior to the beginning of the new year. Before the beginning of each quarter, the budget for that quarter is often prepared in greater detail. During the year, the budget tends to become outdated because of changing conditions, so it is common to revise the budget periodically during the budgetary period.

Many of the values of planning are realized through budgeting. The very process of budgeting forces scrutiny of operations and planning at all levels—steps that are beneficial in most instances. The control function also benefits from the budgetary program, because standards of performance are thereby established. If it appears desirable, certain classes of decisions may be required to conform to the budget—for example, by checking purchase orders with the budgeted amount. Or, performance may be compared with the standard—that is, with the budgeted figures—to discover and analyze out-of-control situations. Corrective action is, then, the final control step in bringing performance back into line. The budget may thus be a comprehensive control tool.

To many people, the term *quality* carries a connotation of *high* quality. They think of Cadillacs and sterling silver as symbolic of quality. To the manufacturer, however, quality refers to the particular quality standards that are desired. In the eyes of customers, they are not necessarily high standards. The Chevrolet Division does not attempt to produce Cadillacs.

Product quality is directly related to the basic objectives of the firm and rests, therefore, upon fundamental policy decisions of management. A number of factors are involved in these basic decisions. One manufacturer, for example, may elect to sell to a segment of the market desiring superior quality, while another may decide to sell to the mass market which accepts a lower quality product. Such decisions entail evaluation of market potential at various levels as well as an evaluation of production capacity to produce at these levels. Production cost is also pertinent. Higher quality typically entails higher production cost. Quality objectives emerge in this way from the general strategy and purposes of the enterprise.

The manufacturer's concept of quality may involve standards for a number of different characteristics, such as physical dimensions, chemical composition, weight, color, strength, and freedom from scratches. In the light of market and cost conditions, the manufacturer chooses a specific quality level, not necessarily the best. But, having chosen it, he or she attempts to meet that standard consistently.

Although inspection is an integral part of quality control, it is not fully synonymous with control of quality. Inspection provides feedback to management by measuring the product to determine the extent to which it conforms to established standards. Control also includes those steps necessary in regulating and correcting the manufacturing process to meet the stipulated standards.

Some type of inspection is required in the quality control process. This inspection may be limited to the finished product and occur at the end of the production process, or it may occur at different stages during the process. A key question, in fact, concerns the number of times the product should be inspected. The ideal is to minimize inspection costs without losing control of the product. Other questions relating to inspection concern the number of items to be inspected—100 percent or some fraction of the items—and the location of the inspection—floor versus central inspection.

In one sense, inspection activities are wasted effort. They are necessary, but they add nothing to the product. Furthermore, inspection is not perfect and seldom catches all defects. Even 100 percent inspection fails to produce perfect results. Inspectors are human and fail to exercise consistently good judgment.

Inspection may be accomplished by operators who check their own work or by full-time inspectors. If inspectors are used, the results must be reported to line managers or operators to permit corrective action.

During recent decades, management has improved the control of quality by the introduction of statistical quality control, which applies the theory of probability to the process of inspection and quality control. Even without statistical quality control, inspection is often conducted on the basis of systematic sam-

Quality Control

Meaning and Purpose of Quality Control

Traditional Quality Control Methods

Statistical Quality Control

pling. Rather than using 100 percent inspection, only a part of a lot is singled out for inspection. The assumption is that the quality of the entire lot will be indicated by the inspected items. Lacking statistical methodology, however, there is little knowledge of the degree of risk involved. The sample may be insufficient or unrepresentative and thus fail to present a true picture. On the other hand, the sample may be unnecessarily large and thus involve unnecessary and wasteful inspection effort.

By the use of statistical quality control methods, management is able to make a choice as to the degree of risk that can be tolerated—that is, the proportion of below-standard items that can be accepted. The extent of risk can be specified by the statistician, and the risk (of accepting defective items) can be reduced with the expenditure of additional time and money. Statistical quality control tells the manager how likely it is that bad products will slip by with a given inspection plan. The manager can then weigh this problem against the increased cost required to reduce that risk.

Statistical quality control also makes it possible for management to maintain control of quality more effectively during the production process. Quality is checked periodically during the processing period. By analyzing the trend in these readings, it is possible to discover an out-of-control condition before it becomes serious. In other words, an analysis may indicate the process to be out of control even though the quality still falls within tolerance limits.

It seems likely that most quality control is still nonstatistical. To the extent that it can be profitably adopted, however, the statistical method offers improvement in the quality control process.

Production Control

Objectives and Values of Production Control

A busy manufacturing department appears to be a beehive of activity. Hundreds or thousands of employees are performing specialized functions, many of them requiring unique skills. Almost miraculously, it appears, their individual efforts blend together to complete products as scheduled. The brain or nervous system behind this bustle of activity is known as *production control.*

Production control basically involves a coordinating function. The various manufacturing activities must be regulated to achieve production in accordance with customer demands. In addition, the manufacturing operations must occur in an orderly and efficient manner to achieve economy of operation. The objectives of production control, then, are both efficiency in operation and customer satisfaction.

Production control is concerned with the orderly flow of materials and work through the production process. At just the right time, the production process begins. Products are shifted from department to department at a rate or at a time that avoids delay in work schedules and at the same time prevents bottlenecks. Subassemblies must be completed on a schedule permitting their efficient combination into finished products. Work must move through the manufacturing process on a schedule that achieves promised delivery dates. Management must keep in touch with progress on individual orders and take corrective action if unusual delays occur. Materials, tooling, and labor must be available at the right place at the right time. Idleness of equipment and of manpower must be avoided.

It is easy to see that production control may become a most complex process. In a large or involved manufacturing process, entire departments are created to maintain surveillance over production activities. This production control department typically reports to a production executive. Although smaller plants may not establish production control departments, the same control functions must be exercised. In any organization, much of the production control function is of necessity performed by first-line supervisors.

It is possible to group production control activities around a number of basic functions. Although different writers on production management differ in functions that they recognize, the following are common to many such analyses:

Functions of Production Control

1. Routing
2. Scheduling
3. Dispatching
4. Followup

Routing refers to the sequence of operations to be performed and the path to be taken by a manufacturing order. It may also include an analysis of materials required and a determination of items to be purchased. In some types of manufacturing, there is a choice in the order and location of work performance. The product may be processed through Department *A*, then to *B*, then to *C*; or it may begin with *A* and then be routed to *C*, then to *B*.

In *scheduling,* the time of performance is determined. This includes the time for beginning work on a given order or project and may also be extended to include the time that individual operations will be performed. Schedulers must observe completion dates and work backward sufficiently to find the appropriate time for beginning operations.

Dispatching refers to the order-giving function. The various departments and operators must be notified as to when they should begin work on particular items. Authorization is also necessary for the issuance of tools and materials, the movement of materials, and so on.

Followup includes those procedures designed to keep track of production operations. As a first step, it is necessary to keep tab on purchase orders and material requisitions. The production orders must also be checked from time to time to see whether they are falling behind schedule. If delays are discovered, action may be required to expedite the order to bring it back up to schedule.

Schematic drawings and graphs have been used extensively in production planning and control. One of the oldest and most widely used devices of this type is the *Gantt Chart.* This tool was originated by one of the pioneers in scientific management and is used in scheduling and controlling the work of particular machines or production centers. There are numerous variations of the Gantt Chart in current use. One example is presented in Figure 16–1.

Methods and Tools of Production Control

In this chart, the light lines and the numbers above them show jobs that are scheduled. The brackets indicate the scheduled beginning and end of each job. The heavy lines show the proportions of jobs completed, and the "V" at the top of the chart indicates the present date. In examining this chart, we can see that work on Machine *A* is running well ahead of schedule while work on Machine *C* has fallen behind.

Figure 16-1   *Gantt Progress Chart*

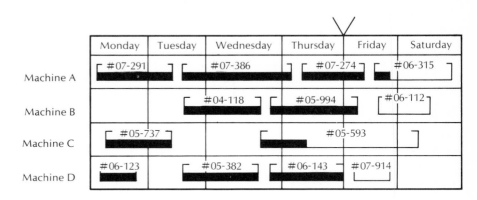

Source: Robert H. Bock and William K. Holstein, *Production Planning and Control: Text and Readings* (Columbus, Ohio: Charles E. Merrill Publishing Co., 1963), p. 8.

One limitation of the Gantt Chart for production planning is its concentration upon the single dimension of time. An important, neglected factor, however, is the relative cost of producing on one machine rather than another. The method of *linear programming* has been used in recent years to assign production to machines or production centers on a least-cost basis. This method takes into account the relative efficiencies of the various production units—differences in maintenance, operation time, and so on.

Data processing equipment is also being applied to the clerical aspects of production control. As orders are received from customers, for example, the computer may be checked to determine availability of materials and facilities to fill the orders by the desired dates. Inventory records and prior commitment of facilities can be quickly checked in this way. Necessary requisitions and shop orders may then be printed automatically. Information on work completed may also be entered in the computer, which can then prepare production reports.

Control With Network Techniques

Two analytical tools of production planning and control originated in the late 1950s and are known as PERT (Program Evaluation Review Technique) and CPM (Critical Path Method). Both techniques are basically similar and are designed to facilitate management of complex projects.[1] PERT was first introduced in 1958 as a system for monitoring development of the Polaris Ballistic Missile, a primary weapon of U.S. nuclear-powered submarines, and is widely credited with saving years of time in making the Polaris operational.

---

[1] Although there are some differences in PERT and CPM, the present discussion will stress features common to both. Numerous variations of these techniques have been developed and carry such labels as LESS, PACT, SCANS, and so on.

The Navy Special Projects Office collaborated with Lockheed Aircraft Corporation and Booz, Allen and Hamilton, a prominent management consulting firm, in developing the PERT approach. The Polaris program was large and extremely complex. Many business and governmental organizations were involved, and the work was widely spread geographically. There was also much uncertainty concerning performance times. CPM was originated by the DuPont Company at about the same time in order to manage major construction projects more efficiently. In both cases, therefore, the tool was devised to help control large, complicated projects.

The interrelationships among the various parts of major projects required a type of control that would regulate the system as a whole. In fact, both PERT and CPM use network analysis, which, as the name indicates, deals explicitly with the network of relationships among the various phases of the total program. The network shows what activities must await completion of other tasks and what activities can be performed concurrently with other tasks. PERT and CPM thus represent an application of the systems concept to managerial control.

The PERT network in Figure 16–2 shows in highly simplified form the basic steps that would be followed by an American manufacturer in marketing a new product. The illustration assumes that the preliminary design work has been completed and that a well-organized plant and distribution setup are available. Numbers on the arrows show the number of days estimated for each activity.

Simplified PERT Network to Introduce New Product   **Figure 16–2**

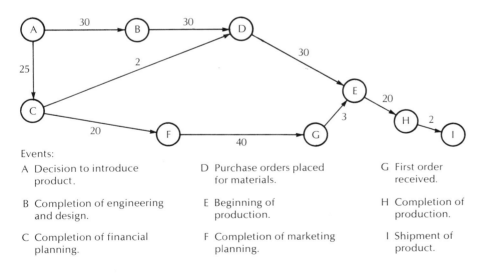

Events:

A Decision to introduce product.

B Completion of engineering and design.

C Completion of financial planning.

D Purchase orders placed for materials.

E Beginning of production.

F Completion of marketing planning.

G First order received.

H Completion of production.

I Shipment of product.

By examining the network, we can locate the *critical path*—the series of related steps that requires the longest time. In this example, we can see that the top path (A–B–D–E–H–I) is the longest and that any delay in this path will delay completion of the project. Other paths have *slack*, and it may be possible to divert personnel or other resources from those paths in order to speed up work on the critical path. In actual practice, the network would be infinitely more complex.

Network techniques are particularly well adapted to control of major, complex, one-time projects. In addition to the preceding applications, they have been used in the following ways:

Retooling program
Revising an accounting system
Timing and placing a new stock issue
Installing a computer system
Installing a new organization structure

These techniques are concerned with time scheduling, but they are also useful in analyzing costs and improving efficiency in usage of resources. For example, the analysis may suggest the desirability of expediting critical jobs at higher cost in order to reduce total cost. Although relatively simple applications of PERT and CPM can be accomplished manually, an electronic computer is essential for network analysis of major projects. The computer may be used, for example, to locate the longest, or critical, path and to determine slack time on noncritical tasks.

Inventory Control

Need for Inventory Control

In many organizations, inventory is the largest current asset. For this and other reasons, inventory control is essential for business success. From a cost standpoint, control of inventory quantity is necessary. If a substantial investment in inventory is required, the expense of maintaining it is great.

From the standpoint of operating efficiency, it is also essential to have effective inventory control. If a production tie-up is caused by an out-of-stock condition, the resulting costs may be staggering. In a retail store, customer dissatisfaction occurs if the shelf is bare when the customer wishes to buy.

The objective of inventory control, then, is an adequate but not excessive inventory. In a marketing institution, this refers to merchandise on the shelf or in the warehouse. In a manufacturing plant, it refers to the inventory of raw materials, supplies, goods in process, and finished goods.

Inventory Turnover Calculations

One technique used by management in controlling inventory is the calculation of an *inventory turnover rate*. This computation compares inventory cost with cost of sales (or with sales) for a given period. For example, assume that the current income statement of a retail department having an inventory of $50,000 (at cost) reports the cost of goods sold for the year as $350,000. In this case, the inventory turnover rate is seven times. It means that the department sold, during the year, seven times as much inventory as it had on its shelf at one time. In a similar manner, the raw materials inventory of a manufacturing plant may be compared with the materials put into production during the year.

By comparing the turnover rate with industry standards or with an earlier turnover rate, we can gain some idea of the effectiveness of inventory control. If the rate is low, the inventory is apparently unnecessarily large relative to usage or sales. Of course, the difficulty may be with either sales or inventory or both. The turnover rate is also an indicator of efficiency of management in the exercise of the control function. A manager whose inventory turnover rate is consistently low is an ineffective manager of this asset. Some caution is necessary in interpreting data of this type. It is possible, for example, to achieve a higher rate of turnover by passing up quantity discounts and purchasing only small amounts at any one time.

Determining Minimum and Maximum Inventory Size

Effective control of regularly stocked inventory items requires an accurate determination of minimum and maximum inventory levels. A number of factors must enter into decisions of this type. If the product is subject to substantial loss in value through obsolescence or physical deterioration, for example, the inventory must be held near the minimum level. If a policy of speculative buying is followed, a maximum size may be attained that is higher than would otherwise be justified. Of course, there are strong arguments against the practice of speculative buying.

In the absence of compelling considerations based upon price fluctuations, obsolescence, or deterioration, the manager has some margin of freedom in determining appropriate inventory levels. Assuming a standardized item, the minimum amount to be carried may be considered a *safety stock* or *minimum reserve stock*. Normally, this level cannot safely be zero. This would be possible, of course, if stock were always replenished by the time the last item was removed. This is not always possible, however, and the safety stock is provided as a "cushion." Lack of precision in estimates and uncertainties in procurement and deliveries explain the need for the safety stock. It allows for such contingencies as unanticipated delays in shipment and unexpected withdrawals from stock.

Given a specified minimum stock level, the maximum is determined by the amount procured at one time. Buying in large quantities increases both the maximum and the average inventory size. To determine the most economical level, the manager must calculate an amount known as the *economic order quantity*. This amount is the purchase quantity that minimizes total costs by properly balancing costs associated with large orders (such as cost of money tied up in inventory and warehouse space) and costs associated with small orders (such as loss of quantity discounts, costs of stockouts, and overhead clerical cost in placing purchase orders). Today many companies use complex mathematical techniques—some employing electronic computers—in deciding how much inventory to carry.

Receiving and Physical Control of Inventory

A receiving procedure is the first step in maintaining physical control of a product. Items coming into inventory from outside the business normally arrive by truck or rail. Personnel in the receiving room open the shipment, examine the material, and prepare receiving reports which are compared with ordering documents. This step assures both the proper quality, by detecting broken or defective items, and the proper quantity.

While awaiting usage, inventory items are typically kept within enclosed stockrooms. This practice and the record keeping associated with it provide physical protection and also assure availability of inventory items as needed. Restricting access to the stockroom tends to eliminate pilfering. Withdrawals are made on the basis of duly authorized requisitions.

Some inventory items are controlled by records known as a *perpetual inventory system.* Such a system requires the entry on the records of every receipt and withdrawal of items from stock. At any time, it is possible to check the inventory level by referring to the appropriate stock card. Another method, that of the *physical inventory,* requires a periodic count of items on hand. Because inventory records customarily involve some errors, even the perpetual inventory records must be checked from time to time by taking a physical inventory.

Summary

The profits realized on business operations provide a general performance measure useful in overall control. The basic conventional statements used in managerial control are the *balance sheet, income statement, statement of retained earnings,* and *statement of application of funds. Internal control* refers to the organization plan and methods used within a company to safeguard its assets, insure accuracy of accounting data, and encourage compliance with policy. One of the major accounting tools for control purposes in business organizations is the budget.

Quality refers to the standards applicable to various characteristics of a product; such standards do not necessarily specify high quality. It is the purpose of *quality control* to assure consistent performance in terms of the quality standards that are accepted. During recent decades, management has improved the function of quality control by the adoption of various *statistical techniques.*

Through *production control,* a manufacturer attempts to meet delivery schedules while maximizing operational efficiency. Of the various functions of production control, those of *routing, scheduling, dispatching,* and *followup* are recognized by most writers. Modern analytical methods used in production control include *linear programming* and *network techniques,* such as PERT and CPM.

Inventory control is designed to minimize operational costs and to assure the presence of inventory items as required for sale or production use. The *inventory turnover rate* provides a measure of the efficiency of inventory management. In controlling inventory levels, managerial decisions concerning *minimum and maximum inventory size* are necessary. The minimum inventory size is determined by the size of the *minimum reserve stock,* and the maximum inventory size involves a calculation of the *economic order quantity.*

Discussion Questions

1. Identify several limitations of conventional financial statements and explain the relevance of each limitation to managerial decision making.

2. What is the basic concept involved in *internal control?*

3. Distinguish between inspection and quality control.

4. Explain the concept of *statistical quality control.*

5. Why does 100 percent inspection fail to produce perfect results?

6. What specifically do production managers wish to accomplish through *production control?*

7. Distinguish between the *routing, scheduling,* and *dispatching* functions of production control.

8. What is the purpose of a *Gantt Chart?* What is a limitation in its use?

9. What is the *critical path* in *PERT?* What is its significance?

10. In computing the rate of *inventory turnover,* should a manager use sales figures or cost-of-sales figures? Why?

Anthony, Robert N.; Dearden, John; and Vancil, Robert F. *Management Control Systems,* Rev. ed. Homewood, Ill.: Richard D. Irwin, Inc., 1972.

Edwards, James Don and Roemmich, Roger A. "Scientific Inventory Management." *MSU Business Topics* (Autumn, 1975): 41–45.

Newman, William H. *Constructive Control: Design and Use of Control Systems,* Chapters 5–6. Englewood Cliffs, N.J.: Prentice-Hall, Inc., 1975.

Schiff, Michael and Lewin, Arie Y. "The Impact of People on Budgets." *The Accounting Review* 45, no. 2 (April, 1970): 259–68.

Supplementary Reading

Case 16

The Case of Matt Hopper*

When Matt Hopper's boss asked him to see if he couldn't straighten out scheduling bottlenecks in his department, Matt got busy right away. He made a thorough analysis of work loads, manpower requirements, and process flow. He designed a form for loading machines and for scheduling work for each operator. And he double-checked his plans with his boss and with the production planning department. Everybody agreed that Matt's work schedules ought to be dependable. Time proved they weren't.

To determine where the difficulty lay, the industrial engineering department sent a methods man in to observe actual practices in Matt's department. Here are some of his observations:

8:00 A.M.: Whistle blows. Of eighteen work places, fifteen are occupied. Only twelve of the fifteen are actually operating.

8:12 A.M.: All work places occupied, fifteen now working.

8:45 A.M.: One work place not occupied, fifteen working, two waiting for material.

9:22 A.M.: Observed one worker watching her neighbor to learn how to work on special job.

11:12 A.M.: Foreman in area. All work places filled, all working.

* Lester R. Bittel, *What Every Supervisor Should Know,* 2nd ed. (New York: McGraw-Hill Book Company, 1968), pp. 320–21.

11:55 A.M.: Fifteen work places occupied, two women putting on makeup. One man eating lunch.

12:30 P.M.: Ten work places occupied.

12:35 P.M.: All work places occupied.

1:15 P.M.: One man reports to nurse with headache.

2:05 P.M.: All work places occupied. Three women talking with material handler.

3:57 P.M.: Two women waiting for mechanic to fix soldering irons.

4:17 P.M.: All work places occupied. Seven men waiting for materials.

Questions
1. What do you think may have been wrong with Matt's plans?

2. What are some of the conclusions you would draw from the engineer's observations?

3. What will Matt have to do to make sure his department meets schedules?

7

Managing in a Changing World

Objectives

1. Summarize the growth and competitive trends in international business.

2. Cite the distinguishing features of multinational corporations and discuss their relationship to host countries and host country cultures.

3. Identify the unique features involved in managing multinational corporations.

Chapter

17

International Management

Growth of International Business
Cultural Context of International Business
The Process of International Management

Case: The Election in Chile

The expansion of world trade and the rise of multinational corporations have added a new dimension to the role and management of business in today's world. Consequently, the management of international business is becoming increasingly difficult and also increasingly important to the economic welfare of society.

Growth of International Business

Growth of a Global Competitive Economy

The international relationships and responsibilities of American business firms are increasing with the growth of international business. In recent years, many companies have acquired an international dimension that has modified their basically domestic character. As part of this development, American firms are expanding exports, increasing imports, establishing foreign subsidiaries, or creating international departments.

American industry must compete in world markets with industrial concerns of other nations. Furthermore, this worldwide competition is growing more severe.

In spite of stiffening foreign competition, however, the United States has succeeded in expanding exports and also in maintaining a favorable balance of trade. Continued success depends upon the efficiency of American industry. American manufactured products must be priced competitively, and this type of competition demands continually rising productivity and declining unit labor costs.

For any company, its technology and operating efficiency determine its competitive market strength. In the early 1970s, U.S. electronics firms used mass-produced integrated-circuit chips to recapture the consumer calculator market from Japan. In the late 1970s, these electronic firms and other watchmakers are expected to bring the watch business back from Switzerland and Japan by production of solid-state digital watches. In both cases, improved technology provides a competitive advantage in international markets.

The American business firm has no monopoly on business transacted in the United States. German steel, Japanese radios, and French autos compete with American industry in its own home territory. Furthermore, foreign competition in the domestic market has expanded significantly during recent years, particularly in certain product areas.

The pressure of foreign competition leads to demands for protective tariffs. Although such tariffs can provide direct protection against low-price imports, the indirect effects are often disastrous. By eliminating "undesirable" imports, we choke off the market for other types of American exports.

Rise of the Multinational Corporation

Expansion of international business involves more than an expansion of foreign trade in the conventional sense. An important development has been the growth of multinational corporations—firms that straddle international boundaries. The direct investment by U.S. firms in manufacturing abroad—a common measure of multinational corporate growth—increased from $3.8 billion in 1950, to $11.2 billion in 1960, and to $32.2 billion in 1970.[1]

---

[1] John Fayerweather, "The Internationalization of Business," *The Annals of the American Academy of Political and Social Science* 403 (September, 1972): 2.

The International Business Machines Corporation is a good example of such a multinational corporation. In addition to its extensive facilities and operations in the United States, IBM operates in 126 other countries with 125,000 employees, does business in 30 languages and more than 100 currencies, operates 23 plants in 13 countries, and has 8 development laboratories in as many countries.[2]

The chairman and chief executive officer of the IBM World Trade Corporation—a part of IBM Corporation—described the interrelationships of world events and conditions within the multinational corporation as follows:

> Despite the company's geographic dispersion, there is scarcely any event, however remote, that does not have some impact on the total company: currency devaluations and revaluations; a variety of international tensions; natural disasters such as floods and earthquakes; strikes; military coups; civil wars; and the like. In addition, a variety of business practices, customs, and national characteristics compound the complexity of our business environment.[3]

American firms are not the only multinationals. Unilever (Pepsodent, Lipton's), Royal Dutch/Shell, and Anglo American (metals, chemicals) are examples of corporations with subsidiaries in the United States. The pace of foreign investment is quickening, and, as of 1975, foreign investors were sending some $2 billion a year into the United States.[4] Some of this investment is going into construction of manufacturing facilities. For example, Volvo is building an auto assembly plant in Virginia; Michelin, a tire plant in South Carolina; Brown Boveri, a turbine testing plant in Virginia; and BASF, a petrochemical plant in Louisiana.

Our world is still organized politically in terms of national entities with specific boundaries. The jurisdiction of one national government extends to its borders, where the jurisdiction of another country begins. The very concept of international business involves crossing these national boundaries for business purposes.

Business Scope and Political Boundaries

Problems of business regulation become more complex as business institutions cross national boundaries. Social scientists recognize the unique features of the present economic structure and the ways in which it differs from earlier economic forms. The noted historian Arnold Toynbee has described this situation as follows:

> What I see is that the multinational corporation fills a vacuum. There is an increasing misfit between the fact of global economic life and the political organization of the world, in 140 local, so-called sovereign states. . . . Most of

---

[2] Jacques G. Maisonrouge, "How a Multinational Corporation Appears to Its Managers," edited for The American Assembly by George W. Ball, *Global Companies: The Political Economy of World Business* (Englewood Cliffs, N.J.: Prentice-Hall, Inc., 1975), p. 15.

[3] *Ibid.*, pp. 15–16.

[4] "The New Immigration," *Forbes* 116, no. 9 (November 1, 1975): 28–31.

the economic troubles of the world are due to this misfit between the anti-
quated political setup of local states and the real, global economic setup.[5]

The incongruity between economic and political realities in the international
realm, therefore, creates questions and problems in business-government relationships. The questions have been sufficiently serious, moreover, to lead to
congressional investigations and even to inquiries by the United Nations.

Cultural Context of International Business

Host Country Relationships with Local Subsidiaries

The sales volume of some corporations exceeds the gross national product of
many countries. This situation makes it appear that multinational corporations
are more powerful than the countries in which some of their facilities are located. Such comparisons tend to exaggerate the power of the corporation,
however, because governments have other types of power—to tax and to raise
armies, for example. The small country, therefore, can take strong action
against a local affiliate if it wishes, even to the point of expropriating its
property.

Nevertheless, small nations are sensitive to displays of corporate power and
concerned with the potential political influence of multinationals. Some host
countries, for example, fear that parent corporations in the United States can
use the U.S. foreign aid program to punish or reward host countries on the
basis of their dealings with local affiliates of the parent company.

Application of U.S. law to multinational corporations may also modify a
host country's foreign policy. For example, a U.S. act prohibited American
firms from trading with China, Cuba, and North Korea. The U.S. headquarters
of multinational corporations were required to regulate their foreign affiliates
accordingly. Thus, manufacturing subsidiaries in Canada could not sell to the
"enemy" countries, even though Canadian law permitted such trade.

Background Cultures of Other Countries

Each country has its distinctive culture—that is, its generally accepted values
and patterns of behavior. These cultural differences interfere with the efforts
of multinational managers to understand and communicate with those in other
cultures.

It is easy to underestimate the significance and implications of cultural differences and their effect upon organizational effectiveness. Often, indeed, we
lack a full awareness of our own culture and the degree to which our behavior
and ways of looking at things are culturally conditioned. To appreciate cultural differences better, we may note the ways some illustrative features of
other cultures differ from our own.

One important feature that varies from country to country is the prevailing
attitude toward time. In the United States, for example, we are particularly
time conscious, having long experience in using clocks and meeting deadlines.
Close adherence to schedules is assumed, and promptness is expected in
meeting appointments.

---

[5] "Arnold Toynbee: Are Businessmen Creating Pax Romana?" *Forbes* 113, no. 8 (April 15, 1974):
68.

Time spent waiting in an American's outer office is a sure indicator of what one person thinks of another or how important he feels the other's business to be. This is so much the case that most Americans cannot help getting angry after waiting 30 minutes; one may even feel such a delay is an insult, and will walk out. In Latin America, on the other hand, one learns that it does not mean anything to wait in an outer office.[6]

In the Middle East, setting deadlines is viewed as being overly demanding, rather than indicating the urgency of a matter, as might be the case in this country. In Japan, there are long delays involved in business negotiations, and the Japanese are often surprised at the tendency of Americans to act too quickly or abruptly and thereby weaken their own position.

In many Latin American cultures, class distinctions are more pronounced than those in our society. The "upper class" manages work performed by the "lower class." There is a distinct absence of the democratic atmosphere that characterizes American industry. Such class distinctions tend to inhibit upward communication and interfere with frank discussion between two levels of management. The subordinate shows deference, rather than speaking up to the boss, even when a clarification of feelings would be desirable.

The Multinational Firm and Other Cultures

The emergence of multinational business firms brings American managers into contact and potential conflict with many foreign cultures. They must, consequently, adapt to many of the prevailing patterns. The American manager in Japan, for example, must understand the ritualistic, snail-paced type of negotiations. He may wait for hours several days in a row to see a Japanese executive. After extensive discussion, he may then discover this executive is not the one who will make the decision! In the discussions that follow, he will find that Japanese rarely get right to the point, thus necessitating much small talk. The American manager, because of his own cultural conditioning, is naturally inclined to hurry the pace, to get to the point, and to speak up during the seemingly interminable periods of silence.

Cultural Inefficiencies

The cultural context of international business has been discussed largely in terms of facilitating understanding and harmonious work relationships. These goals, indeed, are desirable. If a multinational manager can appreciate nuances of other cultures with which he or she works, that manager should be more effective in local organizational relationships. In an attempt to understand and respect the ways of others, however, the manager may gloss over questionable aspects of the culture. A manager may come to regard a practice or belief as good simply because it is a part of the culture. This is not necessarily true.

An understanding and respectful attitude toward another culture, therefore, should not blind one to its possible defects. Some practices, hallowed by culture, may be dysfunctional to the multinational corporation as a whole and even dysfunctional in the efforts of those in the local culture to reach their own objectives. A lackadaisical attitude toward time or a culturally conditioned re-

---

[6] Edward T. Hall, "The Silent Language in Overseas Business," *Harvard Business Review* 38, no. 3 (May–June, 1960): 89.

luctance to speak forthrightly may be less than helpful in the effectiveness of any organization. The manager, while appreciating the difficulties involved, may work toward some modification of those cultural features that create significant problems.[7]

The Process of International Management

Most business firms are affected by the trend toward international operation. Purely domestic concerns, for example, face competition from imports. For multinational corporations, however, the problems and challenges for management are numerous.

High Risk in International Business

A high and often unknown degree of risk is involved in many ventures of the multinational corporation. This risk is particularly true for firms in countries having an unstable political system, although there are problems of controls and taxation even in developed countries. In some countries, multinational firms face a danger of expropriation. Or the terms of the concession—for example, the price of oil—may suddenly change. The company may also be pressured to share ownership locally or restricted in its freedom in transferring funds.

Domestic public opinion may also be adverse to policies of multinational corporations operating abroad. The corporation may be accused, for example, of helping perpetuate a racist government by conducting business in South Africa. Or the corporation may be harassed by pickets at home because it is contemplating construction of a refinery or manufacturing plant in a Communist country.

Evaluating political risk is obviously difficult. Nevertheless, management must logically attempt to assess such dangers if it correctly perceives itself as an open system in an international environment.

Attitudes of Multinational Corporate Managers

Thinking and acting in a truly multinational fashion should eliminate bias in favor of particular countries, particularly the home country. As a matter of fact, time and experience are required to develop a pattern of management thought that is conceptually "pure" in this way.

Three states of mind or attitudes of multinational managers have been identified as follows: [8]

1. *Ethnocentric (home-country oriented)*
   This attitude assumes a superiority of home country nationals over foreigners in headquarters or subsidiaries. Messages of instruction and advice go from headquarters to subsidiaries, and home standards are applied in judging performance.

---

[7] This suggestion obviously has its limits. While an attempt to increase the degree of time consciousness, for example, may be desirable, an effort to change deeply held religious beliefs is a different type of issue.

[8] Howard V. Perlmutter, "The Tortuous Evolution of the Multinational Corporation," *Columbia Journal of World Business* 4, no. 1 (January–February, 1969): 9–18.

2. *Polycentric (host-country oriented)*

This attitude recognizes variations in cultures and holds that local people understand local situations better than do foreigners. Foreign segments of the firm are given considerable latitude, and the corporation is held together by financial controls.

3. *Geocentric (world oriented)*

A world view is taken in deciding questions about raising money, building plants, conducting research, and so on. Foreign subsidiaries are parts of a whole whose focus is on worldwide objectives. A collaborative relationship exists between subsidiaries and headquarters.

The *geocentric* set of attitudes applies naturally to multinational firms. In practice, however, such attitudes are developed over time, and various obstacles interfere with their adoption. Until they accept such viewpoints, multinational managers may be more provincial than multinational. Patterns of thinking, therefore, limit the development of international management skills.

The development and promotion of managers in multinational corporations is complicated by differences in national cultures. Unless managers are broadly experienced in various cultural settings, they tend to be ethnocentric in viewpoint and find it difficult, if not impossible, to appreciate the differing values of others. The ideal multinational manager should possess cultural empathy in addition to other necessary professional and technical qualifications.

Management Development and Progression

Although multinational firms regard themselves as multinational in management staffing, this is more fiction than fact at top executive levels. The headquarters of U.S.-based multinational corporations are staffed primarily with American managers.[9] In offices located abroad, there is a mixture of American and other managers, but American managers still tend to hold the most influential positions. There are exceptions, of course, and many executives recognize the desirability of developing a world-centered management team.[10]

Slowness in advancing foreign managers to corporate headquarters in the United States is not caused entirely by the restricted viewpoint of American executives. Some national managers prefer to stay in key management positions of subsidiaries rather than enter what to them is a foreign culture. We must note, however, that this is by no means a universal desire of national managers.

Use of foreign managers in overseas operations has proceeded much more rapidly. This practice is understandable in view of the national's background and ability to work in the local culture. American managers in overseas branches frequently encounter communications problems because they cannot

---

[9] In a study of top management personnel in the 150 largest U.S. industrial corporations, Simmonds found that only 1.6 percent entered the United States as foreigners after age 25 or held top management positions outside. Kenneth Simmonds, "Multinational? Well Not Quite," *Columbia Journal of World Business* 1, no. 4 (Fall, 1966): 118.

[10] For a discussion of this issue, see Howard V. Perlmutter and David A. Heenan, "How Multinational Should Your Top Managers Be?" *Harvard Business Review* 52, no. 6 (November–December, 1974): 121–32.

speak a foreign language. In Japan, some firms—including Coca-Cola, Japan Company, Ltd., Pfizer—Taito Company, First National City Bank, and American Metal Climax Company—have turned over top management positions to Japanese.[11] Not only did these appointments facilitate internal communications, but they also helped to "open doors a foreigner just can't enter."

On balance, management development and promotion programs in multinational firms appear to be in a primitive stage but are showing signs of improvement. We can expect greater emphasis on the use of foreign managers and flexibility in assignments with the further growth of international business.

Monitoring a Global Environment

Worldwide expansion of the corporate environment makes environmental scanning correspondingly more difficult. Analysts must discern trends in governmental policy at home and also size up political currents and other developments abroad. They must anticipate the likelihood of a Communist takeover, for example, and evaluate the danger of expropriation. Information is also necessary on market opportunities, scientific developments, and financial developments abroad.

Some political risks affect all foreign firms, as occurred with the Castro takeover in Cuba. Other types of risks apply to particular firms because of their specific policies. Extractive industries, for example, are particularly vulnerable because they appear to exploit the natural resources and wealth of the host country.

Political forecasting must be coupled with economic forecasting to provide a realistic picture of significant developments.[12] The former requires an analysis of the governments in power and the political forces at work. Using these forecasts, management must then assess the degree of danger for the corporation.

Summary

A substantial increase in international business has occurred in recent years. As a part of this development, *multinational corporations* have become the dominant business institution in world business.

Because of the global scope of multinational firms, their operations are no longer coextensive with the jurisdiction of governments which regulate them. Tensions exist, therefore, between national governments and multinational firms.

The *cultural context* of international business is significant because of the varied cultures in which multinational corporations operate. Some knowledge of and adaptation to the cultures is essential for effective performance. At the same time, some effort should be devoted to elimination of culturally approved inefficiencies.

---

[11] "When in Japan, Put a Japanese at the Top," *Business Week,* no. 2255 (November 18, 1972): 41.

[12] The way in which one company makes political risk forecasts is described in Stefan H. Robock, "Political Risk: Identification and Assessment," *Columbia Journal of World Business* 6, no. 4 (July–August, 1971): 6–20.

Management processes in the multinational firm possess certain distinctive features. The *political risk* in international business is a part of the high risk multinational firms face. Management should, ideally, take a *geocentric* view of the corporation as a whole. *Management development* and progression involve special challenges, particularly in promotion of nationals into key management positions both in the host countries and in the headquarters country. *Environmental scanning* is particularly difficult, because management must monitor not only the domestic environment but the entire *global environment*.

1. What is the key to success for firms competing in international trade?

Discussion Questions

2. How does a multinational firm differ from an exporter? What are the customary distinguishing features of the multinational firm?

3. What multinational corporations are there, if any, that are not U.S. firms?

4. What unique problems of government regulation are presented by the multinational firm?

5. How did a U.S. law prohibiting trade with the enemy affect the foreign relations of Canada?

6. In what ways do the background cultures of other countries appear to differ from U.S. culture? If you have traveled or lived abroad, give an example from your own experience.

7. How easy or difficult do you think it would be to teach the average Middle Easterner to understand and follow the time schedules and deadlines of the business firm?

8. Should a multinational manager ever try to change some feature of a foreign culture?

9. Explain the difference between an *ethnocentric* attitude and a *geocentric* attitude. How are they related to the multinational corporation?

Supplementary Reading

Ball, George W., ed. *Global Companies: The Political Economy of World Business*, Forty-seventh American Assembly. Englewood Cliffs, N.J.: Prentice-Hall, Inc., 1975.

Haner, F. T. *Multinational Management*. Columbus, Ohio: Charles E. Merrill Publishing Company, 1973.

Kolde, E. J. *The Multinational Company*. Lexington, Mass.: D. C. Heath and Company, 1974.

Mason, R. Hal. "Conflicts Between Host Countries and Multinational Enterprise." *California Management Review* 17, no. 1 (Fall, 1974): 5–14.

Perlmutter, Howard V. and Heenan, David A. "How Multinational Should Your Top Managers Be?" *Harvard Business Review* 52, no. 6 (November–December, 1974): 121–32.

Case 17

The Election in Chile

Testimony before a senate subcommittee in 1973 revealed an apparent attempt by the International Telephone and Telegraph Company to influence the selection of a president in Chile. I.T.T. director John A. McCone, who was a former director of the C.I.A. and still a consultant to the C.I.A. at the time of the incident, testified that he had carried an I.T.T. offer regarding the situation in Chile to top officials of the administration. According to McCone, I.T.T. was willing to contribute $1 million in support of a government plan to prevent the election of Dr. Salvador Allende. Dr. Allende was a Marxist who had campaigned on a platform of nationalization of basic industries. One obvious I.T.T. objective was prevention of expropriation of I.T.T.'s Chilean subsidiary. The offer was authorized by I.T.T. chairman, Harold S. Geneen.

Mr. McCone stated that the million dollars was intended to be used to help unite political factions holding democratic principles in opposition to Allende. Use of the money might have included expenditures for technical assistance, assistance in agriculture, and low-cost housing. This idea, McCone contended, was consistent with the traditional role taken by the United States in combatting communism.

Mr. McCone, in response to a question about proper limits of multinational influence in another country's politics, expressed the opinion that multinational corporations should *support* U.S. government plans but not *initiate* plans of their own. He also said he thought multinational firms "must be very, very careful not to involve themselves in the local domestic politics of the host country."

In the hearings, Senator Case pointed out that, in 1969, U.S. economic assistance to Chile amounted to more than $100 million. He then asked how a person of Mr. Geneen's intelligence could possibly think that a gift of $1 million was going to have any effect in six weeks. Mr. McCone replied that I.T.T. did not intend to carry the whole burden.

Harold S. Geneen, chairman of I.T.T., later argued that there was nothing improper in an American corporation dealing with the C.I.A. since the agency was part of the government and any company had the right to "petition the government" on behalf of its own interests. He was particularly upset because he, with other American businessmen, had been encouraged to invest in Chile as part of the U.S. program of helping to develop the country and keep it democratic.

Following the disclosures in senate hearings, editorials appeared in various publications, deploring the close links between the corporation and the intelligence agency and describing such ties as unhealthy and undesirable.

1. If you were a citizen of Chile, how would you react to the offer of I.T.T. and to the arguments of Mr. McCone?

2. How does Mr. McCone appear to perceive the relationships between a multinational corporation and its home government?

3. Is it appropriate for the government to encourage a multinational corporation to help keep another country democratic—the policy that had apparently motivated Mr. Geneen?

4. What does this case show about the political power of a multinational corporation in relation to host countries?

5. What are the implications of Mr. McCone's background in the public service?

Objectives

1. Identify the types of change occurring in the external world of business.

2. Describe the significant internal changes occurring in business organizations and in their management.

3. Summarize managerial practices that contribute to development of innovative managers and innovative organizations.

Chapter

Trends in Contemporary Management

The Changing World of Business
The Changing Organization
The Managerial Role in Meeting Change

Case: Enlightened Self-Interest

Successful managers must be oriented toward the future. They must be able to solve unusual problems, adapt to novel circumstances, and introduce modifications to traditional management practices. In short, they must face the challenge of change. This chapter emphasizes the changing world of business and its implications for the manager of the future.

The Changing World of Business

The 1970s— Decade of Change

Business managers have always dealt with change, but changes of the 1970s are more extensive than ever before and accelerating at a rate scarcely comprehensible to older managers. A best seller, *Future Shock*, assured us that these changes are not limited to the business world but that they permeate all of society.

> Many of us have a vague "feeling" that things are moving faster. Doctors and executives alike complain that they cannot keep up with the latest developments in their fields. Hardly a meeting or conference takes place today without some ritualistic oratory about "the challenge of change." Among many there is an uneasy mood—a suspicion that change is out of control.[1]

Changes in our society are not only accelerating, but many changes are unprecedented and involve a sharp break with the past. Peter F. Drucker has alluded to the qualitative aspects of change and to shifting foundations in his book, *The Age of Discontinuity*.[2] He suggests four areas in which major discontinuities exist.

1. Introduction of new technologies which will create new industries and render existing industries obsolete.
2. Emergence of a world economy that involves a world market or global shopping center.
3. Development of a changing political and social matrix involving much disenchantment with our major institutions.
4. Creation of a "knowledge economy" in which about one half of our American dollars are spent on procuring ideas and information and in which knowledge has become the central "factor of production."

Some have referred to the 1970s as the beginning of the *post-industrial era*—thereby sharply distinguishing the present and future from the industrial era of the past several decades.[3] This terminology reflects a view similar to that of Drucker, namely that recent changes involve a drastic break with the past and a reversal of past trends. A new type of industrial world is replacing the familiar world of the 1950s and 1960s.

America's managers, therefore, face a future of great uncertainty. On the basis of the observations cited in this section, we realize that they must func-

---

[1] Alvin Toffler, *Future Shock* (New York: Bantam Books, 1970), p. 19. Copyright © Random House, Inc.

[2] Peter F. Drucker, *The Age of Discontinuity: Guidelines to Our Changing Society* (New York: Harper & Row, Publishers, 1969).

[3] See, for example, William Simon, "Management and Man," in Edward C. Bursk, ed., *Challenge to Leadership: Managing in a Changing World* (New York: The Free Press, 1973), pp. 275-97.

tion in a society that is changing more rapidly and more drastically than ever before.

One need not be a prophet to discern a number of environmental trends significant to business. The future is partially evident in changes that are now occurring. Ansoff has stressed the crucial importance of the following external forces.[4]

The Impact of Environmental Change

1. Product dynamics
2. Market dynamics
3. Changing role of the firm in society

The significance of these factors will be discussed in the following section. Recognition of change in these areas, while essential for competent business leadership, is insufficient in itself. Management must both recognize and learn to cope with environmental change. This chapter views the manager in a changing role as an adapter to change and as a change seeker.

Product dynamics and *market dynamics* are closely related forces. The former is concerned with changes in the products sold by a firm and the latter with changes in the marketplace in which those products are sold.

Product and Market Dynamics

A moment's reflection makes apparent the tremendous product changes in the American economy. Products that were unknown a few generations ago—transistor radios, jet aircraft, ball-point pens, Polaroid cameras, computers, Xerox copy machines, and many others—are important in today's economy. Established products, moreover, are constantly being adapted and modified.

Today, the introduction of a new product is followed quickly by the rush of competitors with similar or improved models. In most cases, the competitor has the technology necessary for direct competition. Effective patent protection is rare, and the market becomes flooded with new products.

> In drug and grocery channels alone, there are now some 6,000 new products a year—more than twice the figure of 10 years ago. "The result," says one Chicago industrial designer, "is that companies are facing risk situations they never dreamed of before." [5]

It appears likely that the trend toward an abundance of new products will continue and will affect the market environment in which business firms operate.

The growth of international business and the rise of the multinational firm illustrate the *market dynamics* that affect managerial decision making. Foreign products compete in the domestic market, and the market areas of many firms have become worldwide. American markets also change as the population shifts, industrial changes occur, and levels of income rise.

---

[4] H. Igor Ansoff, "The Firm of the Future," *Harvard Business Review* 43, no. 5 (September-October, 1965): 162-78.

[5] "New Products: The Push is on Marketing," *Business Week*, no. 2218 (March 4, 1972): 72.

An Example of Successful Adaptation: Harris Corporation

An example of successful adaptation to product and market changes is provided by the Harris Corporation, manufacturer of electronic composition equipment for use in printing.[6] Known for most of its history as Harris-Intertype, the firm has produced printing presses and typesetting equipment since its founding in the late 1800s. Until recently, the basic product line had changed little since the early days of the business.

In the 1950s, however, Harris Corporation's management became interested in the relationship of electronics and printing. They made a series of acquisitions to obtain competence in electronic technology and proceeded to work at the blending of the two concepts. Over a period of fifteen years, the company's sales went from 100 percent machinery to 57 percent electronics, with electronics providing two-thirds of the profits.

Harris Corporation was first in the market with electronic editorial equipment in the early 1970s and quickly became the recognized leader. In addition, the corporation planned an even broader penetration into nonpublishing electronics products. For the future, the firm's management anticipates other new products and new technologies. This firm has been highly successful in capitalizing on the new technology.

The Firm and Society

A third major external force is found in the firm's relationship to society. There is no question as to the rising expectations of society concerning business performance. Rightly or wrongly, there is a widespread feeling that business firms should demonstrate responsibility and leadership in areas of social concern.

Many types of social concerns involve the business community. For example, industry must help protect the physical environment and preserve natural resources. Business is also expected to support education and contribute to the nation's goals of equality of opportunity. Unemployment and poor housing in city ghettos are likewise seen as areas of business concern. Change in the nature of social problems calls for change in the relationship of business to society. Consequently, awareness and understanding of social change have become essential for business leadership.

Business managers of the future will be expected to demonstrate an awareness of social concerns, as indicated by the following statement:

> According to the time schedule, a new type of manager should now be emerging to cope with the complexity of factors and forces in a society that is struggling to adapt to changing human values and rapid technological advances. It is probable that the manager of the future will be classified as a "public manager" or a "public oriented executive." [7]

Many business leaders are apparently coming to appreciate the necessary contribution of business to an improved quality of life in America. Statements

---

[6] "A Double-Barreled Overhaul for Harris Corp.," *Business Week*, no. 2354 (October 26, 1974): 78-80.

[7] John F. Mee, "Profiles of the Future: The Manager of the Future," *Business Horizons* 16, no. 3 (June, 1973): 8.

by leading corporate executives reflect such a point of view in assuming that the problems and instabilities of society are likewise problems of the business community. Business concern is likewise evident in corporate participation in conferences on broad social problems. In December 1972, for example, American business was strongly represented in a national conference sponsored by the Urban Research Corporation on "The Changing Work Ethic." Although corporate programs alone are inadequate to alleviate many social problems, the business contribution is seen as a vital part of the total solution.

Another major area of social concern is the corporation's responsibilities in equal employment opportunity. If problems of employment for minority groups are to be solved, the solution must eventually include enlightened employment practices by those corporations who are the nation's major employers. To some extent, the rising expectations concerning business responsibility in this area have been spelled out in law. Some companies are going further than the law requires, however, in aggressively seeking to provide opportunities for minority groups.

The Changing Organization

Increasing Importance of Behavioral Aspects

Organizations have always been staffed with people. Thus, they have always been social or behavioral systems. However, behavioral factors were only dimly understood in past generations. In recent years, the comprehension of the social dimensions of business organizations has been rapidly increasing.

Behavioral aspects of organizations are not only better understood, but they are also increasingly important in the functioning of the enterprise. As physiological and security needs are satisfied, higher-level social and egoistic needs become dominant. As the standard of living continues to rise, members of organizations place greater value upon human relationships and the social environment of business.

The trend in business management appears to lie in the direction of more democratic and participative leadership. The movement toward greater democracy, however, raises questions concerning the proper balance between freedom and authority. At some point, the need for effective coordination and achievement of organizational purpose imposes limits upon democracy in the workplace. Success of participative management efforts indicates that management generally is operating short of this limit and that we may expect further advancement toward participative management.

The success of a manager of the future, therefore, will depend upon his or her ability as a manager of behavioral systems. He or she must possess an ability to work effectively with people and must develop skills in communication and human relations. In short, a greater premium is being placed upon the social skills of management.

Changing Methods and Technology

Another significant area of change is that of technology and methods. Developments in production technology, for example, are constantly changing the nature of the manufacturing process. Development of the sophisticated tools of management science further illustrates the drastic changes in methods of decision making.

The dynamic forces of technological change are reshaping entire industries. The field of communications is typical of those areas experiencing rapid growth and revolutionary change. The combined sales and service revenues of telephone, telegraph, broadcasting, and communications product industries have shown a phenomenal growth rate of 10 percent or more annually over the last twenty years. Future prospects appear even brighter. This growth involves not only a simple expansion of existing facilities and services but also many new developments, such as communications satellites, laser beam transmission systems, and computer networks.

The direction that future change will take is not clear, but it is certain that major changes will occur. The office of the future, for example, will eliminate much of the paper that inundates offices today. Following is a forecast of expected changes:

> Over the next decade, most corporate offices will still be geared to the movement of information on pieces of paper. Office automation will bring improvements in productivity through the use of automatic typewriters and other stand-alone equipment that crank out paper faster. Some inter-office information will move electronically, but what the manager reads and files will be printed on paper.
>
> But during this period, a relatively small but fast-growing group of companies will have moved into the office-of-the-future environment. The leap forward will be led by the "paper-makers"—those companies that are involved primarily in generating, modifying, or moving paper. These pioneers will have hooked together word-processing equipment into office systems to transfer information electronically and to move it into and out of central electronic files. For them, it will be the start of the paperless office.[8]

In describing the office of the future, research specialists have assured us that managers and office workers will be able to call up documents from the file and have them displayed on a screen that sits on the desk. Letters will also be transmitted by wire. The office may be virtually paperless. The magnitude of technological change and its enormous importance in management thinking are clearly evident from this one example.

Growth of the Systems View of Organization

The view of an organization as a group of isolated parts has been replaced with the concept of an integrated whole that is more than the sum of the parts. Within the organizational system, there are centrifugal forces—those that tend to cause the system to disintegrate. There are also centripetal forces that tend to bind the component parts into a functioning organism. One category of factors that can either build or destroy the system as a functioning mechanism is that of managerial policy and decision making. Effective management today demands an awareness of the systems nature of organizations. This requires a breadth of comprehension and understanding not always possessed by managers in the past.

---

[8] "The Office of the Future," *Business Week*, no. 2387 (June 30, 1975): 80.

The manager who grasps the principle of the systems concept will organize in terms of this concept. This will undoubtedly lead to continued deemphasis of traditional functional specialization. Increasingly, the manager must organize in terms of smoothly meshing units of the organization and must recognize social groupings involved in the system. Perhaps the most general way in which the systems approach will affect planning is by the process of integrated planning itself. The logical hierarchy of plans will be understood, and the importance of linking the plans of one unit with those of another will become evident.

As relationships are determined with greater precision, tools of operations research can be applied and the electronic computer used more extensively in decision making. The following examples show the type of systems analysis carried on in industry today:

> At Boise Cascade Corp., Executive Vice-President Stephen B. Moser is experimenting with a computerized model of the Timber & Wood Products Div.—with almost 8,000 equations and 15,000 variables—to take a 15-year forward look at operations and to help decide on the most efficient use of timber lands and where to build new plywood plants.
>
> Sigurd Andersen, manager for marketing planning at DuPont's Development Dept., works with a score of computer models, including one that simulates the dye industry and the company's stake in it. His colleague, Robert Gee, uses a mathematical tool called risk analysis to help DuPont executives assess what the odds are that a new product will produce profits—and how big those profits are likely to be.
>
> Kenneth C. Ponsor, Owens-Illinois vice-president and director of corporate planning, uses a computerized "mechanical adder" to tap financial data from seven far-flung divisions. O-I is about to unveil a corporate financial model that will let executives pretest ideas and strategies, so they can see companywide profit and loss statements and gauge the need for funds before resources are committed.[9]

Control in terms of the entire system is likewise possible. It differs from a control process that regulates one part at a time. Control of one part may leave another part out of control. Control action in one area may call for adjustments in other areas. The network concept of control is pertinent at this point.

The probable increasing emphasis upon systems management in the future is discernible in recent trends. Numerous concepts and tools of a systems nature have been devised and used. Managerial approaches employed in project management and network analysis, for example, illustrate this trend. The increasing use of automation and automated data-processing systems are likewise examples of this approach. The adoption of operations research tools is similarly consistent with the systems concept. It seems likely that these trends will continue and that management will necessarily need to adopt a philosophy and approach compatible with the systems view.

---

[9] "The 'New Management' Finally Takes Over," *Business Week*, no. 2086 (August 23, 1969): 58.

**The Managerial
Role in
Meeting
Change**

**Increasing the
Level of
Managerial
Competence**

The increasing complexity and responsibilities of modern management call for greater skill and sophistication on the part of managerial personnel. The need for greater technical knowledge, conceptual ability, awareness of social issues, and familiarity with the methods of modern professional management necessitates higher staffing standards. To some extent, this requirement is reflected in the need for a broader educational preparation on the part of today's executives. Education and development are also coming to be viewed as a continuing process, receiving a strong emphasis throughout the working life of the manager.

Figure 18–1 contrasts the managerial skills required in the mass-production era (past) with those required in the post-industrial era (present and future).

Figure 18-1   *Required Managerial Skills*

Mass-Production Era Skills	Post-Industrial Era Skills
Experientially acquired	Acquired through career-long education
Familiar problem solver	Novel problem solver
Intuitive problem solver	Analytic problem solver
Conservative risk taker	Entrepreneurial risk taker
Convergent diagnostician	Divergent diagnostician
Lag controller	Lead controller
Extrapolative planner	Entrepreneurial planner
Change control leadership	Change generation leadership

Source: H. Igor Ansoff, "Management in Transition," in Edward C. Bursk, ed., *Challenge to Leadership: Managing in a Changing World* (New York: The Free Press, 1973), p. 41. Copyright © 1973 by The Conference Board, Inc.

The skills of the manager of the future will apparently be concerned with the new and drastically different and will call for an even higher type of professional education than has been necessary in the past.

The plural executive—the executive team or office of the president—offers a possible solution to demands for more sophisticated managerial talents. A variety of management abilities might be combined in this way. Although this approach is a possibility, one panel of management scholars does not believe this approach will be widely used in the near future.[10]

Professional managers often supplement their own experience and abilities by using management consultants. Surrounded by major problems, many leading executives have little reluctance in calling in specialists for research and advice in reaching decisions. The majority of America's largest corporations engage management consultants either continuously or as needed from time to time.

Change Seekers

An even greater problem than managerial competency is the managerial attitude toward change. It is well known that some members of organizations,

---

[10] Robert M. Fulmer, "Profiles of the Future: The Management of Tomorrow," *Business Horizons* 15, no. 4 (August, 1972): 6.

even managerial members, resist change. It is also evident, in view of the changing world and changing organization noted earlier, that such managers are quickly obsolete. The successful organization of the future must be staffed by managers who are change seekers and capable of change.

> By the 1980s, the truly professional manager will emerge; change will be his stock in trade. The qualities that differentiate him will be those of intellect and behavioral flexibility. . . . Selections will be based on behavioral flexibility because the manager will live in continuing change, which will affect him as much as others.[11]

Throughout much of our history, managers responded to competitive challenges by making changes as needed for efficiency in production and marketing. Environmental demands of the future, according to Ansoff, call for an ability to make more drastic and dramatic change and to discern discontinuities which pose threats to and opportunities for the firm.

> The primary focus is no longer on exploiting the firm's business, it is on *changing* the business, including products-markets-industries-technologies which no longer afford the best potential.[12]

How to identify and develop change seekers is a problem. Age is one factor, of course. Although there are exceptions, people become more conservative as they advance in age. This has led to the suggestion that personnel be moved into top level managerial positions at an earlier age than before—for example, thirty-five to forty-five, rather than forty-five to fifty-five.[13]

Age is not the only factor, however. It is important that the organization of the future be able to detect and reward its innovative members. Highly creative people are often individualistic in attitudes and behavior. A tolerance for nonconformity and creativity is, therefore, important for developing change seekers.

There is a common tendency to forget that change is inevitable, even though one recognizes that it has consistently occurred in the past. The organization may, therefore, need to arrange for experiences that will enable managers to recognize and appreciate the nature of change in organizations and in methods of management. Many university programs for business executives are designed to provide this sort of stimulus. When Paul Austin became president of Coca-Cola Company, he began to emphasize continuing education for the Coca-Cola executives. One member of management was quoted as follows:

> When I was graduated from college, I thought I had finished with my education, but since Paul has been president, I've had more education than in my

---

[11] W. J. Reddin, "Profiles of the Future: Management Effectiveness in the 1980s," *Business Horizons* 17, no. 4 (August, 1974): 9.

[12] H. Igor Ansoff, "Management in Transition," in Edward C. Bursk, ed., *Challenge to Leadership: Managing in a Changing World* (New York: The Free Press, 1973), p. 35.

[13] Patrick H. Irwin and Franklin W. Langham, Jr., "The Change Seekers," *Harvard Business Review* 44, no. 1 (January–February, 1966), p. 92.

whole life. He's had us runnin' up to Harvard where he set up these special bottler schools and management programs and we were the first ones to test them out.[14]

Austin himself expressed his philosophy with regard to this point as follows:

> What we do, a lot of us strive for a spirit of self-renewal in management. We have to guard against the pitfalls of size alone. You know, when companies get big and successful, they build Maginot Lines. A swift competitor goes through a Maginot Line, always does. We don't believe in Maginot Lines. We have to keep the flexibility, keep in competition.[15]

The Innovative Organization

As noted, the changing environment is creating a demand for more innovation. Business firms should ideally be innovative, forward-looking, and progressive. Even so, some fear that American business firms have been slowing in their traditional innovative methods.

> Yet from boardroom to research lab, there is a growing sense that something has happened to American innovation. Some say it is in rapid decline. Others claim it is taking new forms. Either way, the country's genius for invention is not what it used to be.[16]

The decline in total spending for basic research since the late 1960s tends to confirm this alleged trend. It is a disturbing change, moreover, in view of the growing need for innovation by business firms.

According to John W. Gardner, organizations have unpredictable life cycles.[17] They may go from youth to old age in two or three decades, or they may last for centuries. The secret to continuation is found in their steps toward organizational renewal. It appears that the need of American business firms for such renewal is acute during the last quarter of the twentieth century.

Let us consider some of the features that make for a viable organization in a world of change.[18] One essential feature is a built-in provision for self-criticism. People and organizations tend to resist criticism. The organization with an eye for the future formulates procedures for critical review of existing practices. To some extent, this is accomplished informally as management tolerates criticism by organization members. More formal arrangements can also be designed to stimulate critical self-examination. Study groups, for example, may be established to review organizational policy, or a management consultant may be engaged to analyze company operations.

---

[14] "The Coca-Cola Co.," *Forbes* 100, no. 3 (August 1, 1967): 32.

[15] *Ibid.*, p. 34.

[16] "The Breakdown of U.S. Innovation," *Business Week*, no. 2419 (February 16, 1976): 56.

[17] John W. Gardner, "How To Prevent Organizational Dry Rot," *Harper's Magazine* 231, no. 1385 (October, 1965): 20.

[18] Many of the characteristics suggested here are based upon those suggested by John W. Gardner in the article cited in note 17.

Closely related to the foregoing is the need for an adequate system of internal communication. Lines of communication need to be established not only internally, on both a horizontal and vertical basis, but also with the external environment in which the company operates. Adequate exchange of information among levels of management and among divisions of an organization does much to eliminate the stagnation that may otherwise occur.

The innovative organization also requires fluidity of structure and flexibility of procedure. Tradition in either structure or procedure makes change difficult, and a vigorous approach is necessary to avoid difficulty in this area. The status quo is always comfortable. However, a firm may fail because of dogmatic adherence to traditional procedures or a structure designed to solve problems that no longer exist. The successful organization, therefore, must develop a flexibility and capacity to change as conditions make such change desirable.

The successful, vigorous organization must also avoid the hazards of catering to vested interests. These exist in every organization and destroy the flexibility necessary for health and vigorous growth. Once again, the achievement of this goal requires a philosophical viewpoint of management that looks to the future of the organization as a whole and avoids the pitfalls of narrow self-interest.

Once again, we should recall the concept of the business firm as an open system. In the context of this view, the firm depends upon its external environment and is subject to the forces imposed by this environment. Any living system, whether biological or social, will die if it fails to maintain a proper relationship to its environment. Management's natural preoccupation with the problems of internal management, however, tends to obscure the vital link between business and its environment.

Management of an Open System

> Thinking of the organization as a closed system, moreover, results in a failure to develop the intelligence or feedback function of obtaining adequate information about the changes in environmental forces. It is remarkable how weak many industrial companies are in their market research departments when they are so dependent upon the market. The prediction can be hazarded that organizations in our society will increasingly move toward the improvement of the facilities for research in assessing environmental forces. The reason is that we are in the process of correcting our misconception of the organization as a closed system.[19]

In the 1960s, the J. C. Penney Company went through the most thorough reorganization of its history. This reorganization was not only successful, but it was based upon a highly perceptive analysis of changes in its business environment. Its management had understood the open system nature of the company and correctly used intelligence concerning environmental forces.

> These changes date back more than a decade—to that now-famous memo Penney's Chairman William M. Batten sent to the board declaring that the

---

[19] Daniel Katz and Robert L. Kahn, *The Social Psychology of Organizations* (New York: John Wiley & Sons, Inc., 1966), p. 27.

world Penney had prospered in was fast disappearing, and that if Penney hoped to survive it would have to change with it. "Want has supplanted need," Batten said. Populations were shifting; the patterns of consumer buying had changed; credit had supplanted cash; affluence, penury; fashion, utility.[20]

The openness of the system necessitates an alertness not only to needs of customers but also to public demand for acceptable business behavior. Business firms have often ignored or misjudged public dissatisfaction with their practices, only to face restrictive regulation a short time later. The ultimate test of business management lies in the degree of wisdom exercised in coping with the openness of the system. Internally, the firm must adjust to meet successfully the changes in its external environment.

Summary

Changes in the business environment are occurring at an accelerating rate and involve discontinuities as well as simple extensions of past trends. As a result, the role and responsibilities of professional managers are likewise constantly changing. Three of the crucially important external forces are (1) product dynamics, (2) market dynamics, and (3) the changing role of the firm in society.

There are also significant internal changes in the business organization as well as changes in its external environment. Behavioral aspects of organizations, for example, are becoming better understood and increasingly important in the functioning of the enterprise. Technological change is constantly reshaping business institutions and their methods. Also, the systems concept is coming to have great value in the proper performance of managerial functions.

Successful management of the changing organization in a changing world requires increasingly competent and better educated managers who are also change seekers. A current problem concerns effective methodology for identifying and developing managers as innovators. Other factors contributing to an innovative organization are (1) a built-in provision for self-criticism, (2) an adequate system of internal communication, (3) a fluidity of structure and flexibility of procedure, and (4) a refusal to cater to vested interests. Business managers must also realize that the firm is an open system and that its management must properly analyze and regulate the firm's relationship with its external environment.

Discussion Questions

1. What is the distinction between *product dynamics* and *market dynamics,* and what is the significance of these forces to the business manager?

2. Discuss the current significance and nature of (1) product dynamics, (2) market dynamics, and (3) the changing role of the firm in society as these apply to a major automobile manufacturer.

3. Early in 1968, a leading businessman associated with a well-known retail organization said that big city retailers cannot wait for the government to solve urban problems. He pointed to the problem of ghetto unemployment and called on stores to recruit and train the hard-core unemployed even if they must "fit the job to the

---

[20] "Can the Last Be First?" *Forbes* 103, no. 6 (March 15, 1969): 30.

man." How do you explain or interpret these comments in the light of the ideas discussed in this chapter? Does this executive appear to be a "hard-headed businessman" or a "soft-headed philanthropist"?

4. What explains the increasing importance of behavioral science in contemporary business organizations?

5. What is meant by the greater requirement for "systems thinking" on the part of future business managers?

6. Consider the most creative, innovative, change-seeking individual whom you know. Does it appear that this person's creativity is an innate quality or an attitude that has been developed? Is it possible to develop an innovative attitude in managerial personnel?

7. Assuming an organization has reasonably creative and innovative individuals on its staff, what feature appears to be most essential in order for this spirit of innovation and change to be properly exercised?

8. What are the values, difficulties, and limitations involved in relieving an executive of customary managerial duties and giving this individual responsibility for considering the broad problem of the firm's future in a changing environment?

9. Consider the case of a company that became stagnant over years of operation. An observer described one such sick company by saying that "its name is 'lethargy.' " In speaking of the problems of correcting this weakness in the same organization, another observer asked, "How do you get an organization to move and accept change when it hasn't done it for years?" What *is* the answer to this latter question?

Bursk, Edward C., ed. *Challenge to Leadership: Managing in a Changing World.* New York: The Free Press, 1973.

Drucker, Peter F. *The Age of Discontinuity: Guidelines to Our Changing Society.* New York: Harper & Row, Publishers, 1969.

Mee, John F. "Profiles of the Future: The Manager of the Future." *Business Horizons* 16, no. 3 (June, 1973): 5-14.

Townsend, Lynn. "Problems and Potentials of the 1970s." *Michigan Business Review* 22, no. 2 (March, 1970): 6-11.

Supplementary Reading

Case 18

Enlightened Self-Interest*

Mr. William Smith, President of Cosmos Chemical Company, was reviewing his company's corporate objectives with his administrative staff. Mr. Smith began, "Although we recognize that business serves society mainly through implementing its basic functions of producing goods and services, it is time we address ourselves to the social responsibilities of business."

*Bernard A. Deitzer and Karl A. Shilliff, *Incidents in Modern Business* (Columbus, Ohio: Charles E. Merrill Publishing Company, 1975), pp. 12-14.

Smith also summarized some interesting statistics: since 1890, the total real national product of the country has almost doubled every twenty years. Real disposable income has more than tripled, and working time has declined by one-third. In generating such economic growth, American business has provided safer employment, rising wages and salaries, and a myriad of employee benefits. More important, the rising standard of living has enabled citizens to develop new, freer life styles coupled with more leisure time. Moreover, business has carried out its basic responsibility of products and services well.

Along with these accomplishments, Mr. Smith pointed out, the expectations of American society have begun to rise at a much faster pace than the nation's economic performance. Society has become increasingly aware of environmental problems, population pressures, mass transportation, equal opportunity, poverty, and crime.

Smith also presented some societal goals, which have been articulated by leaders in politics, labor, education, and business. The goals included:

1. Equal opportunity for each person regardless of race, color, or creed.
2. Good housing, with good cultural and educational opportunities.
3. Elimination of poverty coupled with good health care.
4. Bountiful jobs and career opportunities.
5. Safe streets, pleasant environment.

According to Smith, the public wants business to give a great deal more to help achieve these goals. Smith said, "The contract between business and society is changing rapidly. What shall we do about it?"

Following is a list of Cosmos Company objectives and goals:

Cosmos Company Objectives

To obtain maximum return on investment through technological leadership.

To develop new products to permit maximum profitable growth.

Goals

To realize a before-tax income of 15 percent of sales.

To implement a comprehensive business plan in all divisions within the year.

To reduce inventory by 20 percent throughout the company.

To attain 6 percent average increase in productivity within the year, over all product lines.

To introduce a new, more profitable line of products in Division A.

To increase support to Research and Development to 10 percent of total funding.

Questions

1. Are Cosmos Company's goals and objectives directed to societal problems?

2. What are some specific goals Cosmos could incorporate into its structure?

3. What does the realization of societal goals do to a company's profits?

4. What do we mean by "enlightened self-interest"?

Index

Index